# OUTDOOR LIFE®
# DEER
# HUNTER'S
# YEARBOOK

Outdoor Life® Books
Meredith® Press, New York

Cover photo: Len Rue Jr.

Published by Outdoor Life® Books
150 East 52nd Street
New York, New York 10022

For Meredith® Press:
    Director: Elizabeth P. Rice
    Editorial Project Manager: Maryanne Bannon
    Production Manager: Bill Rose

Produced by Barbara G. Tchabovsky
    Consulting Editor: George H. Haas
    Book Designer: Jeff Fitschen

Special thanks to
    Vin T. Sparano, executive editor of *Outdoor Life* magazine
    Ralph P. Stuart, editor of *Outdoor Life's Deer and Big Game Annual*
    Gerald Bethge, editor of *Outdoor Life's Hunting Guns Annual*
    Jim Eckes, art director, *Outdoor Life*
    Allison Longo, assistant art director, *Outdoor Life*
    Brian Holland, prepress director, Times Mirror Magazines Inc.

ISBN: 0-696-11109-8

Printed in the United States of America

10  9  8  7  6  5  4  3  2  1

# Contents

# PREFACE

# Tenth Anniversary

You're reading the tenth edition of the *Deer Hunter's Yearbook*. The first edition—1983—was intended to satisfy a need felt by many readers of *Outdoor Life* magazine. The editors of the Outdoor Life Book Club knew that the deer hunters among the magazine's readership found many of the articles and narratives of such great interest that they wanted permanent editions. That a very specialized annual hunting publication remains in demand after so many years demonstrates that the editors were correct.

During the years after the first edition, two additional *Outdoor Life* publications were brought out—*Deer and Big Game* and *Hunting Guns*. Once a year, the *Outdoor Life* editors develop these specialized publications to satisfy a need. *Hunting Guns* is unique because it contains articles of interest only to hunters. There's nothing on target shooting, self-defense firearms, military arms and small arms history, or combat shooting. The publication is for hunters only, and there's nothing else quite like it in the United States. A hunter who buys the usual "gun magazine" knows that he's getting a lot of material in the magazine that's of little or no interest to him. *Deer and Big Game* omits bird hunting, fishing, and hunting for small game, and its readers are almost exclusively big-game hunters. Put these two annuals together with a year's worth of *Outdoor Life*, and you have an excellent source of material for a yearbook—though we sometimes include something from the past.

The 1992 yearbook contains 31 articles and narratives. It leads off with an "issue" piece, "Guess Who's Coming to Deer Camp?" by Deborah Morris, and the lead photograph tells the reader who it is—women! More and more, female hunters are participating in the blood sports. Oh yes, Southern gentlewomen have for years fired dainty shotguns at bobwhite quail, and in New England, you'll find tweedy and well-heeled women who have hunted woodcock and grouse all their lives. These women are analogous to the feminine aristocrats of Europe and the British Isles who hunt, often on horseback. But now, in the United States, women in large numbers are hunting deer and other big game. This comes as a distinct shock to some male hunters, who believe that big-game hunting, among its other attractions, is a good way to absent themselves from female influences for a week or two at least once a year. Don't go away, fellas! The author tells us why even the most crusty "males only" hunter should welcome women to deer camp. On their acceptance may depend the very survival of hunting in America. Of course, if a man wants to hunt alone in male isolation, he can always do so, but he now has something to think about.

The other "issue" story is on gun safety. In "I Didn't Have My Figger on the Tringer," Dennis Sandmeier approaches the subject in the form of a first-person narrative about an accidental wounding or death that fortunately did not happen. Read it, and put yourself in the place of the author, and maybe you'll check your rifle or shotgun more carefully before you next go afield.

By the way, the lead photograph of the article on women in deer camp illustrates a very common and very dangerous safety violation. Take a look at it now and see if you can spot it. It came as a shock to me when I first tumbled to it. I'll tell you what it is at the end of this preface—just in case you don't spot it.

The remainder of the yearbook consists of 13 articles and narratives on hunting whitetail deer; five on Western deer (mostly, mule deer, but including one haunting narrative about calling Sitka deer in Alaska that brought on a bear attack); five on bigger game—elk, moose, and caribou; and six on firearms and shooting. This year, articles on cooking game and on accessory equipment have been omitted because we felt that readers would rather have more material on hunting and firearms, as many have said.

We include articles and narratives on bigger antlered game because we have never met a deer hunter who didn't already hunt these animals or want to do so as soon as possible. Besides, these antlered animals actually *are* deer, according to any dictionary or zoology book. Take a look.

Some of the units in this yearbook are first-person, nonfiction narratives, not informational articles. A hunter simply tells the story of his hunt. This is the original form of the "outdoor story," employed by primitive tribesmen as well as many "outdoor writers." Some primitive peoples even tell the stories of their hunts in dances. Narratives are preferred by many readers, but some subjects, particularly those dealing with the selection, care, and use of firearms are best presented in instructional articles. But there's no rule against including some humor and dramatic anecdotes among the useful information. Writers published in *Outdoor Life* are experts at doing just that. This is one reason the magazine has been successful for more than 90 years. (The first issue came out in January 1898.)

I was an *Outdoor Life* editor for 24 years before "retiring," and I've edited this yearbook for several years. It's a very pleasant way to keep up my contacts with writers and editors, though I no longer go to the office, a blessing for any sportsman. I never bring a notebook and pencil when I go hunting and fishing, and that's a blessing too.

Readers often ask me about the changes in American hunting that I've experienced in so many years of editing *Outdoor Life* and the yearbook, and I have no hesitation about citing the biggest change of all. It's something that very few hunters think about because it has happened quite gradually.

The biggest change among hunters is that most of them are no longer traditionalists. Time was when you could tell how a man hunted simply by knowing which part of the country he came from. New England deer hunters, for example, were almost always "stand and drive" enthusiasts or stump sitters, except

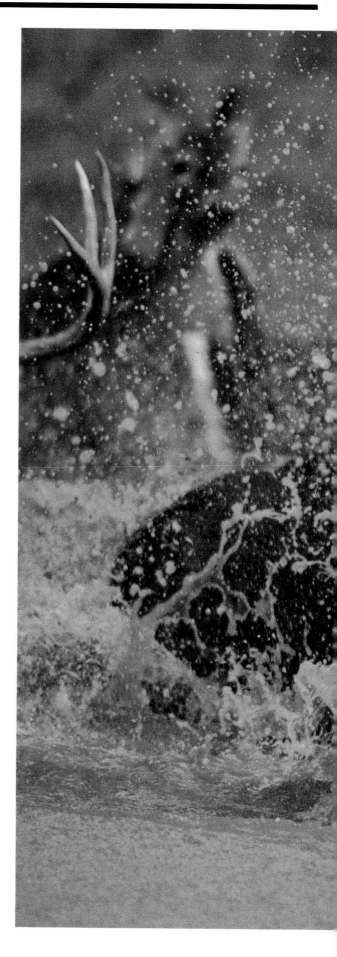

*The yearbook has always included many fine photographs of deer and big game. Here, frequent contributor Leonard Lee Rue has captured a group of whitetails crossing a river. Photograph by Len Rue Jr.*

*Today, hunters use both old and new techniques to hunt mule deer, like this, as well as whitetails and big game. Photograph by Leonard Lee Rue III*

for the few who relied on stillhunting and tracking. Out West, mule-deer hunters almost always glassed big tracts of country and stalked after they spotted the game. This is no longer true. Deer and hunters must adjust to rapidly changing conditions in many parts of the country. The sudden great popularity of muzzleloaders and archery tackle also changed deer hunting a great deal as did the revival or introduction of deer scents, tree stands, calling deer with grunts and bleats, and the scientific study of deer to determine their normal behavior and to adapt hunting methods and arms to those realities. Traditional lore absorbed from fathers and uncles is no longer enough. Deer hunting in a given area does change, and sometimes it changes radically. The South was once the home of men who used short-range lever-action carbines and hunted in thick cover. Now, many Southerners are using finely tuned bolt-action rifles to hunt the enormous soybean fields that have become so common. To kill deer at long range, one must hunt differently and use a different rifle. Many other examples could be cited.

Some changes, however, are really the re-introduction of old methods. Calling deer and luring them to the gun with scents are, after all, both ancient history and very modern. These methods and several others were developed by the American Indian long before the white man arrived. And, Indians were the original American bowhunters too, though what they would think of the wheels and pulleys of a modern compound bow is hard to say. I'll bet on one thing though—they'd like the improved accuracy.

The changing nature of deer hunting and other forms of hunting explains much of the continuing popularity of publications about hunting. If deer hunting did not change, the entire story would have been told in the 1890s, and traditional lore would suffice. Since it does change in common with almost every form of hunting, periodical publications are essential if a sportsman wants to keep up.

Narratives appear in this publication simply because they are a pleasure to read. They are popular not because they instruct—though you can learn a lot from them—but because they bring the hunt, with its dangers and tragedies as well as its pleasures, to the easy chair and the reading lamp. I believe you'll find the narratives in this yearbook just as important as the instructional articles.

Did you discover the safety error in the picture of the young lady entering the well-appointed hunting cabin? One often cited safety "commandment" is not to bring loaded firearms into homes, buildings, or camps. Those who do so and are challenged often say, "Oh, it isn't loaded." But, almost every hunter knows that "unloaded" guns sometimes kill people.

How does one know that another hunter's gun is really safe? We know it is safe if the action is open. Even if there is still a cartridge in the chamber or magazine, a gun with an open action simply cannot fire. You can tell if the action is open at a glance. That is why, for instance, all shotguns must be open at Trap and Skeet ranges, except when the gunner is on post or station and ready to fire at a claybird. This is the polite way of informing everyone that you and your gun are really safe.

Look closely, and if you didn't see it before, you'll find that the rifle's bolt handle is down and that the action is, therefore, closed. There is indeed danger in the situation shown. In my own deer camp and in many others, someone who does this is immediately informed of the serious safety violation. If it happens again, the violator is politely but firmly told to pack up and go home. Any newcomer, man or woman, should be aware of such things. If you have the slightest doubt, ask! Accidentally killing someone is very hard to live with for the rest of one's life. And, all forms of hunting, but deer hunting in particular, are under attack by antihunters, and preventable accidents don't help.

Could it be that the photograph was deliberately conceived to remind us of safety matters that we all should have in mind whenever *any* newcomer comes to camp? Deliberate or not, the picture is very effective.

Safety and other weighty issues aside for the moment, I hope you enjoy this edition of the yearbook, and I'll be back next year with more.

**George H. Haas**
**Consulting Editor**, *Outdoor Life*

# PART 1

# KEY ISSUES FOR HUNTERS

# Guess Who's Coming to Deer Camp

*By Deborah Morris*

Kathy Etling still fumes when she recalls the first time she drew a much-coveted bighorn sheep license in Wyoming—then had to fight for the right to shoot the prize ram she sighted.

"This other hunter kept insisting that he'd 'put it down for me' if I missed, or if it ran," she said. "I told him I'd make my own shot, that I was the one with the license, but he wouldn't listen."

She added with obvious relish: "I dropped the ram from 400 yards with my first shot. But the point is that that guy would never have treated another man like that."

Sugar Ferris, owner of Bass'n Gal, a national women's fishing organization, tells her own story about how a male angler once reacted with open horror to news that she would be his partner during a pro bass tournament in Illinois.

"He turned deathly pale, then ran outside and threw up," she laughed. "He tried to convince the tournament director to let him 'trade' me for a male partner, then got sick again when he refused. Talk about feeling unwanted!"

Although recent years have seen more and more women successfully entering previously all-male environments—patrolling city streets in police cruisers, floating weightless at work in the space shuttle, serving military duty in the Middle East—many female hunters and anglers feel that they have to fight a

*Amid some rumbles, the barriers to those sacred bastions of outdoor tradition are tumbling down. You've come a long way . . .*
*Photograph by Tina Mucci*

constant battle to gain acceptance from their male counterparts.

Take the B.A.S.S. controversy that raged earlier this year. Although other pro bass circuits have welcomed and even encouraged female competitors, the prestigious Bass Anglers Sportsman's Society has never allowed women in the BASSMASTER tours. Still, few outside the sportfishing industry would have predicted the maelstrom of protests that followed the announcement in April 1990 that the BASSMASTER Tournament Trail would be open to women.

Some of the organization's top male pros immediately threatened to boycott the 1990–91 events; others presented a petition asking for a reversal of the ruling. Their objections to having women fish the circuit? There were many, but, oddly enough, few seemed to be the same.

Ray Scott, who wrote the original "men only" rules when he founded B.A.S.S. 23 years ago, insisted that the lack of private toilet facilities in the boats would threaten the "integrity of the rules" because contestants, once paired by random drawings, are required to stay within sight of each other. "If you're fishing with a lady," he said, "that's bound to be a problem."

Many male pros, however, shrugged off the bathroom issue. "That may be a genuine concern with some of the older 'Southern gentleman' types," said Shaw Grigsby, a pro angler from Gainesville, Florida, "but most of us have fished with women before on other circuits. The solution is as simple as turning your head, and that doesn't, in my mind, classify as a rule violation."

Other pros insisted that "family hardships" might result if their wives were left at the dock while they spent the day fishing with another woman. Some questioned whether they might unconsciously "hold back" in certain situations—rough water, bad weather and so on—to "protect" a female partner. But Rick Clunn, four-time winner of the BASSMASTER World Championship, called those objections "absurd."

"The women I've fished with have been as professional, if not *more* professional, than 80 percent of the men I've fished with," he said. "I've always promoted the idea that fishing has the ability to be one of the largest sports in existence; anybody—male or female, 16 or 60—can fish. Why should we limit ourselves, and our sport, by excluding female competitors?

"I suspect," Clunn added, "that the real issue is that some men don't want to risk being publicly beaten by a woman. And that, of course, could happen."

For pro anglers Linda England and Fredda Lee, the opening of B.A.S.S. provided a long-awaited opportunity to compete at the highest level of their profession—in "the big leagues," as Lee put it.

"On the women's circuit, second place earns $2,000 to $3,000," she explained. "But with the expenses involved—entry fees, gas, lodging, travel costs, equipment repairs—you can actually *lose* money if you're not careful.

"BASSMASTERS, on the other hand, pays second place winnings of $20,000 in the Invitationals alone, and it also provides the kind of national exposure that helps attract new sponsors. Needless to say, we were thrilled to finally have the chance to participate."

Lee and England paid their $600 registration fees, then bought maps, made hotel reservations, and rearranged their schedules to accommodate the six B.A.S.S. events that would occur over the next eight months.

What happened next left them stunned—and disgusted.

"We were at a Bass'n Gals tournament in Virginia," England recalled, "and one of our sponsors called us and said, 'I need to tell you something before you hear it on the news. B.A.S.S. just reversed their ruling; women won't be allowed to compete after all.' So just like that, we were out. I couldn't believe it."

B.A.S.S. chairman and chief executive officer Helen Sevier expressed disappointment in the landslide 441 to 133 decision by the all-male Association of B.A.S.S. Professionals to reinstate the ban on women. But, she added, "The mandate of the B.A.S.S. pros—the mainstay of our circuit—is clear. They do not want women to compete on the BASSMASTER Tournament Trail."

*Many women are accomplished bowhunters. Here, Linda Judson draws from her stand. Photograph by Richard P. Smith*

*Kathy Etling, a well-known hunter and angler as well as a respected outdoor writer, holds up her largemouth bass. Photograph by Bob Etling*

Where does this leave women in today's sport-fishing industry? "For now, stuck," admitted Norma Brand, a prominent angler on the Bass'n Gal and Lady Bass circuits. But, she added, B.A.S.S. is only part of the problem.

"Look through the fishing magazines sometime and try to find a single female face," she challenged. "There are an estimated 19 million female fishermen out here, but it's like we're invisible!"

Are women faring any better in the smaller but even more male-dominated hunting industry? Robert Jackson, professor of psychology at the University of Wisconsin in La Crosse, recently concluded an eight-year study of female deer hunters in Wisconsin, Iowa, and Washington.

"The hunting fraternity remains highly segregated," he observed. "There is still an element of sexism there: Many hunting clubs and deer camps either don't allow women to participate, or they restrict their participation to certain times."

But an interesting factor emerged during his study of bowhunting clubs in Wisconsin: While male-only organizations tended to show a steady decline in membership, clubs encouraging family participation were flourishing.

"They felt their longevity, their strength, came from involving the families," Jackson explained. "It had added a very positive aspect to their enjoyment of the sport."

Since the early 1980s, there has been an explosive growth in the ranks of women hunters, now estimated to number more than 1.5 million. In just five years—from 1980 to 1985—the number of female hunters

*Patricia Stewart with her hard-earned caribou, taken in Alaska. Photograph by Roger Stewart*

*Mother and daughter team Bonnie and Ashley Wilkinson pose proudly with their Texas whitetails. Photograph by Bill Wilkinson*

increased by more than 25 percent, compared with a scant 4 percent increase among men. However, with women still representing less than one-tenth of all hunters, the perception of hunting as a man's sport continues to present obstacles for women wishing to participate.

Elaine Kalmbacher, a hunter in Michigan's Upper Peninsula, has felt that in a very personal way. Although her husband is extremely supportive of her interest and participation in the sport, the group of men he often hunts with have made it clear that women aren't welcome in their deer camp.

"I think if it were up to him, he'd like to have me there," Kalmbacher said. "But as a guest, he's in an uncomfortable position. In the last 20 or 30 years, the other men have never invited any of their wives, so he'd feel awkward about being the exception. There's a lot of peer pressure in those situations."

Negative pressure can also come from nonhunters. Sheri Fraker, a Colorado bowhunter, said: "A lot of people still think it's not 'ladylike' to hunt. They say things like, 'Isn't it dangerous for women to go out into the woods alone?' or 'How can you actually *kill* something?' They think women should be nurturing; they don't understand the motivation behind a woman's involvement in the sport."

The "man's sport" perception crops up in other ways. Female hunters are frequently challenged at deer check stations and asked if they're tagging deer killed by their husbands—a question that would never be asked of a man, said Christine Thomas, associate professor at the University of Wisconsin's Stevens Point College of Natural Resources.

"They just automatically assume that a woman's game is suspect," she explained. "It never occurs to them to question whether a *man* might be tagging deer taken by his *wife!*"

Sometimes, male hunters also assume that women won't be able to keep up on long hikes or "pull their own weight" in packing out game. Madleine Kay, an accomplished handgunner and one of the world's top big-game hunters, deals with that concern by being direct with her male counterparts.

"I usually just tell them, 'Hey, I'm no lightweight. I can handle this,'" she said. "It's just a matter of proving yourself the first few times."

Some obstacles women encounter in pursuing their love of hunting are more on a practical level. The old feminine adage "I haven't a thing to wear" is a frustrating reality for female hunters today.

"Stores don't carry serious hunting clothes made to fit women," explained Annie Fabio, a hunter from Houston, Texas. "In one place I asked what they had for women and they just grinned and pointed—to a *man*. But wearing hand-me-downs from a husband or brother—pants that fall down, jackets that leak—makes it hard to enjoy a hunt."

Despite the difficulties, many women are drawn into the sport by the simple desire to share a unique, outdoor experience with a husband, friend, or child.

"We're seeing a growing number of single moms who are anxious to provide a rounded life experience for their children," said Jackson. "They value the natural setting and the companionship on a hunt, as well as the opportunity to learn and use basic hunting and survival skills.

"And where in times past, hunting was sometimes

seen as a disruptive influence in a marriage because of a husband's frequent absences," he added, "more and more couples are now sharing that passion—and growing closer because of it."

Female participation, Jackson said, could very well end up being the key to preserving the right to hunt in the face of growing opposition from the antihunting movement. He insists that the time has come not only to permit women to participate in hunting and fishing clubs and activities, but to actually recruit them.

"It's important to bring women into the fold, to let them become much more visible—especially in the hunting industry," Jackson said. "It's one very positive way to combat the macho 'bloodsport' image portrayed by antihunters, while at the same time actively strengthening family ties.

"We can't continue to perceive this as a man-only sport. If there's going to be a future in hunting, it probably won't be unless women are actively involved in it."

# "I Didn't Have My Figger on the Tringer"

*By Dennis Sandmeier*

In the yellowed newspaper clipping, the boy stands in his father's garage next to his first buck. The deer hangs head-down from the unseen rafters overhead. The newspaper photographer has just asked the boy to pull back on the buck's antlers to raise its head. In the icy light of the popping flashbulb, a hesitant half-smile freezes on the boy's face. That was my face 29 years ago, but the smile on it was no kind of smile at all; it was a confused, tormented expression that ironically resembled a smirk. This clipping has always arrested my progress whenever I've pawed through my files of old papers. For many years now, that hesitant half-smile has urged me to wonder, like Don Quixote, about righting unrightable wrongs.

I was 11 years old then and believed that doing things that men do qualifies the doer of these things as a man. I was only one of many boys in my school who believed similarly, and we hunted as much for access to the status of manhood as for joys of and in the field. Carrying a loaded gun and the responsibility that comes with it transformed us, albeit briefly, into men.

Through the fall, we swapped concoctions of hunting mythology and homely truth during recess on the grassy slope under the classroom windows. The bricks of the building oozed a dry warmth as we pressed our backs to the wall in the late morning sunshine to yarn the stories we'd experienced or only heard about, as well as some we hoped to experience or hear about but told anyway. To every one of these stories, however, a boy named Larry told a grand sequel. For every animal brought to bag, Larry had bagged its grandfather. For every firearm in our houses, Larry owned one in a larger caliber, more highly engraved, more accurate, deadlier. Larry the Liar. He never invited anyone to his home to violate his father's gun closet by hosting permissionless peeks at the fabled shootin' irons therein. The rest of us risked serious punishment to do this for friendship's sake and our own uncertain levels of credibility.

Yet Larry's arsenal had, reckoned through his own accounts, nearly exterminated most species of trophy-class game, in the Midwest. Never so much as hair, hoof, or horn of these behemoths and man-killers ever came to school with him, though some of us at times had offered up ringneck rooster tail feathers stuffed dartlike into an empty 12-gauge hull or an electric-green mallard head filched from the cleaning heap. Such a talisman sometimes charmed skeptics into believing a solemnly sworn scatter-gunning tale that had come down with a mild case of "the doubts."

*Illustrations by David Taylor*

Then I shot "the buck." In all of the years since the buck fell to our Marlin .32 Winchester Special, my family still refers to that particular animal whenever mention is made of "the buck." It had been a pathetic "bucks-only" season, and it was, mercifully, the last day of the season in the hottest November anyone we knew could remember in the Black Hills of South Dakota. The hills were dry; the breaks around the hills were dry; the prairie around the breaks was drier still—the deer loved it. I had secretly given up hope of even seeing a buck this season. The notion I would see one within range was laughable.

The oaks had shed drifts of leaves in the steep but shallow draw I had been directed to walk before we gave up for the morning to caucus at the cars for lunch and yet another plan for the afternoon. The sun, as if to compensate for the pre-dawn numbing my fingers and toes had taken, broiled the flesh of my arms and neck in the windless draw. Keeping the flow of corrosive sweat away from the blued steel of my rifle totally occupied my limited sense of purpose and consumed what energy wasn't demanded to crunch and stumble through dry leaves heaped deep as the Marlin's stock. Dust from the leaves mushroomed up from each footfall, creating a snufflike cloud that cleaved to sweaty skin in an itchy paste that, once scratched, burned like kerosene. A fiery semicircle of it sawed at the back of my neck under my woolen shirt collar.

The buck, old and no doubt a veteran of other such assaults, had been watching for just such a weak link in the approaching enemy line. He held his rush until I was too close to do anything other than stifle a dusty squeak as he boiled out of his cover and past me. Maybe I threw the rifle to my shoulder in an instinctive hunter's reaction to get a shot off. More likely after seeing so much horn at such close quarter, I shot in self-defense. Turning and ratcheting another round into the Marlin, I iron-sighted the deer's flashing tail easily enough. Just forward of it, among the various browns of trees, fallen leaves, and dead grasses, were those antlers. The second bullet, aimed directly at the deer instead of only toward it, stopped in the whitetail's spine, derailing his caboose. He buckled in the middle and augered into the bottom of the draw, dozing up a wave of leaves.

Approaching the spot where he went down took me many steps down the hunter's path I'd chosen to travel toward manhood. Drilling rabbits and gophers with a .22 had been a small step. Bird hunting with a 20-gauge shotgun had been another. In my boyish fantasies of big-game hunting, an animal died in quiet dignity once anchored by a single well-placed bullet from my rifle. If I took my time and did my part right, the .32 Special always punched a bunch of holes among the inner concentric circles on the paper animals I used as fantasy fuel. A boy doesn't imagine a mortal wound happening outside those concentric circles. No one tells a boy how long a great animal can hold to life while trying to regain its feet and sundered stride. No one prepares him for the necessity of taking aim at a forest king lying broken at his feet.

A boy may suspect, but he cannot know and when he does, he will draw his own conclusions in time. This was clearly what the two men who had heard my shots and found me were now waiting for. It was a different boy that fired this shot than the one who had deliriously aimed at an escaping trophy moments before. In the echoes of the second of three shots I fired that day, the buck was still. Respectful of his ebbing power and immense beauty, we stood to take a first clear look at the sheer size of him and the wonderful rack of horns he carried. This was truly the stuff that earns a hunting story's retelling rights.

The last one to find us at the bottom of the draw was Dad. Unmindful of the racket he was making, he hurried around the thicket of chokecherries the buck had lain in and saw the monstrous whitetail in the hands of experienced men who had begun to field-dress it. I was standing back, sheathed hunting knife on my belt, watching to see how this was done.

"Who got it?" Dad huffed.

"Dennis did," one of the kneeling men volunteered. I continued to watch and said nothing. Though I ached to shout my claim to the buck and tell Dad every detail at once, I coveted my grown-up brother Richard's casual dignity even more.

"No. Really. Who got him?"

"Dennis got him, Dad," my brother grinned, shrugging his shoulders with arms extended, palms up. "No kiddin'."

Dad's gaze focused momentarily on me, then on the buck, and then back again, an expression on his face unlike any I'd ever seen before—something I've come to understand only now that I have a son. Then, I simply, childishly, mistook it for surprise.

When the field-dressing was finished, two men tried to drag the carcass but barely budged it out of the bottom of the draw. Dad found a stout tree limb and lashed it through the deer's antlers with parachute cord. Four men working as a team behind the limb could drag the deer well enough. More than a mile separated us from our lunches in the cars, and it was long past lunch time. As

the smallest, I would not take a turn at dragging; I was designated rifle carrier. We stood talking in a circle waiting for the last cigarette to be ground into the bare spot of earth already cleared by Harley's boot toe. I had already set about checking the four additional rifles I was to carry lest one still had a chambered cartridge in it. I opened the action of each in turn to see. Having used each type of rifle often, my hands worked confidently.

It was Dad's boss' rifle that didn't respond properly to my confidence. When I lightly nudged the safety

GOOD-SIZED WHITETAIL — Eleven-year-old Dennis Sandmeier, 507 Meade St., bagged this deer, estimated to weigh about 200 pounds, while shooting near Crooked Oaks in Butte County. It was Sandmeier's first deer. Three other members of his hunting party failed to fill. (Journal Photo)

*"Every time I look at the yellowed newspaper clipping, I'm reminded of my first buck and a lost trust"—Dennis Sandmeier*

toward the "off" position, it grittily resisted. I thumbed it again, harder. With a stunning roar the .270 jumped almost out of my hands, and a spray of dirt and fine gravel leaped from the center of the circle. Tiny stones pattered down on my brother's boots and jeans as they arced back to earth among the leaves. Stupidly, I stared at the rifle pointed at the smoking hole in the soft ground. No one spoke as each of the hunters digested the shock. As my father and brother stepped toward me, someone muttered something about "buck fever," and I distinctly heard a soft but derisive voicing of the word "kid." Dad's eyes scoured me with scorn.

"What happened?" he demanded. The others turned back to the task of getting the buck to the car. It was only too clear to them what had happened. In just a few moments of self-conscious silence, they pulled the buck to the top of the draw and out of sight, leaving Dad, Richard, and me to deal privately with each other.

"Dad, I know how to unload a bolt-action rifle. I was going to push the safety off so I could clear the action. I wanted to be sure Albert hadn't left a shell in the chamber." Taking a long breath in an attempt to keep my voice under control, I said what I believed was the truth: "I pushed on the safety and the gun went off." Dad was far from even appearing to accept the possibility; convincing him was simply out of the question. Richard looked away, shamed by and for me. "Dad, honest! I didn't have my figger on the tringer at all!" That clinched it. Too shaken to even speak without getting my words tangled, I bit my lower lip, afraid I'd cry.

No one mentioned then, or ever, that observing the first rule of safe firearm handling had prevented my accident from turning into a tragedy. Although the rifle fired accidentally, it had been pointed in a safe direction. No matter. The glory in this day was gone. What else was said in the draw has always stayed there.

Monday morning's fractions lesson plodded obliviously past the limit of my endurance. Far from the sound of teacher's voice, I sat in the classroom suspended in yesterday's spoiled glory until recess. Sharp gusts of northerly wind cut at the corners of the building, but in the sunshine huddled near the school's warm south wall were eddies of calm air and excited boys conducting the business of exchanging the last fresh hunting tales of the season. I held my news like a pat poker hand until Larry had, with mock modesty, confessed to taking only one three-point buck on Sunday. He wouldn't have shot it, he told us, but he and his dad, having bagged nicer bucks earlier in the season, had been hunting together on his mom's unfilled tag hoping to get a real monster. But the time had run out on them too, and Larry took the buck rather than have an empty tag at sundown on the last day.

"I got a nice whitetail," I said. "I'll bring the antlers to school with me tomorrow. Bring yours, Lar." The news was out, but the details would have to wait. I needed those horns. Even though the newspaper photographer had come the night before, it would be "a few days before you'll see it in the paper," he'd said. Too long to wait. I'd have antlers tomorrow. Dad promised. Talk turned to other things quickly, yet one or two quizzical glances from Larry and my friends reminded me that this was serious. Larry's bluff, if that's what it was, was called: What would we show up with tomorrow?

The next day I showed up with horns; Larry with words. Teacher insisted I visit the other classrooms in school to show and tell. That evening I was interviewed by the local dean of sportsmen for broadcast on his nightly sportscast. The president and the Pope together could have done no more to sanction my bragging rights. Only those six who were there when the buck was ready to be dragged away knew I was unfit to be honored and totally unworthy of the attention I was being given.

The incident of the bullet from Albert's .270 ripping a gash in the dirt four feet in front of my brother was censored from every version of the story of "the buck" I ever heard. Seemingly, I alone worried at the scab the accident left on the memory of that day, and I picked at it as the awful injustice of it gradually healed over in a scar of acceptance: *In a moment of careless excitement I had come horribly close to committing the unthinkable.* The verdict, of course, was guilty. There seemed but one or two punishments that could fit my crime. I would either be left home next deer season, or I would be allowed to go but allowed to have neither gun nor license. In an agony of anxiety, I waited out Dad's decision. Wasn't it enough that the men whose good opinion of me mattered most were now so obviously and overtly safety conscious around me? Because this was a fair punishment in itself, it was bearable. But to be left home or denied the privilege of a license and a gun would be unbearable public humiliation.

As many months passed and preparations for next season were begun, it appeared that I was to get another chance. Waiting out my father's silence turned out to be the smallest part of the hard lesson I had to learn. I would come to know it was hopeless to try to fully regain a once-broken trust. It is a whiff of something rotting in the space that separates us from each other.

If it is a waste of time and energy to hate a thing that cannot respond to such intensity, then I wasted much of both hating Albert's rifle. That symbol of my sin followed me into the next season until one winter evening, Albert and I shivered in the cab of our pickup waiting for Dad. The truck was parked in a friend's field where we had a good view. To avoid fogging the windows, we kept them rolled down and took turns glassing the near hillside and clearing with binoculars. As dusk deepened, the pines closed ranks

around the snow-rutted road. In the last of the daylight, I passed the binoculars back to Albert and stepped out of the pickup to unload my rifle, which was leaning against the truck.

As I stood to stomp some circulation and feeling back into my legs and feet, I caught a glimpse of Dad trudging toward the truck past a blackened snag at the near edge of a burned-over clearing. After placing my empty rifle in the window rack, I scooted back into the cab. Albert got out and picked up his .270. I uncorked the coffee thermos and poured its plastic cap full of steaming black. Albert got back inside and hunkered over to unload before stowing his rifle in the rack. Dad pulled the pickup door open at the moment Albert pushed the rifle's safety off. With a flash and instantaneous concussive thunderclap, the .270 went off. The blast knocked Dad off balance, even though his right hand had caught the wheel to pull himself up and into the cab. He stumbled backward into the snow. My face and eyes stung from thousands of pinpricks. Smoke and dust whirled in the cab and many moments passed in which I heard nothing but an intense high-pitched whine. The bullet had punched a neat hole in the truck's top—an insurable loss. The muzzle blast punched a neat hole in the range of sounds audible to my right ear—a permanent loss. Albert took his rifle to a gunsmith the next day. The faulty safety catch was repaired.

In the yellowed newspaper clipping the boy still stands in his father's garage next to his first buck. The deer still hangs head-down from the unseen rafters overhead. There is a hesitant half-smile that is no kind of smile at all on both his face and mine. With a small "tick" the clipping drops from my hand to the bottom of the file folder held in an open V on my lap. Momentarily pushing awareness of futility and foolishness to the sidelines of consciousness, I wonder about righting unrightable wrongs and flip on through the remaining papers in the file, hoping to recognize what I was searching for in here in the first place. 🦌

# PART 2

# WHITETAIL DEER

# The Deer Jogger

*By Tom Huggler*

"**A**s I rounded the corner on the last leg of my six-mile run, I suddenly froze in my tracks. There, crossing the road at a fast walk about 70 yards in front of me, was the big buck I had been looking for. For several weeks on my daily jog, I had seen his huge tracks, the front hoofs of which were split wider than normal. One time during pheasant season, I got a good look at the buck. He was carrying 10 or 12 points with at least 20 inches between the main beams. Then, on the opening day of Michigan's gun deer season, I saw his tracks leading from a fresh bed near the road edge of an open weed field. Now, it was the second day of the season, and I was face to face with one of the biggest bucks of my life. An hour earlier, I had had a gun in my hands. I wished I hadn't traded it for running shoes."

That was how Jerry Westover of rural Otisville, Michigan, described a big neighborhood buck he had been hunting . . . and running for. When Westover saw the buck on the second day of hunting season, the animal was crossing a country gravel road a stone's throw from an elementary school where children played at recess. The buck seemed unconcerned, probably because he was used to such human noises. Three days later, Westover was hunting in the afternoon over a fresh snow. After finding the big buck's prints again, he tracked him for two miles—while the animal made a big circle—and finally jumped him from a grassy bed along a creek bottom. The big fellow

*For some, buck scouting is done in the woods. Jerry Westover puts on sneakers and runs the roads.*

was with a doe. The doe leaped into Westover's line of fire. He didn't shoot.

"Many hunters make the big mistake of figuring that a deer is gone for good once he's been jumped," Westover explained. "Too many times bucks have shown me a tail and then walked back to the same area where they were spooked. This one started back toward me, all right, but he caught my scent, turned, and made good his escape. By now it was nearly dark."

Determined more than ever to tag the buck, Westover returned the next morning and tracked him to a field with a low area in the center. After checking the field with his binoculars, he walked into it. As Westover neared the far side, the buck suddenly jumped up 40 yards away and Westover shot him on the run with a slug through the heart. The big 11-pointer sported 11-inch brow tines and a 20½-inch spread between main beams.

That was in 1987. Two years later, Westover shot two more bucks, including a bow-killed eight-pointer and a bruising 16-pointer taken with his shotgun. The 16-pointer scored 153⅛ nontypical Boone and Crockett Club points after deductions. And the jogger/hunter has seen bigger neighborhood deer, including a dandy 12 or 14-pointer with beams the size of a man's forearms and nearly 30 inches of air between them. Westover sees such deer on his daily 4 to 10-mile runs. He takes them by combining inside knowledge of their day-to-day movements and behavior with the skillful use of tactics such as stillhunting and stalking.

His unusual approach to deer hunting can be applied anywhere in the country by anyone who is healthy enough to run. And even by those who aren't.

I have known Jerry Westover, 40, since we went to high school together and ran on the same track and cross-country teams. We live less than two miles apart in rural southeastern Michigan, near Flint. Although I, too, know that big deer live in the area and have hunted for them occasionally, I have yet to spot a monster buck at point-blank range, with or without my shotgun. But Westover, who has been running since he was 14, sees them all the time. Maybe I should take up jogging, too.

The problem, for me and many other American sportsmen, is that we hate to exercise for the sake of exercise. Sure, we'll help a neighbor load hay bales onto the farm wagon; and some of us will cut our own firewood. You won't hear us complain about having to walk miles in the fall, as long as we're toting a gun or bow. But to my mind, a regimen of running holds as much appeal as a Marine boot camp in Georgia in July. Daily running rates right up there with push-ups, chin-ups, and toe-touchers. I hate it. Nor do I want to lace up the Reeboks every day to be a better hunter. On the other hand, I like to walk and occasionally ride a bike in the neighborhood or to my office a couple of miles from home. Westover says that if I took the back way instead of the state highway, I'd likely see more deer.

"I believe that, to be a good hunter, you have to

know your area," Westover explains. "And in order to know your area, you have to be there. When I run every day, I'm actually scouting deer—looking for their tracks and other signs—to figure out their daily patterns of movement. In farm country, deer may move two or three miles each night and up to several miles in a week. That's why I cover 16 sections [64 square miles] in a running schedule that repeats itself every week."

When Westover spots deer or their tracks, he often follows them to look for other evidence of behavior: feeding activity in crop fields, tufts of hair on barbed wire, and deer beds. He keeps a daily notebook of weather conditions, hunting pressure, crop-harvesting activities, and how these variables affect deer behavior. When and where do deer feed, for example? What causes them to move from one area to another, and what are their patterns of movement? The ability to interpret deer behavior is a big part of Westover's success once he swaps his warm-up suit for one of hunter orange.

He has learned, for example, that whitetail wanderings are fairly predictable throughout the year. They change greatly, however, during hunting season because of gunning pressure and the corresponding rut. Then, does and yearlings tend to hang around bean fields and cut cornfields rather than expose themselves in the middle of such open areas. He has learned that deer move little with an easterly wind, perhaps because most of their runways and trails are designed to take advantage of prevailing westerly winds. Why else does he see more deer, whether jogging or hunting, when the wind is westerly?

"Hunting deer anywhere, but especially in the farm country, is like putting together a big puzzle," Westover said. "You have to find all of the pieces, and the pieces can change daily. I have learned, for example, that deer grow more cautious when the air is humid, perhaps because the earth is inhaling and they can't smell as well. Everything I have read says that deer move a great deal before a storm, but I can't prove it by my experience. In my area, at least, deer don't move much at all before a storm."

Westover's third-shift job in an auto factory is ideal for his deer-hunting game plan. Throughout the year, he runs during daylight hours, but in hunting season he will typically jog in the late afternoon after a few midday hours of sleep. Upon arriving home from work each morning, he changes into hunting clothes and takes a stand in areas where he expects to see deer. "That first hour or two each morning is ideal," he explained, "because deer are moving from cornfields either to open fields or swales where they will loaf and bed down." Good spots for an ambush include two-track roads, power lines, and fencerows. Westover will also sit for a half-hour or so before dark to intercept deer moving from beds to feeding areas.

"I've sat all day enough times, while posting deer-crossing areas, to realize that 95 percent of the sightings are made during those twin periods of early morning and evening," he said. "I make every effort to blend into my surroundings. For example, I put a fence post or a tree to my back to break up my profile. When bowhunting, I choose stands in the crotch of trees so that I can shield myself against the tree when deer approach in my direction. I wear camouflage or darker colors to blend in, and I sit or stand absolutely still."

Like many other hunters, Westover used to be a confirmed sitter. He began hunting in 1961 but shot only four bucks during the next 17 years. In 1978, he started stillhunting—the art of walking slowly while following tracks or moving through an area that might hold deer. The first year, he shot a nice buck and saw several others, although they were mostly deer that had spotted him first. In recent years, his prowess as a stillhunter has improved. Instead of averaging only one buck sighted per season, Westover now sees three to five bucks that are within range of his bow or shotgun (rifles are not permitted in southern Michigan). During the 1984–1990 seasons, he killed nine bucks, including a pair of trophies. And, instead of taking the first buck that comes along, Westover now hunts for his buck of choice. Not surprisingly, it is an animal whose habits he knows intimately, thanks to his round-the-calendar scouting approach.

Westover's ability to sneak up on deer was the primary reason he tagged the 16-pointer in the fall of 1989. One Sunday during the second week of the gun season, Westover was dressed for church when he looked out of the bedroom window and spotted a huge buck walking with a doe through an open field on the other side of a swale. It was the same buck he had spotted at least twice before while jogging. The deer appeared to be heading toward some woods behind his house. Westover considered skipping church, but then decided to tell his 19-year-old son, Steve, who also hunts, about the big buck. But Steve was busy tinkering with his car and never chased the buck.

When Westover returned from church, he changed into hunting clothes and stillhunted his way through the swale, where he jumped a doe. The buck, however, was nowhere around. Later that afternoon, while watching a football game on television, Westover kept thinking about the big buck and wondering where he had gone. "I wanted to know if his tracks led into the woods," he said, "so I loaded my 12-gauge Smith & Wesson automatic shotgun with slugs and made a pass through the swale again, and then started across a cut cornfield onto the other side." Halfway through the field, he saw movement from bedded deer, one of which was toting hatrack headgear. Westover recognized it as the buck he had seen earlier.

The stillhunter changed into a stalker. Over the next 45 minutes, Westover crawled 150 yards on his belly while keeping a tree between him and his quarry. When he rose to his knees, the doe was just ambling off, but the buck was still in his bed about 100 yards away. Westover's first shot missed; the buck leaped to his feet, broadside to the hunter. A second slug caught

*According to the author, knowing your area well is important if you want to have a chance at a whitetail like this. Photograph by Marilyn Maring/Leonard Lee Rue Enterprises*

him in the heart and lungs, and the buck ran only 30 yards before falling over. Westover estimated the animal's dressed weight to be about 200 pounds. It topped more than 10 other deer to take first place in the *Woods-N-Waters News* big-buck contest for southern Michigan.

**W**estover believes that stalking is the hardest form of hunting deer, "because the animal has probably already seen you," he explained. "Stalking may require being able to crawl, patiently, and to know when to move with deer that may be traveling or feeding. It takes a lot out of you because you are constantly looking and listening and are tensely on guard. My daily running schedule helps keep me in shape."

One time, Westover was bending low under a limb when he spotted a doe staring at him. He held the awkward position, without flinching, for 10 minutes because startling the doe surely would have spooked a buck that might have been with her. On another occasion, he stalked a spikehorn for nearly four hours. Twice, the deer ran off for 50 yards or so, with Westover in pursuit. When the deer slowed down, the stalker slowed down. When the deer stopped to browse, Westover sat down and waited. Eventually, the spikehorn walked back, and Westover shot him at 30 yards.

Another tip Westover gives is to thoroughly hunt the area you think might hold deer. Many times as he has approached the end of a thicket or swale, he has thought, "Well, there's no deer here," only to kick out one or more.

On the other hand, Westover will sometimes deliberately make loud noises to spook deer from a thick area. While skirting the edge of dense cattails, for example, he may stamp his feet or holler to make deer stand up. If they flee, he follows them. Hunting in a strong wind is another condition when deliberate noise may rout deer into exposing themselves. In suburban and rural areas, where deer are used to the noises of civilization, they can be doubly tough to hunt because they easily disappear into available cover. However, this little trick can sometimes turn the odds in a hunter's favor.

"I believe that deer are easier to hunt in northern forested areas that are more remote," Westover said, "There, you can take a stand and, sooner or later, deer will go by. But in farm country, you are on your own— unless you organize deer drives—and the most successful way to hunt is to know your cover and the individual deer. That takes time and effort." Because farmland deer cover a larger area than most deep-woods whitetails, they might show up in the same place only once each week.

"In Michigan, and I believe in many other states, hunters each season shoot only one-quarter to one-third of the available deer," he said. "When I realized that, I began to hunt harder."

Running, walking and riding bicycles are natural ways for many Americans to exercise. Those activities could also help you to score on a big buck.

*Illustration by David Taylor*

# Cut and Slash Whitetails

*By Joel S. Fawcett*

It was still dark when Earl Rudderham of Bras d'Or Lake Outfitters in Boisdale, Cape Breton, Nova Scotia, pulled his pickup truck off the abandoned logging road.

"This is perhaps as far as we ought to go in the pickup," Earl remarked. "About a quarter-mile down the road there's a small clear-cut, but if we drive any closer, we'll make a lot of racket and more than likely spook any deer that are out in the logging slash. I think that the best way to hunt the cut is to follow this survey trail that's marked by orange spots, and it'll bring you to the top of the cutting.

"Once there, you can skulk along the edge of the clearing, or you might want to find a good vantage point amidst some cover and sit in ambush for a while just after daybreak. There are also several skidder roads leading to the cutting that receive some heavy deer traffic that you may want to investigate. I'll be here at the pickup to help drag out your big buck," he concluded with a grin.

After about a 100-yard hike into the woods, I came to the old logging operation, made myself comfortable on a stump, and waited for daylight. In a distance, a great horned owl hooted, and a few minutes later, closer by, a red squirrel chattered. Then I heard the echo of a lone rifle shot from down in the valley. Shooting light had come to the Boisdale hills.

Before moving, I examined the logging slash carefully with both my naked eyes and a $5\times$ monocular. I spotted four deer—two does, a fawn, and a six-point buck. I raised my Winchester Model 70 in .308, placed the crosshairs of the 2¾ Widefield scope in back of the buck's shoulder, and then slowly lowered the gun.

"Perhaps I'll regret this," I mused to myself, "but I'm going to wait and see if I can't line my sights up on a super buck."

Slowly and quietly, one step at a time, I crept along just inside the forest border and out of sight of the sharp-eyed whitetails out in the cutting. For a while I hunted without further incident. Then, about halfway down the cutting, I came upon a spot where a skidder road entered the clearing. There the area was so pockmarked with tracks that it resembled a sheep pasture, and piles of fresh droppings were everywhere. The road just looked too good to pass up.

A short distance down the lumbering trail, I came upon a debarked and broken sparring sapling, and nearby I spotted a "horning" tree and a recently worked scrape. Suddenly, I heard brush cracking in the woods off to one side of the skidder road. I waited expectantly, gun at the ready, and very shortly a fat and saucy doe accompanied by a husky eight-point buck stepped into the trail. I quickly shouldered my gun, released the safety, settled the scope crosshairs in back of the buck's shoulder, and touched off a shot. Both deer exploded out of there like NFL wide receivers on fly patterns. But after about three jumps, the buck faltered in midstride, stumbled, and skidded on his nose. My Nova Scotia deer season was history.

I was elated but not surprised. Over the years, logging slashes and their connecting network of skidder or tote roads have produced a goodly number of deer for the Fawcett freezer. One reason for this is that abandoned logging operations provide perhaps the most fertile whitetail real estate found in the North Woods. What's more, all of the logging companies that I've come in contact with have been very obliging in allowing me to hunt their lands at no cost or for a negligible fee. Most simply ask hunters to stay out of currently posted logging operation areas.

Despite all this, I have been known to curse, sometimes quite violently, when a logging company bulldozes new roads and provides easy access into some of my favorite remote fishing waters or game covers. I must admit, however, that such practices do improve the game habitat substantially.

A few years after being cut, a forest will begin to regenerate. An abundance of saplings and other browse will spring up, and this will, in turn, provide considerably more fertile forage and cover than the old mature stand of timber offered. A deer herd with a plethora of winter browse will come through the hard months with fewer losses from malnutrition, disease, predation, and fawn deaths. Therefore, the size of the herd will likely increase and its condition will improve after a logging operation is completed.

Back in the "good old days," pulp and lumber operations were conducted with horse and ox-drawn equipment, crosscut saws, and axes. At that time, logging companies practiced selective cutting—they just cut trees 5 inches or more in diameter and left the smaller trees to grow. Most logging operations were conducted near waterways, and when ice-out and the spring freshets occurred, the logs were floated to the mills via river drives.

With the development of mechanized equipment, the river drives were abandoned and all-weather roads were bulldozed into remote areas of the North Country. For a while, logging operators continued to employ selective-cutting methods, but recently most logging companies have switched to clear-cutting techniques, which call for everything in a tract of land to be taken and utilized. The slash, small trees, and low-quality wood are put through the chipper right on location at the cut.

In my opinion, selective cutting or small clear-cuts 10 acres or less in size benefit deer much more than extensive clear cuts, some of which can be several miles across. In large clear-cuts, unless they are reseeded, it often takes a decade or more before the effects of natural reforestation can be observed. Near my home in Down East Maine, there are mammoth clear-cuts that were logged at least 15 years ago and that are just now beginning to provide a smattering of deer browse. The new forage is attractive to the deer,

*Bucks can often be caught feeding or rutting in and around abandoned logging operations. Photograph by Charles J. Alsheimer*

but the lack of cover tends to make the deer apprehensive.

Whitetails are animals of the edges, and they're not very comfortable out in the open far from the thickets. What little browsing they do engage in out in these wide-open clearings is likely to be conducted under the cover of darkness, and even on a dark night rarely will they be more than a few jumps from the bordering woods. Therefore, about the only worthwhile time to hunt a large clear-cut is during the last hour of shooting light in the afternoon and the first hours of daylight in the morning.

In selective-cutting and small clear-cut operations, the slash is often left in the woods. The green tops and branches provide a prolific source of succulent and nutritious forage, and this, of course, draws the deer like a magnet. Thus, it pays for the whitetail hunter to keep abreast of recently abandoned logging operations. Such locations are excellent sites to erect stands, particularly for early morning and late afternoon use.

Probably the best way to hunt a cutting during its green-slash and reforestation stages is to combine stand and stillhunting techniques. A ground blind or tree stand situated where you can view the most heavily trafficked portions of the cutting will be invaluable for early morning and late afternoon hunting, though stillhunting through the thick stuff will likely be more effective during the midday hours. Stands should, of course, be well-concealed or camouflaged because approaching deer will be able to spot and avoid an easily visible stand in or near these openings.

I spent 18 years as a registered Maine guide, and on a number of occasions, my clients left the concealed stands where I had left them. When I returned to pick them up, I'd more often than not find my sports sitting out in the open on a stump where they could get a clear view of the entire slash area. And they could never understand why they hadn't spotted any game, when I'd reported observing an abundance of deer in the same cutting on pre-hunt scouting expeditions.

A year after a cutting, the tops and limbs of the felled trees will have dried out and turned brown, and the logging slash will not be as bountiful a dining area as it was the previous year. Many hunters abandon a logging slash at this time, and that, I can assure you, is a big mistake. The reason is that, though the food value of the area may have dissipated, the site will likely have become a popular cover area for the deer herd. The bone-dry slash will be noisy underfoot, making it almost impossible for a hunter or predator to approach unannounced, and deer will readily bed in these areas for just this reason.

One way to hunt a year-old logging slash successfully is to find a good vantage point—perhaps the tree stand you used the previous season—where you can eyeball a good portion of the slash and sit and wait for the game to come to you. Another effective tactic, providing you have an adequate number of hunters in your party, is to post several hunters around the perimeter of the cutting on known escape routes and then to send a couple of drivers crashing their way through the noisy slash. It won't take much of this sort of commotion to spook any bedded deer to the hunters in the stands.

A few years after an area has been cut, small saplings, grasses, and other vegetation will burgeon, and the natural reforestation process will have begun. This, of course, will again make the logging slash a choice dining spot for deer. Also by this time, the deer herd will have made a network of worn and gullied thoroughfares crisscrossing the logging slash. By sticking to these trails, a careful hunter can now still-hunt the cutting quietly.

I recall not long ago stillhunting my way along a heavily trafficked deer trail that meandered through an area of dry logging slash near my home in Grand Lake Stream, Maine. It was about a week into the season, but the weather had been unseasonably mild, and the deer were not moving. That's why I had decided to hunt the bluff, which was a small knoll that had been lumbered off a few years earlier and was bordered on all sides by a dense cedar swamp. Early and late in the day, I reasoned, the deer might be out feeding on the young evergreen browse.

At dawn I entered the cutting along a main game trail and then proceeded at a snail's pace through the cutting. Twice I heard brush popping out in the swamp, but whatever was making the noise moved away from me. Then, about an hour into the hunt, I picked up the unmistakable sound of an approaching deer. Unfortunately, there was a pile of slash perhaps 8 feet high between us. Several times I caught brief glimpses of the deer through the slash, but there was no reasonable opportunity for a shot. I waited, not moving, gun at the ready, and finally my patience was rewarded: A seven-point buck poked his head and shoulder around the end of the slash pile. A few minutes later, I was attaching my tag to the husky beast.

Sometimes lumber crews, instead of making one mammoth clear-cut, will make several smaller cuts divided by strips of undersized saplings in between. Whenever I discover one of these logging operations, my eyes light up in anticipation. In this situation, the whitetails will often be found out in the slash feeding during the late afternoon, at night, and in the early morning; and they'll spend the midday hours bedded down or checking their scrapes in the patches of cover.

If there are several hunters in your group, these strips of unharvested trees are choice spots to drive. Station one or more hunters, depending upon the strip's length, on each side of the patch to be driven. Then, starting at one end, the drivers can spread out and advance through the strip. When jumped, the deer will likely flee across the slash, giving the waiting hunters excellent opportunities to fill their tags.

Usually I hunt alone; therefore, I frequently spend my midday hours stillhunting my way through these strips of cover. The skulking whitetails don't like to

*Several-year-old slashes are good for glassing early and late and for stillhunting during midday. Photograph by Ralph P. Stuart*

expose themselves in the open slash, and therefore they tend to hold pretty tight, and I'm often able to approach quite close to the hiding whitetails before they spook. If the cover is fairly open, I may be able to tumble a buck while he's still amidst the trees. If I jump a deer in thick growth, though, I make my way post haste to the edge of the cutting, where chances are good that I'll get an open shot before the deer reaches the other side of the clearing.

During the 1989 season, while hunting out of Loon Bay Lodge in St. Stephen, New Brunswick, my guide, Mel Weeks, put me into an old logging slash that had been cut using the strip method. The first morning, while stillhunting one of the slash areas, I caught sight of a humongous buck moseying through one of the unharvested strips of cover. Unfortunately, the impenetrable thicket of alders and jack pines didn't allow me to take an unobstructed poke at the buck before he had passed out of sight.

Two more times during the five-day hunt I jumped the king-size buck, but he always kept to the jungles of heavy cover where I had no chance for a shot. I also pushed out 11 other whitetails in the process, and though each offered me good shot opportunities, I had already eyeballed the jumbo buck and knew that no other deer would satisfy me. As it ended up, the old patriarch outsmarted me, but I went home empty-handed with no regrets.

Over the years, logging slashes have yielded an abundance of whitetails to my gun, but even more productive have been the skidder and tote roads leading to the cuttings. Throughout the whitetail's range, there are few, if any, forest lands that haven't been harvested at least once. Thus, practically all of the prime whitetail woodland real estate of North America is crisscrossed with tote or skidder roads; these roads not only make for superb still-hunting paths or trail-watching posts but also form the backbone of the network of thoroughfares over which deer travel in dense cover. Some of these roads connect small clear-cuts; others lead to yarding areas; and in selective-cutting operations, these roads are byways to harvest locations back on remote conifer ridges. Other heavily trafficked game trails often cross or join the tote and skidder roads, too. Consequently, these logging trails offer the best, and frequently the only, opportunities to harvest heavy-racked bucks back in the bush.

You'll never find a buck scrape out in a clear-cut, but tote and skidder trails are often teeming with scrapes, "horning" trees, and sparring saplings. In addition, though whitetails are not likely to be found in an open cutting except very early or late in the day, they often travel the tote and skidder trails at all hours.

Most nimrods who are hunting abandoned logging operation areas tend to erect their stands at sites that overlook clear-cut areas; but when I was a guide, my most productive stands were located along tote and skidder roads. My prime stand locations were either in the vicinity of a major buck scrape, where a winter tote road crossed a swamp or bog, handy to where a heavily-used deer thoroughfare crossed a tote or skidder road, or were near where a skidder road accessed a clear-cut.

Back when I was a working guide, my *most* productive stand overlooked a site that boasted several of these features. From that stand, my clients could command a view of a tote road swamp crossing and several scrapes as well as a major whitetail thoroughfare that bisected the tote road at that point. There were no mature trees in the area, so downwind of the prevailing northwesterly breezes, I'd made a simple ground stand out of conifer saplings to screen my sports. The only access to the area was by water; and I marked a trail from the lakeshore to the stand, making sure that the hunters wouldn't cross the tote road or the main deer trail and leave deer-spooking scent. Over a period of five years, a buck was taken from that site annually. Included in the harvest was one bruiser that weighed 187 pounds, another that dressed-out at 204 pounds, and a third that tipped the scales at 211 pounds.

Occasionally, I may hunt from a stand during the first and last hour of shooting light; but if conditions permit, I prefer to pussy foot my way through the woods, pausing after each step to inspect the cover in all directions from both a standing and a kneeling position. I don't hike through much territory in a day's hunt, but when I eyeball a buck, he's more often than not serenely standing or walking slowly and offering an opportunity for an easy shot. Sometimes I may slowly stillhunt my way randomly through stands of mature timber, if they're at least somewhat open, but most of the time I hunt the dense conifer woods. The best way, and often the only way, to hunt quietly and effectively through these usually impregnable thickets is to stick to the tote and skidder roads.

How does one go about locating abandoned logging operations in unknown country? To my knowledge, there are no maps that show many of the infinite number of tote and skidder roads that lace the North Country. However, as a starting point, you can find a few logging roads on government topographic maps; and, for a small fee, some logging companies have maps available of their gravel roads and logging operations. Aerial maps will, of course, show some of the more recent logging operations, too. Surprisingly, many of the old tote roads that were in use prior to 1941—they'll be on topographic maps that were surveyed prior to that year—are still relatively clear of debris and receive heavy deer traffic today.

In 1988, I took a 226-pound eight-point buck on one of these ancient lumbering trails. It was the third week of November, the peak of the rut in Maine, and I was skulking along a tote road bordered on one side by a cedar swamp and on the other by a forest of black growth. Suddenly, about 8 A.M., I heard shell ice breaking out in the swamp. I waited, but the animal, just out of sight, remained in the heavy cover. It didn't appear that it was going to come out on its own, so on a hunch I took out my grunt call and blew on it four or five times. That got the critter's immediate attention, and the animal headed my way post haste, snapping and popping brush as it came. Shortly thereafter, I spotted antlers moving through the alders, and then into an open glen stepped the huge buck. I was less than one mile from the lake shore, but it took until dark to drag the heavyweight deer out to my canoe.

The best way, in my opinion, to find these old logging operations is to ride the backcountry-woods roads, until you spot an old lumbering byway that joins the road that you're traveling on. Or, to find primitive tote roads, I just paddle or outboard slowly down a river or lake that has a history of hosting log drives until I come to an old yarding area. This latter strategy is the one that I use to locate remote tote roads that, due to more difficult water access, are not likely to be hunted by anybody but myself. Here in the North Country, most deer hunters don't seem to be very eager to cross a lake or cruise down a river before daylight in November, anyway. In 30-plus years of hunting Maine tote roads in this manner, I've only met one other hunter in the woods.

Another happening that results in an area similar to that left by a logging operation is a forest fire. At first, a fire-ravaged area appears to be devastated and barren and very few species of wildlife inhabit the burn, but in a few years, grasses, saplings, and other deer browse sprout. When this occurs, deer move into the burn edges in low-light situations to forage. Then, in a surprisingly short while, the conifer saplings grow high enough to provide cover, and the burn becomes a popular deer bedding area, too. It takes very little cover to screen a deer—even a big buck—from a passing hunter.

Similar to a cutting, a burn, in the early reforestation stages, is best hunted in lowlight situations from a camouflaged stand where the hunter can either survey areas of prime deer browse or overlook a heavily traveled access trail. Later, after sufficient cover has been produced, a burn is best hunted with a combination of stand hunting early and late in the day and stillhunting during the midday siesta hours. Keep in mind that in October and November whitetails have a propensity for bedding in areas of a burn that have a southern exposure so they can take advantage of the warm midday sun.

I've been hunting whitetails for more than 40 years, and I'd estimate that at least 75 percent of the deer I've shot and seen have been in tote and skidder roads, logging slashes, forest fire burns, and covers bordering each of these. In my opinion, there's no more fertile whitetail real estate, especially for monster bucks, to be found in North America.

# Racks in the Rain

*By Gary Clancy*

What is the word on deer hunting in the rain? For as long as I can recall, older hunters and outdoor writers have been preaching the same gospel when it comes to hunting deer in the rain. Hunting is good and deer are active in a drizzle, but deer seek thick cover and remain inactive during hard showers, and all hunters with an IQ above 10 do the same. Well, if you will forgive my pun, that advice is all wet.

I have spent enough rainy days in the woods to convince myself of three givens when it comes to hunting deer in the rain. The first is that deer do not suffer any discomfort in the rain. The second is that deer are almost always active on rainy days. And the third is that hunters who stay in camp when it's raining are missing the boat.

One problem is that we hunters tend to judge an animal's comfort zones by our own. If we are cold, we assume the deer are cold. If we are wet and miserable, we wrongly assume that the deer are also wet and miserable. But nature doesn't work that way. The nervous system of a whitetail deer is not like our own. Deer are not programmed to seek "comfort." Instead, deer *adapt* to changing weather conditions and go on about their business. If they didn't, and simply sought protection from the elements every time it rained, snowed, or got too warm, they would quickly starve to death.

I say that deer are *almost* always active on rainy days because there are conditions that can accompany rain that will definitely cause deer to severely curtail all movement. Wind is the most common culprit.

Whitetail deer depend most upon their senses of sight, smell, and hearing to survive. Wind interferes with all three senses, making it difficult for deer to detect danger, and thus transforming an already high-strung creature into a real basket case. It doesn't make any difference whether the wind is accompanied by rain or not; deer will move as little as possible during strong winds.

I cannot say how deer react to violent thunderstorms. The reason for this is that during 30 years of tromping around the places where deer live, I've seen a couple of hundred trees that have been struck by lightning. Any force that can split a sturdy oak from crown to trunk has *my* respect, and when forks of lightning begin stabbing at the ridges, I get out of the woods.

I am tempted to climb out on a literary limb and proclaim that, in my estimation, deer are more active on rainy days than they are on days when it is not raining. Indeed, my hunter's log, in which I record all of the pertinent facts of each day's hunt, including the hours hunted and number of deer sighted, backs up that claim. But I have a hunch that the reason I see more deer per hour hunted on rainy days is not solely because the deer are more active, but rather because of my preferred hunting style on rainy days. Conditions for stillhunting are never better than when it is raining. An excellent example of how productive this

wet-weather technique can be was a recent hunt that I enjoyed.

Sometime before the alarm clock rang, I had awakened to the sound of water pouring off the roof of our comfortable cottage at Callaway Gardens in west-central Georgia. I wasn't surprised. It had rained most of the previous day and had still been coming down hard when we had called it a night. By the time the coffee was ready, I had my game plan for the morning figured out. I planned to sit on stand for the first hour of the morning, and then, just as soon as it was light enough to see well, I'd make my way to a particularly long, narrow ridge where the previous afternoon I'd found a dozen whitetails—including two bucks that I'd elected to pass up—busy feeding on a bumper crop of acorns and hickory nuts. I was betting that the deer would be in the same pattern the following morning.

My host, Bill Jordan, wrestled the Suburban down a slick, Georgia-red-clay two-track and dropped me off in the bottom of a hollow.

"I'll pick you up here at 11:30," Bill said as I slid out the door. "Good luck, now."

It never does get full-light on rainy days. It seems to me that daylight just sort of oozes out of the wet blackness, and then you suddenly realize that it's as bright as it's going to get. That particular morning, I had been on stand less than an hour when I came to the realization that it wasn't going to get any lighter. I climbed down from the stand, removed the sling from my rifle—as is my habit when stillhunting—and began the long climb to the top of the ridge.

Near the crest of the ridge I spotted movement. Through my binoculars, I could see that what I originally thought was a doe was really a spike. I waited for the little buck to feed over the crest and then continued my slow ascent.

Conditions were ideal. The rain was coming straight down—heavy at times, then letting up to little more than a drizzle at others. Occasionally, patches of misty fog drifted over the rolling Georgia hills, cutting visibility down to a few yards.

Two hours later I came to a place where a saddle of loblolly pine cut through the hardwood ridge. Bill had erected a ladder stand at the edge formed by the pines and hardwoods, and I stood beneath the platform for long minutes using the binoculars to pry into the dark recesses of the thick stand of trees. A flicker of white caught my attention, and I trained the glasses on the location where I had seen the movement. Again I saw the flash of white, and this time I recognized it as the upturned tail of a deer.

For 20 minutes, I stood under the stand and

*When it rains, stillhunting in known feeding and rutting areas may cause a close encounter with a wet buck. Photograph by Charles J. Alsheimer*

searched for more movement, but there was none. The deer, I was sure, had moved out of the pines and into the hardwoods on the far side of the saddle. I knew that if the other deer were feeding where I expected them to be, I would be close when I crested the ridge. So, to be as quiet as possible, I took off my raingear and proceeded at a crawl—literally.

Fifteen minutes later, I was on my hands and knees covering the last few yards to gain a view of the north slope of the hardwoods. As the slope came into sight, I dropped to my belly and scanned the bleak forest before me. Nothing moved. I reached inside my jacket and pulled out the binoculars. Eighty yards away a doe stepped from a clump of brush and began to feed up the slope. Three more does followed, then a five-point buck, and then another doe. Feeding slowly, as deer tend to do in the rain, the herd took a half-hour to drop over the far side of the ridge and out of sight. I stood up slowly, stretching cramped muscles and debating whether to move on or stay put for a while. A hunch told me to sit tight. I'm glad I did.

A few minutes later, a doe, followed by a very respectable eight-point buck, exited a little draw at the bottom of the slope and began to slowly feed uphill. I put the scope on the buck and studied him carefully. Slightly wider than his ears, the buck's light-colored rack sported short brow tines, but long curved, symmetrical main tines. My mind raced back a week to a hunt in another state when I would have given a week's pay to have seen such a buck. I don't consider myself a trophy hunter, but Bill Jordan had convinced me that the property we were hunting held some real monster bucks. To back up his claim he had shown me a dozen mounts of bucks he had taken from the same hills during the past 10 years. From the 163-point typical down to the "smallest" 10-pointer, they were all beautiful bucks. And the buck that I was scoping was one that in another year should fit in that category. I elected not to take him.

Suddenly the buck and doe both turned and stood staring intently down the hill in the direction from which they had come. When the eight-pointer tucked his tail between his legs and hunch-backed his way slowly up the ridge—a sure sign that a buck higher up in the pecking order was approaching—I knew that I had made the right decision.

Slowly, I wiped both lenses of my scope free of rain and snuggled into the stock while at the same time peering over the top of the scope in the direction that the eight-pointer had been staring. A doe showed first, and then behind her I caught the first show of butter-yellow antlers against the backdrop of wet, black timber. I didn't have to look twice at the heavy nine-point rack to know that this was the buck I had traveled 1,500 miles south to find. When the big bruiser stepped into the clear behind the doe, I touched the trigger and the buck crumpled.

Without the rain, which allowed me to quietly sneak into position on that hardwood ridge, I'm convinced that I never would have seen that buck.

A word of caution about stillhunting in the rain. Many hunters tend to move much too fast when attempting to stillhunt on rainy days. A quick pace is tempting, of course, because of the ease with which you can move silently through damp cover, but though you will certainly be rewarded with a look at more country, I guarantee that you will also be looking at far fewer deer than will the hunter who proceeds slowly. When stillhunting in the rain, I make a conscious effort to move at the same snail's pace that I use when hunting under less ideal conditions. Although it is true that you can move quickly without making alarming sounds when it is raining, whitetail deer are so well-adapted for motion perception that you will rarely escape visual detection when hurrying the hunt.

There are three reasons hunters who venture out in the rain will so often find deer actively feeding during the hours we normally associate with daytime bedding periods.

The first—and most important—reason can be attributed to the type of weather that so often follows a rainy period during the fall of the year. I am speaking of a cold front. Very often when the rain tapers off, it is followed by plenty of wind, a wind-direction switch to the northwest, and high blue skies. Whitetail deer have an excellent internal weather forecasting system that rarely fails them. Because wind, more than any other weather condition, prevents deer from feeding on schedule, whitetails tend to chow down during the rain so that they can go into the windy, cold-front period with a full belly.

The second reason there is often an increase in deer activity on rainy days is because there is a lack of hunting pressure on such days. Simply put: Most hunters don't like to hunt in the rain. Whitetail deer are quick to react to the respite from human intrusion and slip back into their normal routines, which include periods of feeding in late morning and early afternoon.

Yet a third reason hunters will find deer feeding during rainy periods can be traced to the whitetail's well-documented penchant for being most active during periods of poor light. Under normal conditions, this translates into active periods occurring around dusk and dawn. But when it's raining, skies never totally brighten. Deer are comfortable and relaxed under these conditions because their specially structured eyes allow them to see splendidly under what we humans would term poor visibility conditions.

I should also mention that your chances of finding deer feeding at midday in the rain increase in direct proportion to the availability of preferred whitetail fodder at that particular time. For example, in my home stomping grounds of southeastern Minnesota, the deer depend heavily on the acorns of the red and especially the white oak. The best midday hunting in the rain occurs during those years when there is a poor mast crop. It simply takes a deer longer to get its fill in years when acorns do not litter the ground.

From what I've seen, rain does not interfere with a buck's main objective in life: propagation of the species. I have never seen any indication that soggy skies have dampened a buck's enthusiasm for sex. And because it is the doe—and not the buck—that determines when the breeding actually takes place, it is probably safe to assume that nature has not instilled in the female of the species any anti-estrous switch that is tripped by moisture. When a doe enters that 24-hour period during which she is capable of conceiving, you can bet that a buck will try to find her, rain or shine!

On the same morning that I took the big nine-pointer in Georgia, Bill Jordan was occupying a stand overlooking a string of scrapes. The rut was winding down, but Bill had spied a huge 10-point buck working the scrapes earlier in the week, and he was determined to get a shot at the big deer. His determination paid off on that dripping, dreary morning when the big boy came chasing a doe within just a few yards of where Bill was perched. Unfortunately, when Bill tried to get his crosshairs on the moving buck, he discovered that his scope had fogged up during the wet morning vigil. The buck disappeared into the drenched timber, hot on the doe's tail.

The most miserable day I have ever spent in the rain while deer hunting is also vivid testimony that precipitation does not interfere with the rut.

It was mid-November in a northern state, and though it should have been snowing in earnest, it was instead pouring down rain mixed with sloppy flakes of snow and occasional barrages of sleet. I must admit that I thought twice about getting out of bed that morning, but I had drawn a coveted bowhunting permit to hunt a restricted state area with a reputation for harboring some real buster bucks. I had seen a couple of dandy whitetails during the first three days of the hunt, but I had been unable to get a shot. That miserable day was my last chance.

I put my portable stand up in the spreading branches of a twisted maple tree on the southwestern corner of a rectangular-shaped, 40-acre chunk of extremely thick second-growth timber. Most of the buck activity I had witnessed during the previous three days had seemed to be centered around that parcel of woods.

This was back a few years, before I had splurged on a set of quality raingear. And, by the time it got light enough to make out individual trees in the woods, I could already feel the cold dampness around my shoulders and back. By 9 A.M. I had not seen a deer, and I was ready to call it quits; but as so often happens at such times, it was then that a buck made his appearance. He was herding a reluctant doe out of the dark timber and into the belly-high grass on the edge of the woods. At more than 300 pounds with a neck so swollen that his head appeared too small for the rest of his frame, that buck was absolutely magnificent. Just before the doe completed her circle in the grass and took the buck back into the timber, I got the glasses on

him. I heard myself suck wind as the rack came into focus through the rain-splattered lenses. All thoughts of abandoning the stand vanished.

Twice more through the long vigil in that maple, I saw the huge buck. Once the same doe, or perhaps another, brought him out into the grass where the pair had circled earlier; and again in midafternoon, the buck appeared with a small herd of does and fawns on the edge of the timber. When a smaller buck approached, the big boy lowered his head, laid back his ears, and uttered a low, guttural grunt, causing the subordinate eight-pointer to duck quickly back into the woods. Each time the big boy showed, I hoped that a doe would lead him closer to my tree, but he never came closer than a tantalizing 80 yards before melting back into the timber.

Throughout the day, I fought the urge to climb down from the tree and try to sneak in on the buck, even though I was sure that I could move quietly enough. I also knew, from having scouted the woods thoroughly before the season, that my chances of getting an arrow through the thick underbrush were near zero. I hunkered deeper into the ineffective raingear, shivering uncontrollably. My only thought was to hold out for the last hour and hope for one last opportunity at the giant buck.

My chance came while the rain poured down during the last minutes of shooting light. One minute I was staring at an empty field of sopping wet grass, and the next I was watching the buck shaking the water from his heavy coat like my Lab does after retrieving a duck. I didn't notice the doe at first, as she blended in well with the wet grass, and the rain and hour made it difficult to see. When I did pick her out, my heart jumped to my throat and my hand moved slowly for the bow hanging on a broken limb. The doe was walking my way. Surely, the buck would follow.

He did, quickly catching up with the doe and falling into step just behind her, his black nose only inches from her tail. Through the monotonous drone of falling rain, I could hear him grunt with nearly every step. Eighty yards, 60, 50, and the doe stayed right on line. My numb fingers tightened on the arrow nock. At 40 yards the doe stopped and the buck stepped up alongside her. I don't know what he whispered in her ear, but she must not have cared for the idea. She squirted away from the buck, not running flat out, but prancing in that easy manner with which whitetails cover ground in a hurry. In an instant the buck was on her trail. When he passed at 30 yards, I made my draw and released.

Maybe the long vigil in the cold rain had made it impossible for my muscles to function smoothly when the moment came. Maybe my half-frozen fingers had caused me to make a sloppy release. Maybe I had had a touch of buck fever. The arrow wasn't even close.

No, I didn't get that buck. But I see him often. All I have to do is close my eyes on a rainy day in the woods, and there he is. That buck, and a lot more like him, is what keeps me out there looking for racks in the rain.

# Stands That Deliver

*By Gary Clancy*

**M**y friend Dale Chell of Aberdeen, South Dakota, would rank in the better-than-average category of whitetail deer hunters. Although he frequently hunts in his adopted home state, for more than 40 years Dale has returned to a little hunting shack tucked in the timber of northwestern Wisconsin to spend the week of Thanksgiving hunting deer with friends and family. Most years, Dale manages to put his tag on a buck. But, during one recent season when all Dale was seeing were does, hunters from a nearby camp dropped seven bucks during the week, five of them on the first day of the season, and all seven were shot from the *same stand*.

Five hundred miles northwest of where Dale hunts, another friend, Bob Dahl, hunts in the wilderness country that forms the border between Minnesota and Canada. Climbing atop the same stand he has occupied for more seasons than he can remember, Bob chambers a round in his favorite deer rifle and sits back to wait for a buck to show. If you are in the mood for wagering on a long shot, you can bet that Bob *won't* come back into camp with a hefty North Country buck. The more than 50 bucks Bob has taken from his stand stack the odds in his favor.

And then there is the plywood platform strapped in the branches of a spindly pine just in from the edge of a good-size clear-cut; it's the stand my friends and I have come to call "Old Reliable." My longtime hunting partner, John Tidemann, selected the site for the stand in the early 1980s. Since then, the small group of friends who gather at John's cabin for the deer season each year have made certain that someone is always occupying Old Reliable. When someone in our group kills a buck from that well-used perch, he climbs down, and someone else takes his place. Most seasons, half of the bucks hanging from our camp game pole were killed by hunters posted atop that $3 \times 3$ sheet of plywood. On at least one occasion, every buck taken during the season fell to the bark of a rifle echoing from that nondescript pine. None of us can recall just how many bucks have tumbled within rifle shot of Old Reliable over the years.

Those are just three of the many super-stand sites I am familiar with, and I'll bet you know of places like these yourself. These are stands that just seem to provide deer year after year after year. Well, such consistent success has little to do with luck. The fickle and unpredictable rut is also not much of a factor in the success of these stands. And none of the three stands mentioned in the beginning of this article overlooks the highly touted trails that deer travel between feeding areas and bedding sites. Rather, each of the three—and every other super-productive stand site I

*Leaning against the tree trunk helps the hunter break up his silhouette at first hunting light. Photograph by Gary Clancy*

have ever known—is situated to take full advantage of deer movement dictated by hunting pressure.

Unless you are on private, leased, or pay-to-hunt property where the number of hunters on the property can be strictly regulated, hunting pressure is going to be the dominant factor determining when and where deer move.

When whitetails are disturbed by the presence of hunters, the deer forget about eating, drinking, and resting; they even postpone breeding and its associated rituals (what we call the rut), until they are satisfied that danger is no longer present. Whitetails do this in two ways: One, they stay put and let danger pass them by; and two, they move to a place where the danger is not a threat. The first option becomes increasingly difficult as the number of hunters increases. During the first days of the season, most whitetails move to places that instinct or past experience tells them will be safe.

The best stand site is along the route these harried deer will use to move from pressured areas to safety zones. Along the length of that route will be one, sometimes two, locations for a super stand.

## LOCATING THE ROUTE

The premise here is simple: The deer will move from those areas of dense hunter traffic to those areas that attract the fewest hunters.

Fortunately, deer hunters are pretty much alike wherever they hunt. Most of us think that we really get back into the boonies when we hunt, but studies show that most hunters will be found within a half-mile of their camps or vehicles. If you doubt the validity of these studies, I invite you to get into a small plane and fly over a public hunting area on the opening day of the deer season. What you will see is a distinct "line of orange" decorating the ridges nearest roads and camps. From the air it is also apparent that those hunters who do penetrate deeper into the timber most often take advantage of the easy walking provided by logging trails, power line and pipeline rights-of-way, and railroad tracks. It is further apparent that these hunters stay on, or very near, the avenues they used to arrive at their locations. The rest of the terrain will be void of hunters or, at best, harbor only a smattering of orange. Those are the places deer go when pressure puts them on the move.

An airplane survey is the best way I know to quickly pinpoint the areas that receive the most and the least amounts of hunting pressure. The routes deer will use to move from pressured areas to safe areas are also easily recognized from the air. Most of us, however, will not fly over our hunting grounds, especially when it must be done during hunting season to be most beneficial. Instead, boot leather and experience will provide the basis for our strategy.

In farm country, fringe-land habitat and river bottoms—the choices open to a whitetail attempting to get from one place to another—are limited. A deer spooked out of one woodlot that is connected to an-

other by a brushy fenceline will predictably follow that fenceline. Likewise, deer following creek and river bottoms stick tight to the cover the timber affords.

In the big-timber areas of whitetail domain, the process of determining the route or routes used by deer that are on the move due to hunting pressure is not so simple. The often spouted advice, "Hunt the edges; that's where deer travel," is sound counsel indeed, providing that there is some sort of edge for deer to use as they make good their escape. The edges of big woods, however, tend to be scattered and erratic to a degree that often causes deer to ignore the edge in favor of a more direct route and to make detours only when confronted with crossing wide-open spaces.

Most clear-cuts, by the way, do not fall under the category of wide-open spaces. Only the most recent cuts and then only those free of tops and slashing lack enough cover to make whitetails feel at home. To the hunter's eye, accustomed to appraising whitetail habitats by degrees of thickness, clear-cuts—even maturing ones—appear to constitute wide open spaces. From a whitetail's point of view, however, a clear-cut, with its assortment of brush, slashing, and new growth, is cover aplenty.

Even though bucks do not hesitate to cross clear-

*Whoever proclaimed that deer never look up wasn't quite accurate. This buck has obviously spotted something out of place. Photograph by Charles J. Alsheimer*

cuts, expect them to take the route that offers the most cover and to make use of any islands of concealment along the way. And that brings us to the next part of the selection process.

## YOUR SUPER-STAND SITE

In some cases, pressured bucks have no choice but to exit along escape avenues that are so narrow that a stand placed anywhere along their length will do the trick. Hedgerows, treelines, fencelines, skinny creek bottoms, and drainage ditches are all examples of meager escape passages that are easily covered. Selecting the site for a super stand becomes a challenge when the deer have the whole side of a mountain to use or a seemingly endless stretch of forest at their disposal. Then, narrowing down the options that meet the criteria for super-stand sites becomes a matter of ferreting out every funnel along the route. A funnel is any feature of the land, man-made or natural, that restricts the deer's lateral movement.

The most easily recognized funnel is the "hourglass." Picture an hourglass in your mind and then relate that shape to your hunting territory. One wide end of the hourglass is pressured area, the other, the end into which the deer trickle, is the whitetails' safety zone. You are looking for the "waist" in the hourglass; that is where you want to erect your super stand.

Most hourglass funnels are not formed by a manicured forest, but rather from characteristics within the timber. An example is the super stand of a friend of mine who hunts the sprawling hardwood valleys of the upper Mississippi River.

The section of valley Jack hunts is three miles wide by four miles long and is located between two roads. Jack built his stand nearly dead center in that $3 \times 4$ section. That alone would probably be enough to ensure that pressure from all sides would put a deer in Jack's sights. But Jack isn't interested in just filling his tag; he hunts big bucks, and the numerous mounts decorating his office and den are testimony to his success. Most of those big bucks have been taken from that one stand. Jack's stand is in the perfect bottleneck location: in an ancient maple on a 50-yard-wide flat area that lies between a nearly vertical limestone outcropping and a cold, deep trout stream.

Don't, however, expect every funnel to be so obvious. Remember Old Reliable, the stand on the edge of the clear-cut. It overlooks a funnel through which pressured whitetails flow just as assuredly as sand drips through an hourglass. But, even the most imaginative mind would have difficulty conjuring up visions of that classic bottleneck at this location.

Instead, Old Reliable earned its name because John did his homework. He first determined where the most intense hunting pressure originated, and then he went looking for the stand's site. What he found was that hunting pressure was the heaviest on the far side of the big clear-cut where a well-traveled logging road provided easy access. Another area with heavy pressure was a section of low-lying timber bordering a

small creek that twisted through the forest a mile north of where John eventually put the stand. The site that John keyed on was at the opposite end of the clear-cut from the logging road, where a long finger of aspens protruded into the clearing and intersected a gentle ridge that ran the length of the clear-cut.

Then, John hunted from several stand sites before determining that the attraction of the area was the spear of aspens. Deer naturally traveled the ridge when crossing the clear-cut and invariably dropped down into the welcome cover of the aspens. Any deer pushed out of the creek bottom by hunters would also eventually meander out of that tangle of aspens if hunter traffic was sufficient. Finally, John settled on the little clump of leftover pines on the ridge crest as the permanent location for his super stand.

The trial-and-error process that John went through before choosing the right location for the stand is par for the course. In late 1989, I located what I think will eventually earn a reputation as a super-stand site. I know where hunting pressure originates. I have determined where the deer scoot for cover when the action heats up, and I have found the route they use to evacuate the pressured turf. Along that route is a narrow gash in the timber that has recently been logged over. Skirting the gap would mean a one-mile detour for any deer following the escape route. There are two locations, though, one on each end of the gap, where the deer only need to be exposed for 75 yards between protruding jags of timber.

One season I placed my portable stand on the edge of the timber just south of the most southern of the two crossings, and 13 deer crossed that slash in the two days I hunted there. Only one made the crossing within point-blank range. A dozen deer slipped across at the distant narrows. Although I did manage to drop a buck with a long shot as he picked his way across that skinny gap in the forest, for future seasons, an already-trimmed pine that overlooks the crossing is just waiting for my super stand.

## TROPHY TIME

Although a super stand is the place to be whenever hunter traffic is sufficient to have deer on the move, if it's a big boy you're after, don't dilly-dally over that second cup of coffee in the morning. Big bucks will be moving before many hunters have moved at all. A buck that is large enough to sport impressive head gear is also old enough to remember previous hunting seasons. Although spikes and forkhorns may mill around and be confused by all of the activity, a big buck knows what all of the commotion means, and he also knows what he has to do to avoid it.

Having gone through all of the effort of finding a super site, I make absolutely certain that I am on that stand a full half-hour before shooting light. Most of the big bucks that friends and I have taken from super stands have been taken *early*. Hunting from Old Reliable, for example, has nearly always resulted in a downed buck during the first hour of the season. One

*Find a super stand, and more than likely you'll soon be rewarded with a super view. Photograph by Len Rue Jr.*

year, John's son dropped his first buck from the stand when the season had only been open for seven minutes. The single shot from his Uncle Tim's .270, which took the hefty eight-pointer, was the first shot of the morning. The season before, I had the honors on opening morning. Even though day was nothing more than a ragged scar of pink on the eastern horizon, I was ready when the 200-pound 9-pointer came sneaking along the ridge. When he turned to drop downhill and intercept the aspens, I sent a 117-grain Federal Premium boattail through his lungs.

Super stands are only super when hunter traffic is sufficient to prod the deer. After opening weekend's activity, there often is not enough action to make

sitting on a super stand worthwhile. In Wisconsin, for instance, where I hunt each season, and where the season is traditionally held during Thanksgiving week, the opening weekend is great for occupying a super stand. From Monday through Wednesday, though, the woods are quiet, transforming super stands into superduds. I spend those days hunting from alternate stands or stillhunting in places where I can take advantage of the natural movements of deer. On Thanksgiving Day, however, a good share of Wisconsin's one million-member army of orange will be back in the woods, trying to fill unused tags. Pressure will remain sufficient through the close of the season on Sunday to make a super stand, well, just *super.*

# In Thick with Deer

*By James E. Churchill*

I was standing at the foot of the swamp knoll when it became light enough to see. Voles scampered from one clump of moss to another, and a chickadee roosting on a black ash tree limb slowly turned its head from side to side, as if trying to decide whether it was really morning.

Then, I heard him coming and every nerve tightened. It wasn't the steady sound that a deer makes when coming out of a swamp in the late afternoon, but the stop-and-go sounds of a deer heading for his day bed. Suddenly, his dark back appeared above the bearberry shrubs. He was too close. I knew he would see me when I drew, but I drew anyway, and the shaft scraped softly across the bow. My shoulder joints popped in protest as they were suddenly loaded with 80 pounds of string weight. If the buck saw or heard it, he didn't react.

The shot was true and his rack now hangs in my garage with a dozen other large bucks I have collected with a bow. But I will never forget the careless way this deer moved. He was relaxed, off guard, and as much at ease as a whitetail deer ever gets. Conversely, when I had seen him on the uplands a week or so before, he was like a tightly wound spring, paranoid and vigilant. He obviously had never seen a hunter in this thick swamp and didn't ever expect to see one. He almost completely let down his guard.

## A SWAMP HOME

That was the first buck, but since then, in gun and bow seasons over a 16-year period, my son and I have taken 14 bucks from that exact location. All were taken near a certain knoll in a deep swamp. This proves to me that there are certain small areas that bucks favor for bedding grounds, especially when the weather turns cold and hunting pressure is heavy. Further, when one buck is taken, another will take his place in a year or two.

Most of the long-time hunters in this area have such a place that they return to year after year to get their buck. One man I know has bagged 12 bucks from the same stand, and they all were heavy-racked deer with eight and 12 points. Another never fails to get his deer on the first or second day from his favorite swamp stand. I investigated these locations, and they look a lot like ours.

From our stand, you can't see more than 30 feet, except down the shooting lanes we have cut. There are no deer trails. Even in the snow, a few tracks leading in would be all you could find. But look very carefully and you will see deer beds and an unusual collection of deer pellets. The significance of this will be explained later.

The layout could have been purposely designed by a wary old buck to provide an unapproachable hideout. First, it has a dense stand of balsam and spruce trees stunted by the cold marsh soil, so that they grow short and thick. This cuts the visibility to a few feet in most areas. You couldn't see a deer if you happened to walk through except for the first jump or two.

It is also protected by a dense growth of shrubs such as bearberry and willow. Overlaying the shrubs are blown-down trees as well as dense alder stands. It is

*Logging roads and fields are fine for smaller deer, but big bucks are in thick cover. Photograph by Erwin and Peggy Bauer*

impossible for man or animal to go through this barrier without telegraphing his presence far ahead. I have even heard snowshoe hares running through this cover. A deer sounds like a man and a man like an elephant. Bucks don't sleep very soundly in the daytime, if they actually sleep at all; but even if they did, the sounds would wake them.

This cover superbly protects the deer, but the best long-distance warning is created by the tall aspen and pine that grow along its edges so that the swamp forms a corridor. This corridor is almost perfectly aligned east and west. The wind in this part of the world usually blows from the west, southwest, or northwest. Thus, it is usually funnelled down the corridor, bringing with it all of the messages that a breeze can tell a buck

An easterly wind is just as effective, of course, but even during the few times that the wind blows directly from the north or south, it will tumble over the tall trees lining the swamp on either side and will be borne down to ground level, where it will then fan out in both westerly and easterly directions. Only on calm days does a man have a chance of fooling the deer

completely. But even then he has to be standing in the swamp before the deer gets there, or the deer will hear or see him coming.

## ABUNDANT FOOD AND WATER

This almost impenetrable fortress also offers food and water to the buck. Water is available in numerous puddles and rivulets flowing through the swamp. By the time it freezes hard, snow has fallen and the deer can eat snow to quench their thirst.

Food is also in good supply. Deer will eat almost any kind of browse or grass in a pinch, but this location offers preferred foods. A few cedar trees were blown over or have low growing limbs so that cedar needles are within reach of the deer. A deer can live quite well with only cedar needles for food if it has to. But along the southern bank of the swamp, red maple shoots grow in a thick stand. Patches of wintergreen, aspen, sphagnum moss, and dewberry vines also are easy to find around the deer's bedding grounds. A deer literally could live out his days without coming out of his hiding place, if that's what he wanted.

The bucks do come out for food, and it is no wonder. Ringing the swamp is a wide upland area that has grown up to ferns, new aspen shoots, and several species of grasses. Several large red oak trees are scattered through the territory, and they produce a good crop of acorns every three to four years. One huge beech tree also offers a good crop of beechnuts in favorable years.

There is little doubt that this location is more comfortable. The considerable canopy of evergreen limbs keeps the air temperature higher here than in the open areas by retaining some of the radiated ground temperature. The canopy also reduces the velocity of

*A concentration of big-buck sign will help tip off his location. Photograph by Charles J. Alsheimer*

the wind so that the chill factor is less than in more open areas.

I originally found this buck's favorite bedroom by chance, but most everyone can find a place like this if they are willing to put in the time and effort. Experienced deer hunters should study their hunting grounds very carefully, particularly in regard to swamps bordered by large expanses of highland. Probably at least one location will have the accommodations mentioned; maybe several will, but probably only a few will be particularly attractive.

Beginners or veteran hunters going to a new spot to hunt can start to zero in on a buck's hideout by talking to area department of natural resource's employees, experienced local hunters, or clerks in sport shops. Sooner or later, a particular place will be mentioned time and time again as being a good place for big bucks. This will usually be followed by the statement, "But that's rough country. The bucks will head for the swamps the minute the shooting starts. A company of Green Berets couldn't get them out again."

You won't try to get them out. You will literally join them. Study topographical maps to find a place that from the air looks like a square mile or so of upland territory with a swamp somewhere near the center. Mark all such locations on your map and start scouting. If the swamp has considerable deer sign entering or leaving, it is a favorable sign. This doesn't actually mean that it will be a hotspot. In fact, most big-buck hotspots won't be too clearly defined by tracks. Big bucks don't like other deer. They attract the predators. Except during the rut, big bucks would rather be by themselves.

## FAVORITE BEDDING AREA

This bedding location is not the "core area" that has been mentioned many times in literature, but it can be identified by some of the same signs. Before the rut, there may be a "licking branch" nearby. This licking branch is a sign that deer use a scent post to leave their sign. Licking branches are hard to find but are usually maple or other hardwood branches hanging over a deer trail. The dominant buck will lick the branches, and most every deer that goes by that branch will smell it. By this sign, they will know that the dominant buck is still in the area. When he is killed, a subordinate buck will move in and take over his bedding grounds—which makes these choice locations productive year after year.

When the rut starts, the buck will likely make a scrape line nearby. Scrapes, of course, can typically be positively identified because of the broken branch tip hanging above them. The deer will lick and chew this.

If few hunters are about, the buck may sleep on the uplands. He won't be too far from his hideout, however, and should patrol through once in a while for this reason.

Before they come into estrus, does will frequently hide from overeager bucks. They will sulk in thick cover, and the bucks soon learn to go into the swamps

*A whitetail buck chewing on a licking branch. Photograph by Marilyn Maring/Leonard Lee Rue Enterprises*

looking for them. Therefore, the buck might come by his bedding grounds as he looks for does.

After the rut, the buck will be tired and gun hunting season will be open. The woods will fill with hunters and the buck will home in on his favorite bedding ground like a fox chased by hounds. Although it might have been difficult to find the bedding area earlier, tracks in the snow should divulge his hangout now. I rely heavily on finding and analyzing the beds and droppings, whether on snow or not.

A big-buck bed, of course, will be big. No mistaking the size of his bed for that of a yearling or even an average-size doe. He will usually bed down for about two or three hours, get up and move about a bit, and then lie down again. He may or may not lie down in exactly the same place the second time.

A well-fed buck will probably defecate a dozen times during the day and almost always when he first stands up after bedding for a long time. By studying the location of the droppings, the hunter can often find where the deer commonly beds even if the signs of the bed have disappeared.

A large buck commonly has large droppings, so the number and size of the droppings indicate the size of the deer and the amount of use a deer is giving to a certain area.

If you are not successful in finding the buck's favorite bedding grounds before or during the deer season, keep looking after the season closes. The buck will probably stay around this preferred bedding ground for weeks after the season has ended. By that time, it will be so well-marked that it will be easy to find.

The next year, if that buck is still alive, he will likely use it again. Only if he is chased out three or four times during a short period of time will he abandon the hideout permanently.

After you have found a big buck's preferred bedding grounds, try to do all of your set-up work in one trip. Cut out shooting lanes if necessary, but don't change the cover too much. A large amount of cutting and altering might spook the deer into leaving the location permanently.

You will probably have to hunt from a good blind. A tree blind will be hard to find in most of these areas and, even if a large enough tree can be located overlooking the hunting territory, the cover will be too thick to see the ground. Usually very little altering needs to be done to make a ground blind. Just stand beside a short thick evergreen tree or inside a pile of blown-over tree trunks.

## MARK AN ENTRY TRAIL

Your entry trail must be marked with care. You will likely be coming in to hunt before daylight in the morning, because that is about the only time you can catch him out of his fortress. There is nothing wrong with marking the trail with small reflectors that will reflect the light from your flashlight, so that you can walk directly to the stand with as little commotion as possible. Just remember to remove the reflectors when you finish hunting.

Try not to walk across the buck's trail when you go into the stand. He might pick up the odor from your tracks and be warned. Try to determine where he will come from and stand downwind if there is any moving air. Avoid wearing any type of scent at all. You don't want him to be interested in your exact location even if it is an attractor scent. When you see him coming, you will have to move slightly to shoot; and if he is looking directly at you, this might give enough warning to spoil the shot.

Bowhunters need a clear area for the arrow's flight, and it should connect to a portion of the trail that will reveal the entire deer if possible. This will cut down on the possibility that a branch or shrub will deflect the arrow. No special equipment is needed by the gun hunter. A shotgun and slugs or buckshot will work just fine. I use my scope-sighted rifle because I am used to it. A scope gathers light and makes an accurate shot more likely in the dim light of the early morning. Also, if the deer stops in thick cover, you can often determine parts of his body through the scope better than with an open sight. I use 180-grain, soft-point bullets in my .308.

Hunting deer in the swamps is an excellent way to get lost if you don't use some precautions. When there is a snow cover, of course, you can backtrack yourself out. But it is surprising how few people do that. Instead, they try to get out by walking farther and faster, often in the wrong direction. Always carry a compass for this type of hunting. Know the general direction in which you would have to walk to get out. If you forget your compass and the sun isn't shining, listen for traffic or, after dark, for signal shots. Walk in a straight line by lining up a tree or other landmark. Walk directly to it and then line up another and so on, until you get out. If you can't hear anything, you can still walk out of most areas in an hour or two by walking in a straight line as explained.

Try hunting the swamps this fall. You might find a location that will provide point-blank shots at wall-hanging bucks for the rest of your days.

# Hooked on
# Deer Calls

*By Kathy Etling*

It was a miserable day. Light fog mixed with a bone-chilling drizzle to thoroughly dampen both my spirits and my gear. The only bright spot stood on the hillside in front of my stand where, through binoculars, I watched a small spike buck trailing a doe. It was midmorning on the second day of Missouri's firearms deer season, and I was trying to hold out for a good buck. "Why couldn't that spike have bigger antlers?" I thought to myself. As I shifted my weight in the tree stand, I remembered the buck grunter hanging around my neck. With that spike so close on the doe's heels it just might work, I reasoned.

This was my third season using my favorite deer call—one that imitates a buck's tending grunt. The first year I'd been amazed when I called up two small bucks during a December hunt in Tennessee. The following year I'd added some rattling horns and called in two good bucks during our archery season. All of these experiences were exciting and got me hooked on deer calling.

So I pulled my buck grunter out and blew on it three times. The sound it produced was low and guttural, with a distinctive clicking background beat. And it worked, even at 200 yards away. I watched in astonishment as a heavy-antlered buck charged off the hilltop. With ears laid flat back, he rocketed at the spike. I dropped the call, picked up my rifle, and found the buck in my scope. I fired just as the spike squirted out of my field of view, his plans for the doe forgotten.

The bullet found its mark, and the buck went down, rolling end over end off a 20-foot bluff. When I finally reached the spot where he came to rest, I still couldn't believe that I had managed to lure the big deer out of hiding in such a spectacular manner.

Anyone who hasn't tried calling deer is missing out on some of the most exciting hunting action there is. For years, hunters with calls have issued vocal invitations to flocks of geese and ducks. Ditto hunters who take to fields and forests with slate, cedar box, or diaphragm calls, their minds set on fooling birds with their own style of turkey talk. But I think that the biggest hunting thrill of all is having a whitetail buck, probably one of the smartest animals alive, come looking for you because of a call you made.

My husband, Bob, is hooked on calling too. The weekend before firearms season, he arrowed a dandy buck that just missed the Pope and Young Club record book. The deer had been on a trail that wasn't even within sight of his stand. When Bob heard the sound of walking in the dry leaves, he figured that it was a deer and blew on the call. The walking stopped. He blew on his call again, and the animal turned around and came right in—passing within 10 yards of his stand.

That same year, he called in and passed up yet another good eight-pointer on the first day of our firearms season. Perhaps a tad too confident, Bob thought that he'd be able to call in an even bigger one later. Unfortunately, he learned the hard way not to be so choosy.

*Photograph by Erwin and Peggy Bauer*

With more than three years of calling behind me, I've had some interesting experiences with the buck grunter, the call I usually use. Until the 1989–90 season, I'd never scared a deer using this call. But the week before gun season, I, too, was out with my bow. I applied some matrix scent to some drag lines that I tied to my boot laces. As I walked down the power cut near my stand, the drags bounced behind me, dispensing scent. I climbed up in the tree and waited.

Within 15 minutes, I could see a small buck following my trail, nose to the ground. He hesitated where I'd left the power line to get to my stand. There he stood, nosing the ground. To hurry him up, I blew softly into my buck grunter. Instead of encouraging him, however, the call had the opposite effect. He turned, arched his back, put his head down, and clamped his tail tightly between his legs, slinking back across the power cut and into a heavy sumac thicket.

This particular buck would have been an eight-pointer were it not for a missing antler. As I watched, the buck peered anxiously out of the thicket. He looked up at the power cut, and then he turned and looked back down the power cut. Then he'd back into the thicket, hide a little longer, and then look around some more. I was puzzled by this behavior, until I finally realized that this buck must have had a run-in with a more dominant buck. He probably had been pushed around, probably getting his antler knocked off in the process. The buck grunt brought back unpleasant memories. Not eager to repeat the experience, he hid while keeping a lookout for the bigger buck at the same time. That's why I never could get a bow shot at him.

Even with this experience, I would never hesitate to use the tending buck grunt to try to call in deer. I've had super luck with it. And other hunters have, too. Hunters like Bill McDonald of Indianapolis, who was hooked on deer calling even before he tried any commercially produced calls. After hearing bucks grunting in the woods, he decided to try to call them in himself. He did, too, but he really became addicted in 1988. Using a Knight & Hale call, he grunted in 17 different bucks from four different stand locations, including the biggest buck he's ever seen in the woods. He estimated that the buck would have scored between 160 and 170 Boone and Crockett Club points.

Randy Tillary, of Bonner Springs, Kansas, is another firm believer in grunt calls. Tillary killed a monster whitetail in 1988 while using a tending buck grunt call. Tillary's trophy scored 223⅞ Boone and Crockett Club points as a nontypical and nets 199 points as a typical. Tillary took his buck the hard way, with a bow.

Although you may not always call in bunches of deer like Billy McDonald did, you should be able to call in a few during the course of a season. And one of the new, improved versions of the buck grunter overcomes the main problem hunters had with earlier models. Harold Knight and David Hale, of Cadiz, Kentucky, realized that their original call, the E-Z Grunter would often freeze up in cold weather. When hunters blew onto the call, moisture froze on the reed, preventing it from vibrating and producing sound.

They solved this problem with the E-Z Grunter Plus, a new patented design that makes four different tones of buck grunt because it works when you blow out or inhale on either end of the call. It duplicates the sound of a buck grunting when air is inhaled through the call, and there's no moisture to freeze the reed in a stationary position.

Better yet, the E-Z Grunter Plus now allows hunters to duplicate the sound of a truly excited whitetail buck, the sound Hale called "hyperventilation." A buck, when he's hot on the trail of a doe, will often grunt as he exhales. As he inhales, it's sort of grunting in double time or hyperventilation.

"Hyperventilation is a series of grunts where the buck speeds the rhythm way up because he's so excited," Hale explained. "He's excited because it's mating season, and it only comes around once a year."

Hale used hyperventilation to entice a 134-point (Pope and Young) Kentucky whitetail to his bow last year.

"I called him 20 yards off the trail he normally used," he said. "With new techniques like this, deer calling is entering a new phase. I like to compare it to turkey calling. The very first tending buck grunts were like the basic yelps those first turkey hunters used. Early turkey hunters didn't use a lot of calls because they didn't know a lot about them. But turkey calling soon became more complex when hunters started using cackling and cutting. These later calls are to turkey calling what hyperventilation is to deer calling."

Knight and Hale aren't the only manufacturers making quantum leaps in the deer calling field. Jerry Peterson, of Woods Wise Products in Franklin, Tennessee, helped lead his team to victory in the 1988 Buckmaster Classic, an Alabama deer hunt that benefits charity, by supplying his teammates with Buc-N-Doe double-reed calls. Inhale on one end and you get the buck tending grunt. Inhale on the other and the result is a doe bleat. It's possible to produce six basic calls on the Buc-N-Doe, including contact calls and fawn distress bawls. In addition, each reed cartridge—on either end of the call—can be used without the tube for zero-movement calling or to free your hands so you can draw your bow.

David Westmoreland, of Columbia, Missouri, a hunting advisor for PSE, was Peterson's team captain at the Buckmaster Classic.

"It was my first experience using a doe bleat," he said. "Before then I didn't have much faith in any deer calls. But during the Classic I saw one buck going directly away from me in some real thick brush. With no shot at all at that point and nothing to lose, I made a doe bleat. The buck stopped. I waited 15 seconds and bleated again. The buck turned 180 degrees and walked right back to me. At 50 yards, I shot the six-point.

"Ninety percent of the bleat calls on the market

today produce high-pitched fawn bleats only," Peterson explained. "And while fawn bleats work great on lactating does, they usually won't work for a buck. To call a buck you must sound like a doe. And a doe's bleat sounds like a goat's. It's much lower and coarser sounding."

Peterson graduated from college with a minor in wildlife biology, helping him gain the knowledge that has been immensely important in his hunting strategies.

"I knew about the various studies in deer vocalizations made by different universities [such as those conducted at the University of Georgia and Mississippi State University in Starkville], but I wanted to find out for myself how many sounds whitetails can make."

Peterson presents some good arguments for sticking with either a doe bleat or a doe contact call.

"The buck's tending grunt was very successful at first because bucks are so aggressive," he explained. "Because it was successful, natural selection was speeded up. The most aggressive, eager bucks—the ones most likely to respond to a tending grunt—were harvested, leaving the more cautious ones. That's why so many hunters can call bucks in to 100 yards or so with their grunt calls and no closer. This is a buck that has been wised up by hunters."

While developing his calls, Peterson listened to both wild and penned deer.

"Whenever we separated the does from the bucks during the rut, the does would bleat as if they were calling to the bucks. This reinforced what I'd once seen in the wild when an estrous doe came into a scrape, assumed the classic stimulated posture, and began to bleat quite loudly. It didn't take long for a buck to find her. So I figure that if an estrous doe is ready to breed and isn't tended by a buck, she'll try to find one. And one way she'll do this is by using either the contact call or bleat.

"A fawn's bleat is often called a 'mew' because it sounds like a cat," Peterson continued. "A doe bleats like a goat—*baaa*. And a doe's contact call is a longer, more drawn-out, intense bleat that rises in tone as the doe becomes more stressed. The sound is *neeyatt*—a flat sound with each syllable pronounced and with minor emphasis on the last one. All of these calls are duplicated on the audio tape, 'The Vocabulary of Deer.'"

Peterson is a firm believer in yet another call— the doe grunt. "The very first sound a fawn hears is the sound its doe makes when it calls the fawn to nurse," he explained. "When the fawn responds, it gets groomed and fed, it's rewarded with everything good in its life. So from early on deer are conditioned to come to a doe's maternal grunt. It means, 'Come here.' And, since a doe's grunt isn't an aggressive call, you needn't worry whether a big buck, smaller buck, or a doe hears it. It won't frighten any of them."

According to Peterson, a doe's grunt is higher

*Bob Etling's buck charged to within 10 yards of his stand after the hunter grunted on his deer call. The peak of the rut is also the peak time to grunt to territory-defending bucks. Photograph by Kathy Etling*

pitched than a buck's grunt and difficult, if not impossible, to duplicate on reed-type calls (those that are blown with the mouth). Peterson uses a sonogram to analyze actual deer sounds and then compares them to sonograms of his manufactured calls to determine just how realistic each is. "Since we weren't able to duplicate a doe grunt with a reed call to our satisfaction, we designed the Woods Wise All Weather Friction Grunt Call," he said. "This call is ideal for making the soft, random doe grunts that whitetail bucks find so hard to ignore. Doe grunts are always the first deer sounds I make when I'm out hunting."

To use this call you just hold the striker in one hand and the body of the call in the other. The edge of the striker then fits into the grooved ribs of the call, while the hunter makes downward slicing motions with it. The call can also be clipped to your belt for one-handed operation.

Will Primos, of Primos Wild Game Call in Jackson, Mississippi, is also sold on the doe grunt as a great way to call in nearly any deer.

"Both subordinate and dominant bucks respond readily to this call," he said. "And so do does. In 1989, I called in over 20 deer while I was still experimenting

with it. The call is so new that I'm still learning about it. The main difference in sound between these two calls is that a buck's grunt sounds more piglike; a doe's is higher pitched. The main difference in the animals that come in is that deer responding to a doe grunt come in either hopefully or casually. They aren't worried or fearful. When I use a tending buck grunt dominant bucks will often come in aggressively while subordinates come in quite cautiously."

Primos calls his reed-type call the Doe Grunter, and he says that he uses it two different ways. "First, I've used it sort of sparingly, grunting just two or three times every once in a while," he explained. "Using the call like that says, 'I'm a doe; I'm here.' The second way I'll use it is fairly urgently. I'll call more often and really let any nearby deer know that I'm around. When I use the call like this it's saying, 'I'm ready, I'm here; where are you?'"

I don't know about other whitetail hunters, but I do know that I'll be trying several new calls this deer season. I have to, you see, because I'm a whitetail junkie who's hooked on deer calling. If you try calling and it works, it'll get in your blood too. And once it does, it's a hard habit to break.

# New Fall Call

*By Jeff Murray*

Gary Cook's soft, sexy deer talk had reached the buck's ears, all right. The passing whitetail reversed direction and pulled to a stop well within gun range. Problem was Cook's bow wasn't set up for 50-yard shots. More soft calling didn't move the buck, so Cook, a biologist with the Tennessee Wildlife Resources Agency, waited patiently. The buck held his ground while he stared intently in Cook's direction and sniffed the air.

As the sun melted over the horizon, Cook realized he'd have to make a move or wait for another day. So he switched to another call reserved for situations like this. Sure enough, one toot was all it took. Without hesitating, the buck walked directly into the lap of the Tennessee bowhunter, and a clean lung shot put the six-pointer down.

What made Cook's hunt successful was the fact that bucks and does talk to each other during the fall. More than a dozen deer vocalizations have been documented by researchers, although the number likely approaches three dozen.

Sounding like a sexy doe, as Cook did, instead of like a fightin' buck, could well be the next craze in deer hunting.

## SOUND LIKE A SEXY DOE

"It makes biological sense," says Dr. David Samuel, a wildlife professor at the University of West Virginia, "Bucks are looking for does, not other bucks, and everybody knows it. After all, doe estrous scents outsell buck scents 100 to one."

"Bucks would rather be lovers than fighters," according to Jerry Peterson, an expert call manufacturer from Franklin, Tennessee. The main purpose of the rut is to bring bucks and does together, not to pit bucks against bucks. And, for it to be to the hunter's advantage, the calling must be done efficiently; a doe goes in and out of heat in a matter of 24 hours.

"It's not that buck grunting never works," Peterson said. "But timing is critical. [With grunt calls] you've got to have a shortage of receptive does, and the bucks have to be in that fevered pitch going into the rut. It's just not going to happen that often for the average hunter."

Dr. Samuel agrees. Of the four bucks he called in last year, none responded to a buck grunt. All fell for seductive doe talk.

As logical as this all sounds, the whitetail hunting community has largely ignored this avenue, even though it's the main route to success for hunters of other game. For example, turkey hunters rely mainly on hen talk, not gobbling, to draw toms within range. And elk and moose hunters know that cow calling is more versatile than bugling or grunting. So why do the opposite for deer?

Ironically, it was Peterson who probably started the current rage in buck grunting. In 1985, he was the first to market a grunt call. An overnight revolution

*When bucks start getting hot for does, a bleat call can be close to a sure thing. Photograph by Lee Kline*

followed, and a glut of buck grunt calls flooded the marketplace. Most, however, sported a deep, guttural pitch—the opposite of Peterson's doe/young buck call. As a result, doe talk has taken a back seat to buck grunting in most hunting circles.

That could be changing. Doe grunts, along with another doe sound, are on a roll. The other sound? The oldest known to deer callers: the bleat.

## THE HEAT BLEAT

What first pointed Peterson in this direction was a vivid hunting experience with a doe in 1974. Whitetails in central Tennessee were just entering the so-called early rut in October—scrapes were freshly turned and pungent with buck odor. Peterson had been monitoring a scrape line when he noticed a doe trot across a distant ridge and jam to a sudden halt on top of a scrape. Her behavior was itchy. Her tail was cocked to one side, and her tarsal glands were jet-black. It was obvious that she was in heat.

After a brief moment, she cut loose with a loud, one-second bleat. Then another.

"She seemed to wait intensely between bleats for a response." Peterson recalled. Failing to get one after six or seven tries, she urinated in the scrape and disappeared over the ridge.

There's more. Peterson's hunting buddy, Jerry Holcomb, sat three ridges away and witnessed a repeat performance of this strange ritual. Holcomb, like Peterson, wasn't interested in harvesting an antlerless deer, so he settled back in his tree stand to see what might happen next. He didn't have to wait long. Within a couple of minutes, a six-point buck showed up, and the two deer consummated their relationship.

Doe grunts and this unique "heat bleat," unlike buck grunts, are rarely heard by hunters. Although researchers have analyzed the former with a sound spectograph, the heat bleat has yet to be recorded. There are several reasons for this. For one, penned deer forced into small spaces represent an artificial breeding situation that doesn't always reflect the real world. Although bucks continue to express their dominance, does don't have to attract bucks.

Cook shares another perspective. Having been a biologist for 15 years and a conservation officer for seven years prior to that, he's spent a lot of time in the woods. But it wasn't until he became aware of a commercially made call that he started *listening* for an estrous bleat.

"I think I've heard it on two separate occasions," he said. "But I wonder how prevalent the call is during the day. Most breeding probably occurs after dark, and I have a theory that the estrous bleat might be a pre-copulation vocalization. I mean, breeding is imminent, say 30 seconds to two minutes away."

What does the heat bleat mean? At present, no one is sure. Whether a doe is actually soliciting a buck or is just expressing her stressed condition is still up to the scientific community to decide.

"I don't know what the doe is saying." Cook added. "But the bucks sure do."

## BUCKS RESPOND

Bucks respond to doe talk in a variety of ways, but they're usually more relaxed than when the grunt call of a mature buck is involved. Therein lies a big advan-

---

### MAKING THE SOUNDS

Deer calling is simple, but confusing. Simple, because the sounds are basic and easily reproduced. Confusing, because there's a lack of reliable scientific information on the subject. Deer may talk to each other, but they rarely are vocal in front of a researcher with a microphone in his hand. Expert call manufacturer Jerry Peterson offers these tips:
- Doe grunts are soft, high-pitched calls—higher than those made by a young buck. They're difficult to achieve with a reed call: either you get a deep, guttural burping sound like a pig (or dominant buck) or a higher quacky sound like a duck. The most accurate calls are friction calls.
- Doe bleats are easily produced with a reed call. However, don't confuse the estrous bleat of a mature doe with the catlike "mewing" fawn bleat commonly used by predator hunters. A good estrous bleat should sound similar to a sheep: nee-eeh. Bucks also bleat, but they sound goatlike: bah-bah.
- Hunters often make two mistakes when calling deer. Either they call too loudly, or they call too often. Fact is what humans can barely hear at 50 yards a whitetail can pick up at twice or even three times that range. Practice

so that a hunting buddy can barely hear your calls at 40 to 50 yards.
- Doe grunts say "Come here" or "Where is everybody?" and should generally precede heat bleats. Make random, one-quarter-second "urps" in a three or four-call sequence. Wait at least five minutes to give deer time to work toward you. Repeat but don't overdo it.
- The heat bleat says "Come here right now" with definite sexual overtones. Hold the call for a full second; make two to five "nee-eehs" before waiting five to 10 minutes. This is a louder call. Again, don't overdo it.
- Don't get dogmatic. No need to duplicate exact pauses between calls, or their number, or duration.
- Never call to a sighted buck that's approaching you. It's working! Resist the temptation to hurry him along.
- Always try the soft-sell approach before getting aggressive with a deer call. Deer express the gamut of feelings—from extreme aggression to passive sociality—by changing pitch, tone, volume, and intensity. For sexy doe talk, think passive, not aggressive. If that fails, consider increasing the volume and intensity of the call. Hopefully, the pitch and tone will be set properly at the factory.

*A combination of doe grunts and heat bleats is often successful in attracting a buck—but be flexible in calling. Photograph by Len Rue Jr.*

tage for hunters. Wary bucks, especially those concerned about getting whipped by a larger, dominant animal, often circle the immediate area, winding the calling hunter in the process. But a buck that hears a doe saying, "Why not come over and see me sometime?" often walks, trots, or bolts right in.

Testimonies abound from hunters across the nation. In Minnesota, Shank Scharmach, co-owner of Winona Camo Systems, has called in four Pope and Young record-class whitetails. None was tricked with aggressive tactics, such as buck grunting or rattling. All were seduced into range with the sexy imitation of a whitetail doe.

"When I first tried doe calling, I was skeptical," Scharmach admitted. "But what really sold me was when a six-pointer came in and I let him wander off, only to call him back again. Would you believe I did this three times?"

A Wisconsin bowhunter, Dennis Giannini, arrowed a big nine-pointer that literally crossed an open field—past two young bucks that were sparring—to get to the doe bleat. Giannini couldn't clear several tree branches with his bow the first time the animal walked by his stand, but three short notes on a call brought the buck back again, this time 12 yards away.

And in Florida, Tom Spence used mostly doe bleats to call in a yearling buck. Spence's broadhead dropped the animal 10 yards from his stand, so he continued to experiment with his calling. Shortly, a big 10-pointer materialized from behind a thick tangle of grapevines. After a stare down, in which the deer sized up Spence and his downed buck, the trophy quartered away "looking over his shoulder as he disappeared," Spence said.

## BE FLEXIBLE WHEN CALLING

The heat bleat isn't difficult to master, although it's no panacea and certainly no replacement for dedication and woods savvy. Its chief limitation is that it shouldn't be used alone (soft doe grunts are the perfect prelude); it works best when bucks and does are actively looking for each other.

Heat bleats are deadly when called "broadcast" style—when you advertise the allure of a receptive doe but haven't seen any deer. Begin by examining the terrain and thinking like a turkey hunter. For example, don't try to call a buck across an open field. Also, pick a spot with thick cover that attracts or constricts deer. Edges and bottlenecks are two examples.

Drawing deer within range, especially for bowhunters, requires that you remain totally motionless while calling. Camouflage clothing is another big advantage. The deer are riveting their attention on you, and they could show up anytime without warning.

Peterson, like many turkey hunters, remains flexible with his calling. If he glasses or spots a deer first, he'll go with what seems to be working—doe grunts, doe bleats, or a combination of the two. With visual contact, it's easier to tell if you're hitting the right buttons.

Watch the deer's body language. If a deer gives you a quick tail wag, stop calling. That gesture means "come here." It also means that the deer probably isn't alone. He wants you to join the party. Wait to see if the herd starts moving in your direction. If they don't, try soft grunts that say, "I'm lost and can't see you." Then put the frosting on the cake with a heat bleat that says "I'm the one for you, not them."

What if deer call back? If they're moving closer, you better cool it. If you can't see them, build suspense and anxiety by waiting at least one minute. Then try the specific vocalization that preceded theirs.

Successful estrous bleating, like deer hunting in general, is most productive just prior to breeding activity. If a doe in estrus isn't actively courted, she'll go looking. Now is the time to make good use of this call and not to worry too much about overuse.

Conversely, if the rut is between actual estrous periods (recent research indicates that there may be up to six such breeding cycles, fewer in the North, more in the South), do the opposite: Stick mainly with soft doe grunts, wait longer between calls, and use the heat bleat sparingly.

So knowing at what stage in the breeding cycle the does are in is a prerequisite to seducing a buck with sexy doe talk. Peterson offers two insights that might simplify this chore.

"First, scrutinize every doe that walks past you," he says. "Besides body language, look at her tarsal gland (found on the hind leg). If it's black and matted, not brown or tan, she's ready for action. Second, carefully inspect scrapes. Fresh ones—moist and rank—mean that bucks and does are on the move. The opposite is true if the scrapes in your area are full of leaves (or snow) or dried out."

Even if the rut period isn't in your favor, don't leave the doe bleat at home. Once dominant bucks hook up with does, subordinate bucks are more likely to sneak into heat bleats. Another time to consider doe bleats is during a stalk or stillhunt. Should you spook a deer, quickly give a fairly loud bleat. Peterson says that a doe bleat often short-circuits a deer's strong desire to bolt.

There are no guarantees with deer calling, but one that's close involves a buck on the trail of a hot doe. Should you see a buck sauntering stiff-legged, nose to the ground, try the heat bleat. If the doe he's following is out of view, he'll be on top of you before you can draw your bow! Finally, add heat bleats as a "convincer" to your buck grunting and rattling repertoire. Bleats inject believability to the fight and might sway a standoffish buck. The first time Peterson tried this ploy, he ended up taking a buck with an 18-inch spread.

Two bucks responded immediately to his rattling after he had positioned himself in an area where buck fighting had occurred only moments earlier. The first one had a nice rack, but the outline of the second buck could barely be seen in the bushes. The bucks were too close to make a move, so Peterson gave a heat bleat to see if the second deer would come out. He did, but he was smaller. "Fortunately, the bigger buck turned and zipped by me in a dead run," Peterson said. "I shot him with my .270 at a distance of 3 feet. Now that's what I call a close call."

Frankly, there are a lot of myths surrounding the art of calling deer, and several call manufacturers offer conflicting advice. Purchasing an accurate doe call can be confusing. Ideally, try to match a prospective call to the real-life recording *before* you purchase it. This is possible at the many sport shows held annually across the country. Additional sources include Bob McGuire's deer vocalization video that reportedly draws upon the work of University of Georgia researchers; Larry Richardson's (4037 Beauchamp Cove, Memphis, TN 38118) new audio cassette; and Jerry Peterson's instructional two-tape series.

Before laying any money down, personally check out the call's delivery and steer clear of loud "magnum" calls. Gary Cook warns that the most realistic deer calls have a precontrolled volume and precontrolled pitch to avoid misuse. Two such calls include Roger Wyant's Varitone deer call (Wyant's Original Hunting Products, Box 1325, Harrisonburg, VA 22801) and Peterson's WW Buc-N-Doe Supreme (Woods Wise Products, Box 1552, Franklin, TN, 37064).

If you buy a doe call and learn how to use it, you'll be joining a chorus of doe talkers who no longer sing the no-buck blues.

# The Smell of Success

*By Peter Fiduccia*

The buck was 25 yards away. His massive body arched violently as his wide, heavy rack swayed menacingly from side to side. He pawed the earth purposefully with his hoof and slowly, but defiantly, approached the hunter.

With a grunt-snort-wheeze, the buck lunged forward to face down what he thought was a challenge from another buck. The hunter shot the "possessed animal" 10 feet from his stand!

Olaf Hellstrom shot the aggressive buck in New York State in 1987. Unknowingly, he issued an olfactory challenge to all mature bucks within smelling distance of his stand. The imitation pheromone Hellstrom used was tarsal scent—a pheromone that can agitate aggressive bucks during the rut.

For years, hunters have used the glands of deer as attracting or covering scents to help them take more deer. The gland scents you use and how you use them will affect how successfully you hunt whitetails. You, too, can become a more successful deer hunter by understanding and knowing how to use scents emitted by deer glands. In creating these responses, you will be able to attract or roust deer even when other hunters are having a hard time locating or seeing game.

Whitetail deer have four external glands that play a major role in their communication and behavior. These glands are the tarsal, interdigital, metatarsal, and preorbital. Pheromones created by these glands are received and interpreted by the animal. These scent messages will calm, alert, spook, attract, identify, and even dominate other deer. By knowing when and where to use scent from these glands, hunters can increase their hunting opportunities.

Deer use all of their senses to survive. Their sense of smell, however, is the keenest and most relied upon of them all. A hunter who gets by this line of defense will increase his success dramatically and immediately.

## GLOSSARY

**Atrophying:** Decreasing in size or wasting away of a body part or tissue; arrested development of a part or organ of an animal.

**Cape:** The process of removing the entire deer hide from the brisket forward, carefully peeling and skinning the hide from around the ears, eyes, nose, skull, antlers, and lips. This process is used by taxidermists before they can flesh, clean, tan, and stretch the deer hide to mount on a form.

**Olfactory:** Relating to or connected with the sense of smell.

**Pheromone:** A chemical substance that is produced by an animal and serves as a stimulus to other individuals of the same species, for one or more behavioral responses.

## TARSAL GLAND SCENT

The tarsal gland is on the inside of a buck's hind leg. A tan color during most of the year, the gland turns darker as he continually urinates on it throughout the rut. By late December, the urine-stained gland is almost black. Deer use tarsal gland pheromones in several ways: as an alarm to warn other deer of danger; to identify individual deer; and in mature deer, to function in breeding behavior during the rut. All deer urinate on the tarsal gland, but older deer urinate on, sniff, and lick at it more frequently during the rut. The tarsal gland's pungent odor often instigates aggressive behavior in mature deer during the height of the breeding season—like the buck at the beginning of this article.

To obtain optimum response from tarsal scent during the rut, take several drops of commercially made scent and apply it with an eyedropper to a scent pad or rag. When you are close to your stand, remove the pad and hang it from a sapling. Its pheromones will permeate the area and act as an attracting scent for deer within smelling distance. Do not apply it to your clothing. You don't want the deer to zero in on you. You want him to focus his attention 10 or 15 yards from you.

Last season, my wife, Kate, had an interesting experience using a tarsal gland from a recently harvested doe. Knowing that she would be walking through a swamp, Kate applied the scent to long rags tied around her thighs, and left a trail of scent on foliage a few feet off the ground. She walked a few hundred yards to her tree stand at the opposite end of the swamp. After 30 minutes, several young bucks followed her trail. In one instance, two bucks were one behind the other. Once the bucks reached the end of the scent-marked trail, they became confused and belligerent. Two bucks waited at the base of Kate's tree stand for about 20 minutes. In fact, she watched the young bucks spar with each other several times before they walked away.

The scent did exactly what it was supposed to. However, because Kate didn't remove the rags from her thighs, the bucks followed the scent directly to her. Whenever you are trying to attract deer with scent, it's wise to leave the scent-marked pads or rags 15 to 25 yards from your stand.

Although the scent from tarsal glands of dead does will attract bucks, many hunters have had more success attracting bucks with commercially made buck tarsal scent. This pheromone will often bring in a belligerent buck who thinks another mature buck is working his area. It agitates the bucks; sometimes they respond within minutes.

## INTERDIGITAL GLAND SCENT

The interdigital gland, another external gland, is between the deer's hoofs and emits a glandular secretion with a potent odor. Interdigital scent is like a human fingerprint; it is individual to each deer. And I would speculate that the interdigital scent from mature bucks and does is more potent than the scent from immature deer. It is how a doe will track a lost fawn or how a lone deer will find its way back to the right herd.

I started using interdigital gland scent in 1986. A bowhunting companion shot a yearling doe. I helped him field-dress the animal and took the deer's hoofs for an experiment. I wanted to find out more about the interdigital gland and the scent it emits. The next day I

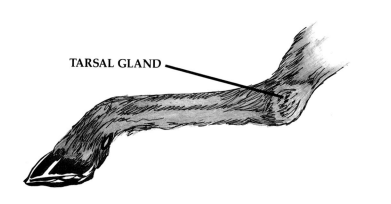

TARSAL GLAND

*The tarsal, or hock, gland releases pheromones that become stronger during the rut in bucks and does.*

INTERDIGITAL GLAND

*The interdigital gland is located between a deer's hoof. Individual to deer, the scent is like a fingerprint.*

*A whitetail buck rubbing scent on a bush near a scrape. Photograph by Len Rue Jr.*

took my knife and inserted it between the deer's toes and extracted a small amount of the whitish-gray substance. I rubbed the scent sparingly on the bottom of my boots and walked to where my friend had taken the yearling doe the day before. Making several large circles around my stand, I hid behind a large oak and waited.

Within 10 minutes, a large doe with twin fawns walked over my exact trail several times. Her nose never left the ground. She acted like a buck on the trail of a hot doe. After wandering off, she returned and walked my entire trail again. This time, she left the way I walked in. Could this doe have given birth to the yearling my friend had taken the evening before? If so, she was obviously trying to locate it through the interdigital scent trail I laid down. Several other deer followed the interdigital scent trail that day. None of the other deer reacted like the first doe; but one deer, a spike, passed close enough for me to reach out and touch him.

Larry Rickard, general manager of Pete Rickard Inc., a scent manufacturer, knows the success hunters can have when using this scent. He sent me several letters from hunters who had taken bucks while using interdigital scent.

Al Biely of Wisconsin wrote, "I used the interdigital by itself." After he applied interdigital scent to his boot pads, Biely walked to his favorite bowhunting stand and waited. Several minutes later he had a buck follow his interdigital scent trail directly to his stand. "Amazingly, I shot the buck at three yards, no bull!" Biely wrote, "I intend to use this scent with my camera this season as well."

"I'm never surprised when hunters tell me how effective interdigital scent has been for them," said Rickard. "It is a pure essence and is potent; three or four drops of interdigital scent will attract deer along your trail. Any time a well-made manufactured scent duplicates a natural glandular aroma it will attract deer."

## PREORBITAL GLAND SCENT

The preorbital gland is in the corner of a deer's eye. Its main function is to act as a tear duct. Deer, however, will continually rub the gland on bushes, branches, and tree limbs—especially during the rut. Biologists speculate that the gland is used to deposit a specific pheromone as a marker.

I know an avid bowhunter who regularly removes the preorbital gland from caped deer, preferably bucks. Once he has caped the hide from the skull, he turns the hide inside out and, with a razor blade, cuts the entire eye section free, including the tear duct (which is the preorbital gland). Wearing rubber surgeon gloves, he rubs the tear duct on branches that are in the shooting lanes around his tree stand.

**PREORBITAL GLAND**

*The preorbital gland is located in the corner of a deer's eye.*

"Over the years," he said, "I've seen deer stop and raise their noses trying to locate the odor. They slowly approach a branch I rubbed the scent on, and then mouth and rub their eyes on it. It has often given me the chance to shoot a deer that might have gone by."

I do not know of a manufacturer who makes a preorbital scent. If you intend to try it, you'll have to gather it from harvested deer, a job that may require considerable effort and work. I haven't used the pheromone from this gland myself, but it sounds like it would work. I plan to try it this fall.

*Preorbital gland secretions are believed to act as scent markers. Photograph by William H. Lea*

## METATARSAL GLAND SCENT

The metatarsal gland is within a white tuft of hair on the outside hind legs just above the dewclaws. Some naturalists and biologists believe that the gland is

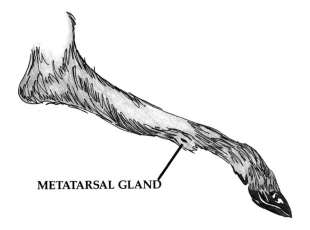

**METATARSAL GLAND**

*Although biologists are unsure of the importance of metatarsal gland scent, many hunters claim hunting success when using it.*

atrophying, and therefore, has no real purpose. Others believe that the gland emits a pheromone and is used by deer for identification and as a warning signal. In any event, this gland is not well understood. When using metatarsal scent, be ready for anything. You may be fortunate enough to attract deer, or unfortunate enough to spook them.

Many old-timers swear by metatarsal scent. They tie the gland to a boot and drag it through the woods. Many claim that they have attracted deer to their stands using this gland and method. For now, the jury is still out on its effectiveness. My suggestion coincides with my philosophy about deer hunting: Innovate. Give metatarsal a try and experiment with it.

## USE SCENTS CAREFULLY

When using scents, especially gland scents, take care not to mix conflicting pheromones. For example, don't use excess interdigital with attracting scents. Excess interdigital scent is meant to warn deer of danger, not attract them. You can, however, use one or two drops of interdigital with an estrous scent; both are attracting scents.

In my early deer hunting days, I tried all types of scents: cover, glandular, sex, food, and attracting. I learned the hard way not to mix and match contradictory pheromone messages. During a hunt on a local farm, I put gray fox cover scent on one boot pad and estrous scent on the other. I climbed into my tree stand on the edge of the field and waited for deer to make their way from the second growth to the alfalfa field. The only deer I saw that evening were a doe, her yearling, and two fawns. The doe repeatedly left the second growth, reached my scent trail, spun around, and quickly returned to the overgrown woodlot. She did this several times. Finally, she took a different route and left.

I was disgusted; I thought that the scents had spooked her. I was half right. Moments later, a red fox emerged from the undergrowth and started across the field. When he hit my scent trail, he literally jumped several feet into the air. He was on the run before he landed!

The lesson learned during that experience was that I had used the wrong cover scent. Gray fox traditionally inhabit mature hardwood forests, while red fox generally inhabit farm fields, brush areas, and young woodlots. The two animals seldom cohabit; they are antagonistic toward each other and will avoid each other's territory whenever possible. When either fox happens to enter the other's territory, it doesn't take the residing fox long to recognize the intruder's urine scent. In this case, the doe obviously found the gray fox scent foreign and reacted accordingly. She paid attention to the foreign odor and removed herself from possible danger. The red fox recognized the urine scent from the gray fox and panicked; the scent clearly told him he was in trouble.

Another caution—if you use gland scents collected from recently harvested deer, be careful not to use too much; the concentration of scent from bagged game is more potent than is commercially made scent. Some glands or even the urine from bladders can be overused and lead to problems. I stick to glandular scents made by reliable scent manufacturers. Most commercial brands are reliable and require a lot less work.

Scientists and hunters have just begun to scratch the surface of the entire scent phenomenon. New information about deer glands is constantly being researched. I believe that during the next few years hunters will learn more about deer's physical and behavioral characteristics and, in doing so, will enjoy hunting in its highest degree.

Pheromones, from external glands, are natural odors in the deer woods. Used properly, they will add to your overall deer hunting experience. They will create opportunities that you may never have had otherwise. Aside from that, you will see deer behavior that you may have never observed before. In addition, you will have opportunities to witness the amusing and interesting reactions of raccoons, coyotes, foxes, bears, and elk when they stop, smell, and react to scents laid out for deer. ⇥

## OTHER OLFACTORY SIGNPOSTS

There are two other glands that deer use as markers during the rut: one is on the forehead and the other is in the roof of the mouth. And, there may also be other deer scent glands.

**Orbital gland:** The forehead gland, sometimes called the orbital, is used when deer rub against saplings and twigs. Both bucks and does use the orbital gland to scent-mark saplings. Some bucks develop a very dark patch of hair on their forehead during this period. After rubbing and depositing forehead scent, does and bucks will smell and lick at the rubbed areas. The rubbed area will often carry the odor for several days.

**Mouth gland:** The gland in the deer's mouth is used in a similar manner. Bucks marking scrapes will mouth the overhanging branch, depositing scent from the gland inside the mouth. They also often mouth licking sticks. Researchers at the University of Georgia have documented this behavior and are continuing their research of these glands.

**Other glands:** The gland found under the tail produces pheromones, too. According to some biologists, there may also be glands just inside the nose of deer. Researchers are studying both glands to determine how deer use and react to these scents.

## HORMONAL GLANDS

**Adrenal glands:** A pair of complex endocrine organs near the kidneys. During stressful—for example, during overpopulation—situations, deer will secrete cortisol from these glands.

**Thyroid gland:** Lies in the neck and produces a hormone called thyroxin. Biologists have used this gland to determine the nutritional state of deer.

**Thymus gland:** Lies near the base of the neck and is most visible in yearlings. The size of the gland is controlled by photoperiodism.

**ORBITAL GLAND**

*Both bucks and does scent-mark saplings with forehead orbital glands.*

# Big Buck Date Book

*By Kathy Etling*

A whitetail deer lives a structured life. Depending on the month—and even the week of the month—the whitetail is both environmentally and genetically preprogrammed to do certain things at a certain time. Doing so helps guarantee the survival of both individual deer and the species as a whole.

During the rut, a whitetail's preprogramming is readily apparent to those of us who hunt. We know that as sure as the sun will rise each morning, the whitetail buck will lose antler velvet, begin making rubs, and start making scrapes. He'll become interested in does, chasing them as they near estrus to the exclusion of nearly everything else. A whitetail buck will be more careless early on in the pre-rut period, while still in his bachelor patterns. And during the rut's peak, a buck will let his guard down once again. Both are ideal times to bag a trophy.

A second rut occurs 28 days after the primary rut. That's when does not bred the first time around come into estrus again. And the bucks—more cautious now—prowl fields and forests once more.

Scientists used to believe that the rut was totally dependent on the amount of light reaching the whitetail's eye and activating the animal's pineal gland. Simply put, lessening amounts of daylight and increasing amounts of testosterone in a buck's blood would start the rut cycle. Because the earth is curved, less light reaches more northern latitudes each day as autumn progresses. So, if the start of rut behavior depended totally on light, during a given week, all deer at the same degree of latitude would behave the same. But that's not the way it is—at least not exactly.

Whitetails living at identical latitudes will often rut at slightly different times. With 15 different subspecies of whitetail deer inhabiting the United States and Canada—and with several species often occurring at the same latitude—genetic differences can also affect the determination of the rut. A few differences exist even among the *same* whitetail subspecies inhabiting states lying within the same latitude.

When trying to predict whitetail behavior, there's another variable to consider: whether or not your hunting area was stocked with whitetails from a different geographic location. Rather than adopting a new internal rut timetable based on the amount of available light at the latitude to which they are transplanted, stocked animals are likely to rut closer to the time that their cousins back home do.

In other words, there's no cut-and-dried formula to predict rut behavior for whitetails in every part of the country.

However, by interpolating the rut data that is available from state fish and game agencies, I was able to come up with an average rut calendar by latitude. And though it's not infallible, this calendar will give you a good idea of what rut behavior to expect when hunting in your neck of the woods. Following are some specifics on what you can expect in the three different rut zones.

## THE NORTHERN ZONE

The whitetail deer's biological clock is fairly well synchronized throughout the Northern Zone of U.S. states and Canadian provinces (see accompanying map for details). Though the peak of the northern rut may vary somewhat, the behavior of deer in the Northern Zone can be more easily predicted than that of deer from either the Central Zone or the Southern Zone.

Northern deer herds were the source of many stocking populations for the other states. Yet, few northern deer herds were stocked themselves, so whitetail strains are pure and rut timetables similar.

One major timetable difference within the state of Michigan does exist, however. Although there's only one subspecies of whitetail—*Odocoileus virginianus borealis*—in the state's deer herd, the peak of the rut for the northern segment of the herd is later than that for the southern herd: exactly opposite of what should be true. Scientists believe that this is a survival adaptation made by the northern herd over many years of late spring green-up. If fawns were born any earlier, northern does wouldn't have enough of the succulent green forage that's needed to produce nourishing milk.

Overall, the accompanying is an average rut calendar for the Northern Zone. And, though it's not infallible, it does provide a good idea of what rut behavior to expect—and when to expect it—in this region.

## THE CENTRAL ZONE

In the Central Zone, the rut timetable is not quite as predictable as it is in the Northern Zone, yet it is still much more predictable than in the Southern Zone. Peak rutting dates across this zone vary from the last week of October and the first week of November in Indiana to the last two weeks of November in both Kansas and Kentucky.

Arriving at a median date for each basic whitetail rutting behavior required the analysis and interpolation of each state's reported rutting dates. Though some variations within the Central Zone do exist, they aren't generally extreme. The calendar should provide a good idea of what rut behavior to expect—and when to expect it—throughout the Central Zone.

## THE SOUTHERN ZONE

Whitetails range from Canada all the way to the equator, and the most predictable thing about these animals is that the farther south they live, the more unpredictable their rut cycles become. First, there's more

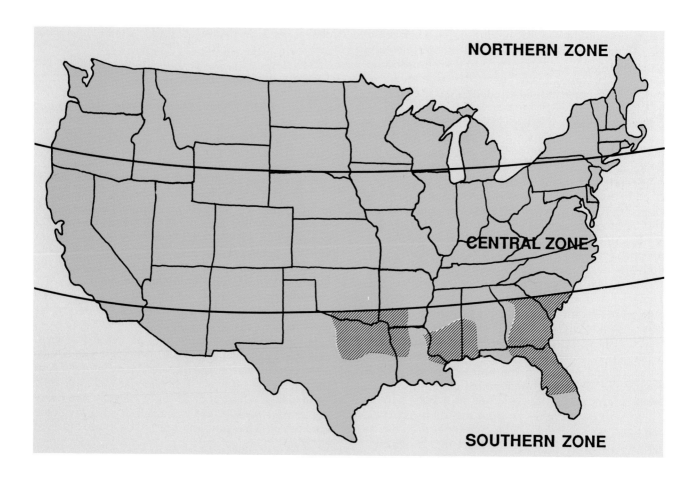

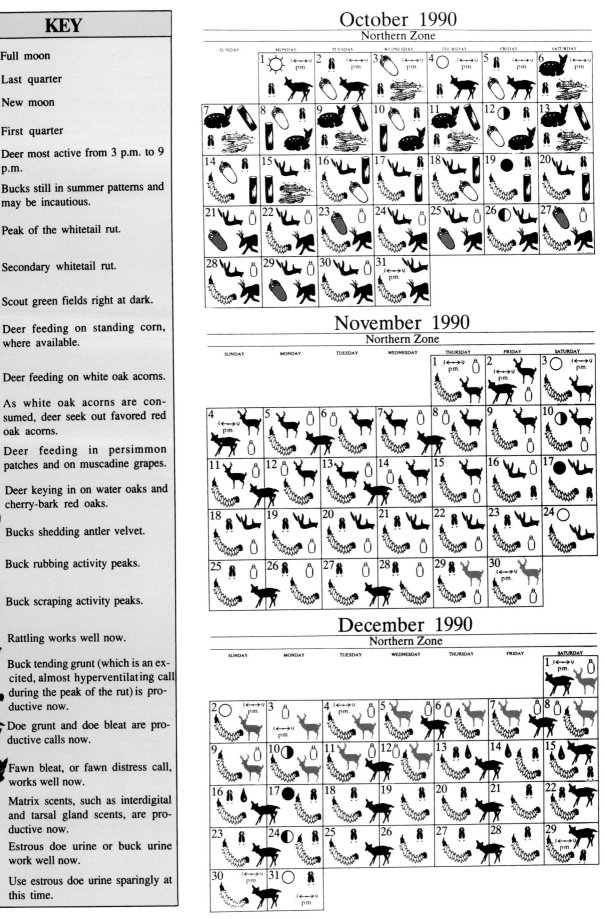

## October 1990
### Central Zone

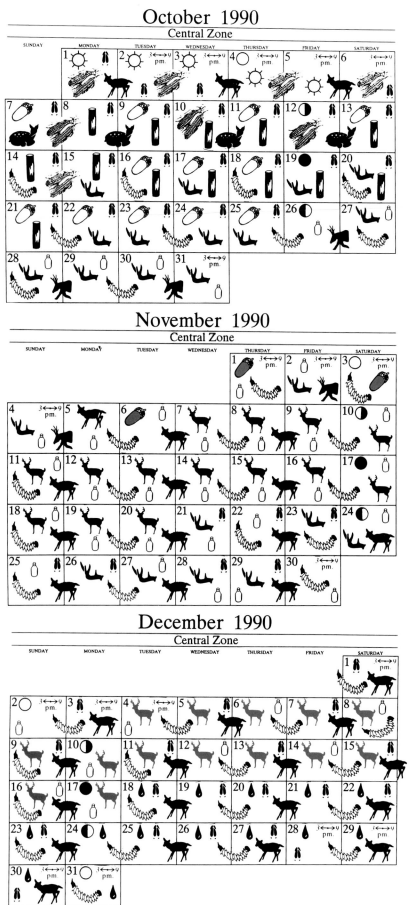

## November 1990
### Central Zone

## December 1990
### Central Zone

*The average rut calendars shown here provide a great deal of information for the hunter. Check with local game agencies about weather and other variables that may affect the average behavior. Adapt the calendars as necessary—and increase your chances of hunting success.*

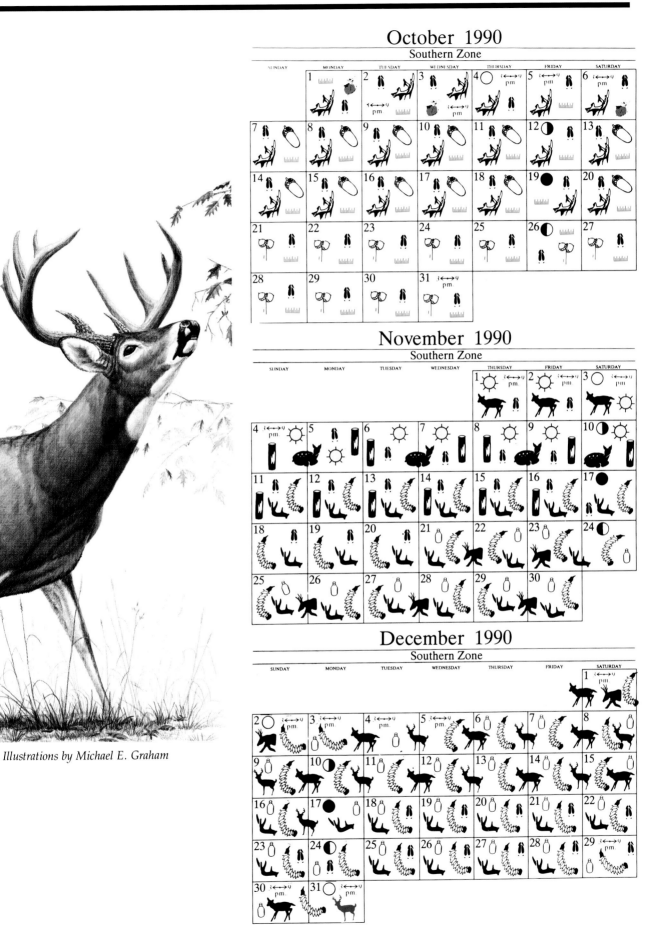

*Illustrations by Michael E. Graham*

*Knowing what behavior to expect when is a great help in getting your buck. Here a buck chases a doe. Photograph by Len Rue Jr.*

daylight year-round farther south. And, with more available light, antler growth cycles—and, therefore, rut behavior—can get totally out of sync.

Next, many different whitetail subspecies inhabit the Southern Zone—and each has its own slightly different internal rut timetable. Whitetails that were imported from other locations have helped throw the region's rut schedule off balance. In Georgia, for example, Wisconsin whitetails were brought in to repopulate certain areas of the state. But, rather than adapting a new rut timetable based on the amount of daylight in their new home, animals from Wisconsin stock are more likely to rut when their northern cousins do, in early November.

Mississippi, with stockings from both Texas and Michigan, has animals rutting from November to mid-March. One southern Florida population of deer lives close enough to the equator that at any given time, some animals may be rutting. Louisiana has several different populations of whitetail. Some rut in late September, but others rut in late February—an adaptation that scientists theorize may have developed after Mississippi River floodwaters pushed the whitetails regularly from their home ranges each year

at fawning time. In other words, the unpredictable whitetail is *most* unpredictable in the Southern Zone.

The Southern Zone calendar was derived from the rut data available from various state game and fish agencies. Look it over to discover when particular rut behaviors are likely to occur. Some regional variations are a fact of life in the Southern Zone, however, so be sure to check with local officials to verify peak rut dates in your particular area. (Shaded areas on the map are locations where the widest range of rutting behavior will be exhibited.)

On each of the regional rut calendars, you'll notice that, in addition to rut information, I've also given hints on food preferences and vocalizations, as well as optimum times to use the various types of scents during the pre-rut and post-rut periods. I hope this will help you narrow down what strategy to use at specific times during the season.

Overall, the most challenging part of whitetail hunting is trying to figure out what these cagey animals will be doing at any given time. With luck, these calendars may help you do just that.

# Stay in a Hunting Rut

*By John Weiss*

There are eight gals at the University of Georgia who have recently shed a good deal of light upon deer behavior. Their names are Heather, Krishna, Madonna, Scarlett, Athena, Flirt, Dutch, and Tina. But they're not the usual coeds that one might expect to find on a college campus.

They are whitetail does that acclaimed deer biologists William Knox, Karl Miller, and Larry Marchington have been intensely studying to learn more about the annual rutting period of that species.

For deer hunters, the rut is unquestionably the most exciting highlight of the season, because just thinking about bucks clashing their antlers together, tending fresh scrapes, and chasing does makes the adrenaline surge.

Yet, though most hunters have long thought of the rutting period as a brief span of time occurring in mid-November and generally lasting no more than two weeks, we're now learning that this is entirely untrue. The *peak* of the rut—when mating activity intensifies to its highest level of the year—is indeed of approximately two weeks duration in November, but breeding certainly isn't confined to this narrow time frame.

We now have evidence that whitetails engage in mating behavior over a period of time believed to be as long as six months! Moreover, this startling new information is enabling enterprising hunters to pursue rutting whitetails as late into the winter season as state regulations allow.

When Larry Marchington recently dropped this bombshell on me, which incidentally was published in the *Journal of Mammalogy* in 1988, it was like he had supplied several key words to a crossword puzzle that I hadn't been able to solve for many years.

For example, it caused me to remember the numerous occasions when I've successfully rattled in bucks during Ohio's muzzleloader season. Although I've always been pleased with this accomplishment, it has been a source of continual bewilderment, too. You see, Ohio's black-powder season takes place in January, when bucks are not "supposed" to be fighting with each other in defense of breeding territories or for the privilege of mating with nearby does.

But perhaps the most perplexing experience I've had occurred in 1990. I was drinking my morning coffee while staring out the kitchen window of our farmhouse when suddenly a doe emerged from a distant thicket and bolted across one of our hay meadows. Scant yards behind the doe, an impressive eight-point buck was trailing with his nose tight to the ground. The buck repeatedly closed the distance and attempted to mount the doe, and eventually the pair disappeared over a knoll. Whether the buck ultimately mated with the doe I don't know, but they were unquestionably engaged in rutting behavior. The significance of this event is that it took place in March, a full three months later than I would have ever expected to witness whitetail mating activities in progress.

When it comes to whitetails, such mysteries abound, sometimes I think for the singular purpose of keeping research biologists happily and gainfully employed. Yet, on behalf of deer hunters, each year sees more and more of these riddles solved.

The unusual incidents described above, which involved the courtship rituals of deer quite late into the winter season, actually have very plausible explanations. This goes back to biologists Knox, Miller, and Marchington and their published findings titled "Recurrent Estrous Cycles in Whitetailed Deer."

Many hunters may already be aware of the fact that whitetail does that are not bred for one reason or another, or that do not successfully conceive after mating has taken place, recycle 28 days later. In other words, those female deer that are not impregnated within the 24-hour period that they're in heat experience a follow-up estrous cycle approximately four weeks later.

What most hunters—and even biologists—were never aware of until just recently is that a given doe does not merely experience one follow-up estrous cycle. Rather, a doe that remains unbred may come back into heat as many as *seven* different times in succeeding months. Naturally, as one might expect, this state of affairs continues to draw the attention of amorous bucks for as long as the does continue to come into estrus.

Biologists Knox, Miller, and Marchington made this discovery in a unique way. Their eight does were housed in individual pens from October through May. Every day, each female was allowed to associate with a mature, sexually experienced buck for a period of 10 minutes.

Whenever a particular doe permitted the introduced buck to mount her, it was apparent that she was experiencing an estrous cycle, because a doe not in heat will rarely allow a buck to take such liberties. To confirm the observations of behavior, whenever a given doe permitted herself to be mounted, she was then subjected to a sophisticated blood test known as a reproductive steroid serology examination to positively confirm that she was indeed in estrus.

Incredibly, the scientists documented the onset of whitetail doe estrous cycles as early as October 17 and as *late* as April 7, indicating a rutting "season" of 172 days!

The implications that all of this may have upon hunting the so-called "rut" are incalculable. Take the technique of antler rattling, for example.

## ANTLER RATTLING

In the past, hunters have generally restricted antler rattling to the mid-November peak breeding period,

*During the late season, a buck may return to a scrape that's been doused with "hot" doe scent. Photograph by Mike Biggs*

but we now know that this can be a big mistake and that they may be missing out on plenty of action late in the year.

According to Noel Feather, who has begun experimenting with late-season rut-hunting techniques, rattling is effective through the entire month of January. Rattling may even be effective in February and March, but it's a moot point because no deer hunting seasons are open at that time. Regardless, Feather, who is from Sterling, Illinois, is the only hunter to have ever rattled in and harvested three Boone and Crockett Club whitetails, two of which were taken with bowhunting equipment. And the bitter late-winter months are his favorite time to be afield.

"When the sounds of antler rattling punctuate the cold silence, any buck within earshot is easily convinced that a still-unbred doe is experiencing a recurring estrous cycle and that two other bucks already are on the scene, fighting to determine who will be granted the privilege of doing the mating," Feather explained. "Naturally, if there's a dominant buck in the area, he'll have none of this and will race to the scene to settle the dispute on his own behalf. But even a subordinate buck is likely to approach in the hopes that while the two superior animals are jousting, he might be able to sneak off with the doe in question."

Feather strongly recommends using a grunt call in conjunction with antler rattling. And he likewise emphasizes the importance of placing a stand behind a screen of brush or in a tree that has plenty of branches to afford ample concealment.

*Even late in the year, antler rattling may be an effective way of getting a buck's attention. Photograph by Leonard Lee Rue III*

"With most of the foliage gone late in the year, a buck can see a long way," Feather said. "Moreover, whitetails are easily able to pinpoint the precise location where they hear antlers clashing together. As a result, if your presence is too conspicuous, they'll detect you and dope out your scheme in an instant."

Keep in mind that when a buck responds to antler rattling, his foremost intent is to determine hierarchical rankings of the animals that he thinks are doing the fighting. Because of this, he is not likely to approach too closely until he can actually make visual contact with the deer in question.

Obviously, there will be no other deer around. But, by rattling in a location where surrounding cover restricts an approaching buck's long-range vision, a hunter can create the illusion that the fighting bucks are simply hidden from view.

If the responding buck nevertheless becomes suspicious and hangs up in the distance, using the grunt call may be what it takes to coax him in just a little closer. The grunt call mimics the sound that a buck makes when his nostrils are filled with the heady odor of a doe in estrus.

## SCRAPE HUNTING

On the subject of late-season scrape hunting, it can be an exasperating experience to select a nearby stand location and then wait for days or even weeks on end and never have the pleasure of seeing the scrape's creator return.

This type of situation, according to Gene Wensel of Hamilton, Montana, commonly occurs in regions where there is a great imbalance in the herd's sex ratio. Wensel is the author of the book *Hunting Rutting Whitetails*, which has long been considered the definitive work on the subject.

"The function of a scrape is not as complicated as many hunters believe," Wensel said. "It is simply a place that serves as a catalyst for a buck to meet a doe for the purpose of mating. Yet this well-defined role on the part of nature presumes that everything is in harmony and that there is a balanced sex ratio of one doe for each buck. Unfortunately, there are many areas of the country where deer herds are poorly managed and the does are allowed to far outnumber the available bucks.

"When this happens," Wensel continued, "the function of the scrape becomes no longer necessary. Early in the season, bucks may initially begin making a few scrapes out of pure instinct alone. But as soon as the region's overpopulation of does begin coming into estrus, each buck has far more female companionship than he can possibly handle."

Such an imbalance in a local deer herd explains why a large percentage of the does are not bred when they come into heat for the first time in October or November. It also is precisely the reason why nature has programmed them to experience recurring estrous cycles late into the dead of winter and even into early spring.

There are several solutions to this enigma that can allow late-season scrape-hunters to at least slightly tilt the odds in their favor.

First, a hunter should be in an area where antlerless deer may be legally taken, even if it means traveling to a different county or even another state. In regions where does are annually harvested in large numbers, there will be a more balanced sex ratio of males to females. Also, it is this very situation that fosters a high level of competition among bucks to find those fewer numbers of does that they might be able to breed with.

Consequently, the bucks will advertise heavily by laying down far more scrapes than they otherwise would, and they'll regularly return to previously made scrapes to see whether a doe has been there during their absence. They'll also be far more responsive to antler rattling.

If a hunter must content himself with hunting in a region where the sex ratio of the herd is imbalanced in favor of too many does, a couple of other options are worth considering.

One January on our farm, where we have too many does, I knew in advance that bucks wouldn't be revisiting their former scrapes with a high level of frequency. This was confirmed by quickly checking the scrapes that I had located back in November. As I expected, most of the scrapes had long been abandoned and had become dried out, weathered, and partially covered with leaves and other windblown debris.

I did, however, find one scrape that seemed to be far cleaner than all of the others, its slightly muddy texture indicating that it was being revisited perhaps once a week. As a result, that was where I decided to install my portable tree stand. Then, to further boost my hopes, I attempted to increase the buck's frequency of revisitation by liberally dousing the scrape with doe-in-heat scent.

Within only two days, I had the buck—a heavy six-pointer—coming back to his scrape both morning and night for four consecutive days in a row. Unfortunately, as such things typically happen when bowhunting, an acceptable shot never presented itself.

Nevertheless, the lesson learned is that if does number high in a particular region, the hunter should know in advance that bucks will not be inclined to regularly tend their scrapes, but that they can be induced into doing so through the use of an estrous doe scent to present the illusion that a "hot" doe is in the immediate vicinity and that she's eager to breed. The premise upon which this technique is based is the simple fact that mature bucks are relatively lazy. Therefore, we can infer that no matter how many still-unbred does may be in a buck's bailiwick, any female that aggressively solicits the buck's attention—rather

*There is now evidence that whitetails engage in mating behavior for up to six months. Photograph by Charles J. Alsheimer*

than requiring him to pursue her—is going to draw his most interested response.

## TRAIL WATCHING

Yet another technique that I'm confident will pay handsome dividends late in the season is trail watching—but with a unique twist that most hunters never consider.

Keep in mind that throughout much of the year, bucks and does do not associate with one another but rather cling to their own separate social groups. Accordingly, as they travel throughout their familiar home ranges to engage in a myriad of activities, bucks and does establish their own different networks of trails. Yet, when does begin coming into estrus in October and then periodically recycle late into the dead of winter, bucks engage in what is known as *trail transference*, a behavioral change that sees them frequently detouring from their own routes onto doe trails.

By way of illustration, let's say that a buck is walking along one of his usual routes with some particular destination in mind. It's almost a certainty that at some point his trail will intersect with a doe trail. If the buck detects the lingering odor of an estrous doe that recently traveled that trail, he will immediately abandon his own route and follow the doe trail until he eventually catches up with the female and attempts to breed her.

If the doe is not quite ready to breed and will not submit to the buck's advances, the buck will follow immediately behind the doe in what is known as a *tending bond*. Eventually, the doe will permit mating to take place, after which she'll lose heat. At that time the buck will once again engage in trail transference, but now it will involve him reverting back to his own travel routes. This will only be a temporary state of affairs, however, because within a matter of hours—or in some cases only minutes—the buck's travels will likely see him cross another doe trail where he may detect the residual estrous odor of another female and again engage in trail transference.

The intriguing thing about all of this is that for generations hunters have been advised to concentrate their scouting efforts on locating so-called "buck trails" and then situating their stands or blinds nearby. Sometimes this pays off, particularly if the month is November, the sex ratio of the herd is in balance, and the bucks are energetically checking and re-checking the scrapes that they've laid down.

Late in the year, however, I much prefer to watch doe trails. Does do not engage in trail transference; they cling to their own routes on pretty much a year-round basis. Therefore, as each doe in the local population experiences a recurring estrous cycle, you can bet the grocery money that the resident buck will quickly become aware of her body chemistry change and deviate from his own line of travel onto hers.

There are several sure ways to distinguish between buck trails and doe trails. Late in the season, does seem to have a penchant for the lowest elevations in a given region, especially bottomlands where meandering creeks are present. Look also for gently sloping sidehills facing to the south where there are thick stands of evergreens. Bucks continue to spend most of their time on higher ground, but they frequently travel downhill to cross the bottomland to gain access to the higher ground on the opposite side, and it's during the course of traveling downhill or crossing the bottom that they're most likely to come upon a doe trail.

Buck trails invariably reveal evidence of tree saplings that have been rubbed in recent months as well as scarred and weathered remains of rubs from previous years.

Yet, as noted previously, I much prefer to find doe trails, which are equally easy to identify. Simply examine the tracks. Large sets of imprints intermingled with small tracks should be evident because until a doe comes into estrus, she'll be accompanied by her current offspring.

Although a doe rapidly approaching the onset of estrus will chase her offspring away, the young will continue to utilize the very same travel routes that their mother showed them during the previous months. They'll often bleat and blat in the hope that the doe will sympathetically allow them to rejoin her, which she will eventually do, but not until after she's been impregnated or loses heat.

Similar to scrape hunting late in the season, hunting a doe trail is far more likely to prove successful when the hunter uses an estrous doe scent. And because late-season hunting opportunities in most states are generally established for bowhunters, black-powder enthusiasts, and in some cases shot-gunners—all of which are afforded shorter-range shots—there's a very specific way in which a doe-in-heat scent should be used.

First, the hunter must locate a frequently used doe trail. Wherever that trail intersects with a buck trail is the spot to begin laying down estrous doe scent by means of a saturated drag-rag tied to a boot. The hunter should then simply hike to some specific vantage point where a tree stand or ground blind will permit a close-range shot. Because does have a tendency to meander, especially when they are nervous and anxious due to the onset of heat, hunters shouldn't worry about getting off the doe trail. Besides, when a buck engages in trail transference, he'll determinedly follow the estrous doe scent no matter where it leads.

To be sure, we're just learning about the late-rutting behavior of whitetails, and therefore do not yet have concrete answers to every conceivable situation that might arise. Yet, thanks to a team of biologists at the University of Georgia, we now have conclusive evidence that deer mate over a span of many more months than anyone previously believed. Understand the slightly different habits of late-rutting deer, and you can effectively use rattling, scrape hunting and other savvy rut-hunting methods well into the tail end of the deer season.

# Hunt the Rut Places

*By John Weiss*

**M**emories are the product of your experiences; every serious whitetail hunter can undoubtedly recall incidents that are forever chiseled in his memory bank. In my own case, one particular incident involved a pre-season scouting mission in southeastern Ohio, where I discovered 27 buck scrapes. In itself, that might not sound too unusual, but consider this: All of those scrapes were laid down within proximity of each other and within a scant *two acres* of second-growth timber.

Upon making this find, still another revelation became apparent. For the first time in my hunting career, it seemed ridiculous to determine whether the many mating invitations should be classified as primary scrapes, secondary scrapes, boundary scrapes, and so on. It just didn't make any difference what label a human might attach to them. In terms of whitetail communication, they all stood for the same thing: a very special place where a buck's most vigorous rutting activity was getting under way.

I wasted no time in hanging a portable stand in a strategic location within shooting range of six of the scrapes. Only an hour later, a splendid 10-pointer made his appearance. Something had the buck on edge, however, and after briefly checking only two of the scrapes, he departed for parts elsewhere.

During the next three days, I saw the same buck seven more times before the animal finally provided an acceptable shot. Upon releasing my bowstring, I watched the arrow pass through the deer's chest, and the buck ran only yards before piling up.

Aside from this memorable experience, I also gained a renewed appreciation for the axiom that enterprising deer hunters who consistently enjoy success aren't just plain lucky. Rather, they are observant and keep abreast of the latest research on deer behavior. Just as important, however, they take their new-gained knowledge and learn how to adapt the information to practical field use.

For example, though bucks make scrapes throughout their home ranges, biologists using radio-telemetry studies are now attempting to explain why some of those scrapes are frequently visited and others are soon abandoned. Obviously, when we obtain the answer to this puzzling question, it will be of tremendous value to deer hunters. Meanwhile, one of the few things that we do know about buck scraping behavior is that it is far from a happenstance occurrence.

**A** buck's scrapes are systematically strung out in linear fashion; the actual length of each scrape line is determined by the population density of animals in the immediate area. Understandably, in regions where deer numbers are relatively low, bucks must travel farther during the rut to find females. As a consequence, the scrape lines made by these bucks may cross many miles of terrain. On the other hand, where deer numbers are high and bucks don't have

*Find where does are bedding, and it's likely that a major rutting area will be nearby. Photograph by Charles J. Alsheimer*

to aggressively advertise for does, scrape lines are far shorter.

Despite differences in length, researchers have found something that the two types of scrape lines have in common. When Larry Marchington, head of the University of Georgia's deer research program, radio-collared deer to plot their movements on maps, he discovered that most scrape lines usually resembled a "star" or "cross" pattern. In other words, a given buck was found to put down two scrape lines: one running north/south and the other appearing on an east/west axis. Interestingly, the two lines crossed each other at their midpoints.

Exactly why this is so is not now known. One school of thought believes that one of the scrape lines is designated for daytime use and the other is reserved for nighttime activity. An even more likely explanation, however, is that by laying down his scrapes so that they are linear in direction and in accordance with compass points, a crafty buck engineers many different travel options for checking his scrapes, depending upon a given day's wind direction.

In any event, several years ago I attempted to use this insight to pattern bucks in my favorite hunting area. It seemed logical to assume that if I intensely scouted the terrain, found all of the scrapes in existence, and then plotted their exact locations on a map, I could ascertain scrape lines forming the correct configuration. From that point on, I figured, taking a nice buck would amount to little more than child's play.

Alas, a hunter's best laid plans often fizzle. With many bucks sharing the same range and each laying down his own scrape lines, I quickly realized the futility of attempting to identify the scrape lines made by one buck. Larry Marchington, however, came to the rescue again.

"For reasons we do not fully understand, not all of a buck's scrapes are of equal value to him," Larry explained. "So don't worry about trying to dope out the star or cross configurations. Just keep in mind that at intermittent locations along the length of his two scrape lines, a mature buck establishes several core rutting areas that occupy most of his attention.

"On the north/south axis of a scrape line, for example, there may be a lone, insignificant scrape every 100 yards for a distance of a half-mile," he continued. "Then suddenly, for no apparent reason, there may be 10 to 20 scrapes clustered in an area the size of a football field. A similar situation may exist along the east/west scrape line. If a hunter can key in on one of these major rutting areas, his tag is as good as filled."

In hindsight, the anecdote at the start of this article saw me chance upon just such a rutting area. I've since learned, though, that hunters can make their own luck and save a good deal of boot leather. The key is in knowing how to find the active areas along the scrape lines. Fortunately for hunters, these rutting areas have well-defined characteristics that seem to hold true throughout whitetail country.

One essential tool for finding these hotspots is a topographic map or an aerial photo of your hunting area; using either of these can reduce your scouting time afield by up to 90 percent. When looking at your map or photo, remember that whitetail bucks very rarely make scrapes on steep hillsides or on similar sloping terrain. Try to recall the scrapes you've found in the past. I'll bet this month's grocery money that the vast majority of them—even those in mountain

*Set up in a heavily scraped area, and you might catch a buck refreshening things. Photograph by Mark Kayser*

areas—were found on predominantly level ground. That flat terrain may have consisted of not much more than a narrow, terraced, hillside bench, but it was probably relatively level.

My friend Harvey Wilcourt, who is an expert in locating major rutting areas, advises hunters to also eliminate the edges of large croplands and meadows.

"It's quite common to find scrapes dotting the perimeters of such landforms," Harvey said. "But these scrapes will lie to you. They are only sporadically visited; usually a buck checks them only after dark. They are not where he engages in intense rutting activity."

In addition to noting the areas that are not worth pursuing, you also need to mark the landscapes that bucks prefer. Whitetails usually put down scrape lines in areas that invariably offer a mix of mature and immature trees and successive understory brush and vegetation. They tend to scrape infrequently in large, endless tracts of mature forest land.

When studying a topographical map or aerial photo, a hunter can, therefore, easily and quickly discount three areas: those with any appreciable slope, those where mature forests predominate, and those that are the perimeters of croplands. This elimination process should then allow the hunter to relatively easily identify the areas worth an on-the-spot investigation.

One time, Harvey and I were hunting gently rolling farmlands in central New York where we found a textbook-perfect illustration of a major rutting area. Ten years earlier, our landowner host had logged 100 acres of mature timber, but he had harvested only the choice trees, such as walnut and oak, and many species were left standing.

During the 10-year interim, the absence of a shade-producing high canopy had allowed a profusion of saplings and woody plant life to spring up, creating the diverse habitat that cover-loving whitetails favor. In addition, despite occasional dips and rises, the topography of the countryside was basically flat.

Although an onlooker might have interpreted our rather casual hike through the area as a sloppy, half-hearted scouting endeavor, we knew precisely what we were doing. We had already studied a map and eliminated the perimeters of the farmer's two pastures and cornfield and alfalfa meadows. We also discounted a steep ridgeline of oaks he hadn't yet harvested. At other times of year, these food sources would have been worth a look. We, however, were intent on scrape hunting, and because the area's does were approaching the start of their estrous cycles, we were certain the region's bucks would be devoting their energies to mating, rather than to feeding. Moreover, the former logging area was the only place on the farmer's several hundred acres where all the elements necessary for a buck's rutting area existed.

We began searching for scrapes and duly plotted each one on our map, hoping to eventually discern some type of pattern. As the morning wore on, we finally pieced together what appeared to be at least

one leg of a cross configuration running in a north/south direction. We were not able, however, to identify the east/west scrape line, so we were left with only one course of action.

*Scrapes are often found in level areas with mixed-age trees, brush, and vegetation. Photograph by Charles J. Alsheimer*

"You follow this scrape line heading north," Harvey suggested, "and I'll work it to the south. We'll meet back at the Jeep in an hour."

It was Harvey who had the good fortune to make a terrific discovery.

"I was heading south beyond the last scrape marked on our map," he explained when we met later. "Scrape lines are never perfectly straight, so I was zigzagging slightly to cover a 50-yard swath of ground, and I was finding a random scrape every 75 yards or so. Suddenly the breeze shifted a bit, and I detected a pungent aroma in the air. I headed toward the source, and moments later stepped into a clearing where the odor was so raunchy it was like being downwind from a privy."

In that one-acre opening, which was surrounded by cover so thick it would have strangled a gopher, Harvey found the ground peppered with one scrape after another. He counted nine of them and then beat a hasty retreat so that he wouldn't disturb the area.

After lunch, Harvey quickly hustled back to the rutting area carrying a portable stand. Two hours later—in the middle of the afternoon—he took an impressive eight-pointer.

Although it's quite possible to follow a scrape line as Harvey did and eventually discover a large concentration of scrapes, exasperation often defeats a hunter's best efforts. As mentioned earlier, trying to sort out which scrapes are part of a pattern can be confusing at best. That's why it's so important to use a map or photograph to identify areas where bucks are most likely to concentrate their scrapes before you go afield. In addition to using these tools, there are a few other shortcuts you can use to make scouting easier and more efficient.

Remember that for much of the year, adult bucks and does live in different areas of their shared home ranges and seldom mingle. As the rut approaches, however, they become inseparable. Therefore, keeping tabs on the whereabouts of does can play a key role in locating a buck's major rutting area.

Time and again, I've bird-dogged a scrape line for several hundred yards, eventually discovered a major rutting area and then, upon closer investigation, found a doe bedding area nearby. Now, when I'm having a tough time following a scrape line or finding a rut area, I try to recall where I have found doe beds in the past. Once I've found a doe bed, it's then easy to study the surrounding 200 or 300 yards for the terrains where bucks like to establish their prime breeding grounds.

If you are hunting in unfamiliar terrain, finding doe bedding areas is not difficult. Does generally prefer to bed in thickets midway up a slope, instead of in bottomlands or along ridge crests. The beds can be easily identified by the matted ovals of varying sizes that are indented in the grass and leaf litter, and by large and small tracks leading in and out of the area. (The smaller tracks are those of the doe's youngest offspring, which will stay with their mother until she drives them off when her estrous cycle begins.)

A more scientific way to identify a doe bed is to bring along a tape measure. According to Dr. Ken Nordberg, a noted Minnesota deer biologist, beds that

*Aerial photos can help pinpoint areas where bucks are likely to lay down scrapes. Photograph by John Weiss*

*The author uses his knowledge of rut areas to get close to trophy bucks. Photograph by John Weiss*

are 40 inches or less in length usually belong to does, yearlings, or fawns. Beds that measure 45 inches long typically indicate a 2½-year-old buck, says Nordberg, and 50 to 56-inch beds have likely been made by 3½ to 6½-year-old bucks. It should also be noted that mature bucks will most often bed alone.

Essential to remember, too, is that mature bucks seem to favor the same major rutting area each year; they will even make scrapes in the exact same spots that they did the previous season. Telltale evidence of this can be seen by closely examining scrapes to see if they have a dished-out saucerlike appearance from repeated use. You're also likely to find rubs on nearby saplings that are in various stages of healing.

Interestingly, these major rutting areas are so valued by deer that even if you take a buck in one of them, another buck will almost certainly take over the same area the next year. It is, therefore, always wise to investigate any prime rutting area you have found in the past because of the likelihood that it will be used again.

On a tract of national forest land that I hunt in South Carolina, for example, I hunt the same major rutting area every fall. I've taken seven bucks there, and every one of them has been taken within a few hours of my first day of hunting. I have even placed my portable stand in the same tree every year.

Finally, it's important to note that, though finding a major rutting area is a virtual guarantee of deer hunting excitement, such strategy does not work throughout the season.

Hunting major scrape areas is best early in the season. Virtually all major rutting scrapes are created and most actively tended during the pre-rut as a buck attempts to interest does. The rut itself doesn't begin until the does come into estrus; from that point on, bucks spend less and less time monitoring their scrapes and more and more time traveling in the company of receptive females.

It is always an excellent idea to ask a local biologist when the peak of the rut will occur in the area you intend to hunt. Then, using that information as a guide, plan to invest actual hunting time during the two to three weeks prior to that date.

Hunters should no longer get overly excited when they find a lone scrape—no matter how large or fresh it may be. Search instead for concentrated activity in small, isolated areas that boast a large number of clustered scrapes. These are the spots where a buck is diligently advertising for female companionship.

Find one of these major areas, and your only lament will be that your deer hunting season is over all too quickly.

# Bucks in Over-Drive

*By John Weiss*

**M**ost of what you've read about deer drives is not true. And the maps you've seen published, with arrows indicating the directions deer will travel when pushed by drivers, bear little resemblance to real-life situations in today's deer woods. As a result, I'd be willing to bet this week's grocery money that the traditional, worn-out driving tactics you and your partners are currently using are largely ineffective.

In the least, the rather standardized deer drives so prevalent among today's whitetail hunters don't have much relevance when it comes to taking big bucks that have become programmed to react to drive situations in an entirely different manner than naive younger deer. In short, today's big deer are panic-proof, and that means they're not likely to get up and flee directly away from a conventional drive line.

Yet it took the unraveling of some unforeseen events one year for my own group of hunters to realize just how often mature bucks had undoubtedly been making fools of us.

These events took place in southern Ohio, where it's common for small groups of hunters to stage drives all day, every day. Only a small percentage of hunters in this area patiently sit in tree stands and still fewer attempt stillhunting. Making drives is the name of the game, and the driving typically begins at first light in the morning and continues until evening dusk settles in.

Well, as it happened one day, the six of us planned the logistics for 14 different drives, and by early after-

noon we had attached our tags to one doe and two small bucks. Trouble was that, by that time, we had also completed all 14 drives. Because we didn't have permission to hunt on adjacent lands, there were only two alternatives: Quit for the day, or return to the location of the first drive that we had staged that morning and begin driving each cover a second time.

**W**ith our standers in place, the spreadout drive line began working through the cover exactly as had been the case earlier. However, after he had progressed only about one-third of the way through the cover being driven, Tom Tomlinson popped a bootlace, requiring him to squat down to initiate a repair. It only took a few minutes, but in the meantime, the drive line had advanced more than a hundred yards, leaving Tomlinson far behind.

When the hunter finally stood and took only a few short steps, he heard a slight rustling in the leaves behind him and a quick glance revealed a splendid eight-point buck slinking along in a head-lowered, sway-backed posture. Probably more by spontaneous reflex than conscious effort, Tomlinson snapped off a quick shot at almost pointblank range, and the deer went down in a heap.

As Tomlinson admired his buck, he considered the hairy situation that might have presented itself had the buck jumped up in front of, instead of behind, him, because that would have required shooting in the direction of his departing friends—which is absolutely *verboten*. Right then, he realized the importance

*Careful driving techniques can get deer to abandon their favorite hiding places. Photograph by Len Rue Jr.*

of every hunter exercising the utmost restraint when it comes to staging drives—to always ensure safe shooting at close range, at fully identified targets, and with no intervening cover even partially blocking the gunner's view.

When the group later rejoined for a confab to discuss the unusual happening, voiced opinions differed widely. Several hunters speculated that the buck had moved into the cover sometime after we had driven the location earlier that morning, but this opinion didn't account for the buck somehow being behind the drive line during the second attempt to push the cover.

Finally, we came to a consensus that the big deer had been there all along and that he had simply refused to leave his chosen security cover, preferring instead to repeatedly circle and dodge any human intruders.

About then, Tomlinson stated his future intentions.

"Next time we hunt together," he said, "I'd like to volunteer to be on the drive line all day. And I hope you don't mind if I occasionally lag behind a bit!"

Of course, Tom Tomlinson is only one of many hunters who have recently begun to accept the tenet that, aside from hunting scrapes during the rutting period, enacting a forced movement is just about the only way to take truly big bucks.

The reason is because most big bucks become nocturnal in their behavior due to conditions that tend to inhibit their daytime activities. Common examples of conditions that suppress daytime movements include

*Bucks may try to vacate small patches quickly, so standers must be prepared. Photograph by William Lea*

the existence of a full moon (which allows for safer, nighttime feeding), strong daytime winds, unseasonably warm temperatures, and hunting pressure. Whenever one or more of these conditions exist—a situation that occurs more often than not—maintaining a vigil on stand is futile, with drives being the most viable alternative.

Obviously, the key to the success of any drive is learning how to predict the most likely escape routes the animals will attempt to use. Yet, what most hunters fail to understand, especially if the terrain being driven is relatively large, is that though immature deer will likely vacate the premises posthaste, mature bucks probably won't come out at all.

Big bucks are extremely security conscious. Moreover, they select their hiding places with craft and cunning and seem to instinctively know that rising from their beds and exposing themselves to full view increases their vulnerability. Consequently, when a hunter filters through a big buck's area, the buck will quite often lower his chin right down onto the ground and then not even blink!

Georgia deer biologist Larry Marchington once told me about a time he was hiking through a wooded area on a routine survey of habitat types when he spotted a whitetail buck bedded in a brushy thicket. The buck quickly lowered his head, and Larry decided to have some fun by attempting to get as close as possible to the animal.

"I made no pretense about my intentions," Larry explained, "and simply began walking straight toward the animal. He was facing in a quartering-away direction, and I got so close that I could have reached out with a stick and prodded the buck in the rump. But, he never budged an inch. Finally I walked around him in a semicircle in order to directly face him. Only after we eventually made eye contact with each other from only scant feet away did the buck explode out of the cover like he'd been scalded!"

Recurring incidents like this make me wonder how many times each year hunters walk right past huge bucks. Therefore, after a drive has been concluded, if members of your group have reason to believe that there is still a buck in the cover somewhere, there's only one thing to do. Drive the cover a second time, or even a third, until the buck is either routed out or everyone is convinced that he wasn't there in the first place.

Yet don't make the mistake of driving the cover in the same manner the second time, because the only thing that this will accomplish is to educate the deer in that particular area. Try something different, such as driving the cover in the opposite direction, with your standers placed in the vicinity of where the drivers started out the first time.

Take a plantation of thick pines, for example. This type of cover offers a buck a myriad of hiding possibilities, and if your drivers repeatedly approach from the west, it won't take very long for all of the deer in residence to learn from the experience.

Therefore, good advice the second time you drive

the pines would be for the drivers to approach from the south, the next time from the east, and so on. That way, especially if you are the lucky beneficiaries of windy weather, the deer will remain totally confused and not know which direction to expect danger from. Nor will they ever know either the surest escape route to take to avoid blundering into hunters on stand or the intended travel routes of the drivers.

In going back to my friend Tom Tomlinson and how he had to credit a broken bootlace in the successful taking of a nice buck, it's now a standard practice for every member of our drive line to make a fishhook pattern. This strategy capitalizes upon a wary buck's preference to hide rather than run.

Draw upon your own gut-level instincts, for example, and imagine yourself trying to elude someone in a jungle. If your pursuer passed close by, but you knew that you were well concealed, chances are you'd hunker down and freeze. Later, after that person had passed and continued on for some distance, you'd undoubtedly reason "this spot is no longer safe." Then, you'd probably begin sneaking in the opposite direction to increase the distance separating you and your adversary while simultaneously looking for a new and better hiding place where you wouldn't again have to risk such a close confrontation.

A whitetail buck behaves much the same by first holding tight in his bed, allowing the driver to pass, and then rising to his feet in an attempt to slip out the back door. Because he is so closely tied to his chosen security cover, it's not likely that the buck will leave the region entirely. Yet, he will indeed feel his safety has been jeopardized and that it's time to relocate his bed a slight distance away—but still in the same immediate area.

It was understanding this behavioral trait of whitetails that prompted Tomlinson to invent his novel fishhook drive. For the purpose of illustration, imagine a brushy river bottom thicket. One or two hunters have been placed on stand along the far edge of the thicket several hundred yards from the drivers. At the near edge, two hunters enter the thicket and begin a routine drive, making their presence well-known by carrying on a casual conversation as they work their way through the cover.

However, instead of the drivers actually proceeding all the way through the length of the thicket to where their partners are stationed on stand, they only travel perhaps two-thirds of the way through the thicket and then reverse their line of travel. Ever so quietly, they begin sneak-hunting in the opposite direction toward their starting points. Naturally, they both wear bright-orange safety clothing and always keep track of each other's location.

Quite often, one of the drivers will have an almost ridiculously easy, close-range shot at a buck slipping way. But here's what makes this drive so super-effective. Any buck that initially stayed put until the drivers had passed and then began slinking away in the opposite direction will invariably find a new place to quickly bed down. If one of the drivers does not get a shot when the buck is on his feet, the buck will predictably hold tight in his bed once again when the drivers approach during the course of making their fishhook pattern. Then, when the drivers pass the second time, the buck will again rise from his bed and begin moving away from the drivers; this will take him squarely in the direction where the stand hunters are waiting!

A similar technique is known as "back standing"; in this technique, hunters are placed on stand both ahead of and *behind* the drive line, with the drivers purposely spreading themselves far apart to actually encourage deer to slip back between them so that the rearmost stand hunters may have shots. Here again, it is imperative that all participants keep close tabs on their partners' whereabouts to avoid any possibility of risky shooting.

The intriguing thing about the fishhook drive is that it can be counted on to produce bucks even on crowded public hunting lands. There have even been several instances in which our group has seen hunters piling into trucks shortly after they had just completed a drive somewhere, has stopped to chat with them briefly, and has then driven the same exact cover and taken a buck that had cleverly eluded the first drive party.

However, one thing that we've noticed about the fishhook drive is that it works best in level-terrain situations, and especially if the hunting party is relatively small, and only if two or three individuals are able to act as drivers.

If the group is small but is hunting in hill country, a still better drive strategy is one that I learned in Tennessee from John Marcks. He dubbed his innovation "the diagonal shift."

"We rarely have enough hunters in our group to place several on stands and designate still others as drivers," Marcks explained, "so we don't use hunters on stand at all."

If you were to have a bird's-eye view of a diagonal shift drive, it would look like a line of individuals marching up and across the crest of a ridge, down through the next hollow, up the opposite facing slope, down the next and so on. The most obvious feature of the drive line, however, is that it is not straight but angular, like the longest leg of a right triangle. Thereby, the lead hunter at the forward end of the drive line may be as much as several hundred yards ahead of the trailing hunter at the opposite end of the drive line.

What makes this strategy so productive is that when a buck holds tight until a driver has passed and then rises from his bed and begins sneaking in the opposite direction, the deer has no idea that he might be skulking right into the lap of another driver trailing behind the first.

Moreover, this tactic is a very safe way to stage a drive, because, due to the way in which the drivers are staggered diagonally across the rolling terrain, a hunter presented with a shot can shoot straight ahead or straight back or to his immediate right or left—assuming that he knows that another driver isn't directly in front of, or in back of, him and that the hunter "ahead" of him hasn't lagged behind, nor the hunter "behind" him speeded up. (In a conventional drive, shooting in any direction other than behind the driver would be very unsafe because of standers placed up ahead and other drivers lined up to one's right and left.)

A few other tips also are in order when it comes to driving today's well-educated bucks. I've been describing how panic-proof bucks generally prefer to hold tight in their beds rather than make like jackrabbits and head for the next county. But this usually only applies to bucks in large, unbroken tracts of real estate where the animals have plenty of room to circle and dodge intruders.

In small or broken segments of terrain, just the opposite often applies, and the deer seem to know that their survival depends upon their ability to get out of a tight space as quickly as possible and into distant cover. My group has had many experiences, for example, in which members began driving a 10-acre woodlot and heard shooting from the standers within only one minute of beginning to push the cover.

This type of situation makes timing crucial to success. If the drive begins only five minutes too early, before the standers are well situated at their intercept locations, the effort is almost certain to be doomed to failure.

By the same token, a hunter who is instructed to take a stand must exercise great care in hiking to his designated waiting location. If a buck is bedded close by and hears the hunter moving into position, he'll undoubtedly attempt to skirt the hunter and thereby vacate the immediate area.

A hunter moving to his stand should therefore take the long, roundabout way, if necessary, and sneak into position as quietly as possible. Also of critical importance is that once the stander has selected his vantage point, it is imperative that he not budge an inch. Many standers, after being in position for a few minutes and having an opportunity to survey their surroundings, decide that they'd be better off 50 yards to their right or left. In not knowing that their partners may have already started the drive, they begin walking to the "better" location; and any buck coming their way instantly spots their movement and veers sharply to avoid them.

Finally, strive to maintain a degree of flexibility in engineering various types of drives. Today's whitetail buck lives in closer proximity to mankind than his predecessors, and this has fostered in him the ability to quickly pattern man's various activities.

It is for this reason that big bucks find it quite easy to outfox unimaginative hunters who always work drives in the same manner day after day and year after year. Conversely, those big bucks that ultimately find themselves packaged away in someone's freezer are deer that never expected the unexpected.

# Taking Aim
# and Trailing Game

*By Norm Nelson*

When you're fighting midday drowsiness on a very dull deer stand, nothing wakes you faster than the roar of a shot not far away. The blast that jolted me was from my younger brother's carbine. After an alert wait, I hiked to Alan's stand. It covered a dense alder swamp, and Al had fired at a whitetail bounding its way through it. Our father, whose approach along the ridge pushed that buck past Al, joined us.

The dry swamp was a mess of thick alders, tall grass, and tub-size potholes big enough to hide a deer. The wet soil held too many fresh-looking deer tracks to pick which ones might have been made by Al's buck. Al could only tell us that when he fired "quite a ways out there," the next thing he'd seen was a flash of white. After that, no more buck.

This sounded as if the buck had taken a midair hit, which flipped it, showing lots of white underhair. Was it dead? If so, where? Fourteen-year-old Al couldn't pinpoint the spot in that featureless sea of gray alder brush. He and I looked fruitlessly for some time.

Then our father took over. From the tree stand, he reconstructed the shot. He looked over his left shoulder as Al said he was doing when the running buck appeared. Next, my father snapped his rifle to his shoulder, took a swinging aim at an imaginary bounding deer, and dry-fired. He froze there, then raised his head to find a reference point on an opposite timbered ridge.

"OK," he said, "you two head into the swamp on that bearing, side by side, 10 feet apart—no more. When I call, come back about 20 feet apart." That meant a systematic pattern, which beat blind groping. It provided some overlap, which was good. From the stand, he could keep us aligned to avoid missing spots.

When far enough out that he couldn't see our shoulders, we were called back. His logic was that a buck could have been no farther in the alder maze or Al never would have seen even the peak of its bounds. A whitetail at full speed normally bounds no higher than a man's shoulders (if that), unless clearing an obstacle.

Headed back to the ridge, I almost stepped on the deer. It's always amazing how little space a dead deer takes. Killed by a bullet in the spinal column, the deer had crashed steeply into one of the little dry potholes full of 3-to-4 foot swamp grass. After stepping back only two paces, the deer was virtually invisible. Our first random search had missed him by more than 25 yards.

Without my father's shrewd replay of Al's shot that led to an accurate and methodical search pattern, we could have looked a long time and still left a fine game animal. Here's why. Young Al's vague recall of the buck's location when shot at boiled down to a $30 \times 40$-yard area—one that would measure 10,800 square feet. Crumpled in his pothole, the buck occupied no

*The antelope offers a fine, behind-the-shoulder shot at a slight, quartering-away angle. Good bullet placement here will likely take out the lungs, making recovery fairly easy. Photograph by Erwin and Peggy Bauer*

more than a $3 \times 5$-foot space, or 15 square feet—$\frac{1}{720}$th of the presumed area. This meant that the theoretical odds for a blind search start at 720 to 1 against the searchers! Maybe not that bad in actual practice but still by no means good odds in thick cover.

Crippled or lost-game situations are not common for good hunters and rare for good marksmen—but they can happen. There are three important factors in preventing or solving these problems. One is making a good shot to begin with. The second is taking action to look in the right place for a possible downed animal, as my father had wisely done. Third is knowing how to trail and locate wounded game.

## MAKING A GOOD SHOT

Let's start with the shooting factor. If done right, it eliminates the wounded-game problem. Many once-a-year shooters think that the increased power, flat trajectory, and accuracy of modern rifles lessen the importance of shooting skill. They're wrong. An ounce of accurate shooting beats 10 pounds of superb tracking skill.

Game-getting marksmanship is not hard to learn. In just two lessons, my daughter was able to put five shots in a 10-inch circle at 100 yards, shooting offhand with a big-game rifle. Such things as rabbit hunting or bird shooting help teach the fundamentals of hitting moving targets. If you're a once-a-year shooter, at least do some familiarization firing before the season, if for no other reason than to check your scope or sights and relearn your trigger pull.

Today, most big-game rifles offer plenty of power. Where problems can occur is in bullet choice. Those designed for bigger game, such as elk or bears, sometimes don't expand well on the smaller deer, particularly if large bones are not hit. For example, I once took a neck shot at a whitetail buck at 20 yards with a .284 Winchester. The shot flattened the buck, but before I could get out of my tree stand, he started scrambling to his feet. The 140-grain Nosler bullet, excellent for elk, hardly expanded going through the deer's neck and missed both the carotid arteries and spinal section. A fast second shot killed him, or he would have been long gone.

As a rule, medium-weight bullets in given calibers kill deer faster than heavier, usually slower-expanding, bullets. The lighter bullets, in expanding faster, apply most or all of their lethal energy in the animal. Heavier slugs all too often apply much of their energy to the landscape on the far side of the game after penetrating through with insufficient expansion. Of course, for bigger animals the heavier bullets, such as the classic 180-grain loads in the popular .30/06, come into their own.

Shot placement is critical to quick kills. Many hunters argue hotly about the best places to hit sizable game. Here's what I've discovered about bullet placement through years of research and from speaking to other big-game hunters.
• The neck shot is unreliable on deer and even less desirable on bigger game like elk and moose. The problem is that only a small part of the neck is occupied by the spinal column and the two carotid (jugular) arteries. A nonvital hit in the neck may only stun the animal (as my first .284 bullet did to the whitetail cited). The neck is also a small target and one subject to erratically quick movement any time the animal moves its head.
• The brain shot is even harder to make than the neck shot. Misplaced shots can hit the animal in the nose or jaw, which may allow it to escape to die later.
• A big-game bullet in the shoulder area is the most reliable one to both immobilize and kill North American big game. First, the shoulder area is a good-size target. Second, a hit almost anywhere in that area with a bullet of reasonable power will do lethal damage. Unlike with a neck shot, precision is not as crucial. Hitting low, a bullet in the shoulder area breaks the upper leg and strikes the heart. If placed a bit higher, the bullet has a good chance to sever the aorta, the major "freeway" of the blood circulatory system; this often drops the animal more quickly than a heart shot because blood pressure collapses instantly with the severing of the aorta—something that may not happen as rapidly with a heart shot. (Heart-shot game often runs all-out for 100 yards or more.)

Higher yet, a shoulder shot smashes the scapula (shoulder blade) and likely fatally severs the spinal column. Between spine and brisket, a bullet already expanded by passage through upper leg bone or shoulder does maximum lung damage, part of it from a shower of bone/cartilage splinters as secondary missiles. True, the shoulder shot does wreck some meat and thus is avoided by some penny-wise, pound-foolish hunters. Would you rather lose a few pounds of second-rate shoulder roast or the entire animal? Next to the very difficult brain shot, the shoulder shot is the quickest and most humane hit. It's the easiest, too.

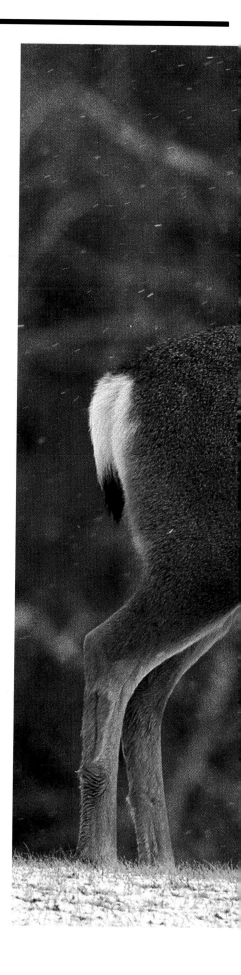

*The mule deer is in perfect position for a shoulder hit. Photograph by Erwin and Peggy Bauer*

Even if not killed outright, a big-game animal with one or both shoulders broken is usually knocked off its feet if standing and almost always knocked down if running.

• Second best is a hit behind the shoulder. It may offer better penetration with an arrow or low-velocity muzzleloader slugs, particularly on bigger game such as elk. Unless the bullet is angling sharply, it's likely to miss both the heart and opposite shoulder. If the bullet expands properly (which it sometimes doesn't when passing between ribs), lung destruction is lethal. But death may not occur for several minutes or longer. Meanwhile, the animal is likely to have full leg mobility to run at top speed into escape cover.

A young friend of mine once drilled an elk broadside through the lungs behind the shoulder ("to save meat") at less than 100 yards with a .30/06 180-grain factory load. The elk immediately darted into thick timber and vanished. This was in the Cascade Mountains where cover can be very dense. A search in driving rain failed to turn up blood sign; and there were too many conflicting tracks to piece out a likely trail. Ravens revealed the wasted elk's location two days later. It was only 75 yards away.

• A hit farther back behind the lungs and boundary diaphragm becomes a gut shot. Hitting high, it can cause fatal hemorrhaging of the liver. But quick kills are rare. Game hit here may travel far enough to pose a recovery problem. A lower paunch wound is even worse.

Despite what a lot of gun writers say, you do have a better chance of recovering a gut-shot animal hit with a high-energy bullet (which means good expansion, among other things) than one hit with a significantly milder load. There's no medical mystery to that. Even so, the milder bullet in a vital place such as the lungs/aorta will kill game much more quickly than twice as much bullet energy to the paunch. Again, there's no substitute for good marksmanship.

• Never write off a shot as a miss because the animal vanished or kept going with no sign of a hit. Running game often reacts less visibly to bullet impact than standing game. An animal on the run is already scared (or it wouldn't be running) and thus full of adrenaline. Hyped by that powerful stimulant, the animal may take a serious wound without even slowing down at first. Furthermore, a running animal such as a bounding whitetail undergoes some violent body contortions that can mask any flinch it may make when hit.

*The neck shot is unreliable and can easily result in lost game. (Left) Be precise with broadside shot placement. A hit even a tad too far back of the whitetail will result in a gut-shot animal. Recovery is difficult. (Upper right) To some, this facing shot may seem like a good one, but your margin for error makes it one that is best avoided. (Right) Photographs by Erwin and Peggy Bauer*

## EYEBALLING THE TARGET SPOT

This brings us to the second golden rule: Mark or remember where the game was when you shot it. Never take your eyes off the target. If the game vanishes at the shot, *immediately* memorize where it was. Pick a tree, brush clump, or horizon feature as a reference point. Immediately taking a compass bearing is a good idea.

Before leaving your location, mark it with a knife-blaze on a tree or by hanging a hat or handkerchief on a branch. You'll need this exact reference point when you look back from out yonder to where the game is supposed to be.

If you don't find the animal down, try to find tracks where it approached the shot scene. With luck, they may be easily discernible. Often there are other tracks, particularly if several animals were present or if your animal was on a well-used game trail, so look carefully. Look hard for hair. Shotgun slugs and large-caliber bullets (for example, muzzleloader balls or minis) blast loose a lot of hair on entrance. On exit, all bullets cut off a wad of hair.

The color and texture of the hair found allows educated guessing on where the animal was hit. Elk hair is tawny on the upper torso; dark on the neck, belly, and legs; and cream-colored or yellowish on the rump. Deer hair is hollow and coarse over much of the animal's body and lighter colored on the belly. Hair along the spine is darker at the tip and is almost black in the brisket area. On the inside of the legs, hair is white, not hollow and finer.

Search thoroughly for hair because you may not find blood where the animal was hit. On one hunt, I recall my 12-year-old son's voice quavering with disappointment when he told me of an apparent miss on a trotting whitetail. But a large amount of impact-shorn hair (his 12-gauge slug never exited) said otherwise, even though no blood hit the ground for the first 50 yards of tracking. A bit farther lay a lung-shot, dead deer.

## TRAILING WOUNDED GAME

"I looked for blood but couldn't find any, so I must have missed," is the common statement made by confused or careless hunters. A fatally wounded big-game animal may not bleed immediately and may never bleed very much externally at all. A high lung hit or a shot in the liver will cause the animal to bleed heavily, but most of the blood accumulates inside the body cavity with little external leakage.

When you find it, blood tells a lot. Very bright red blood—sometimes almost pinkish in color—with bubbles or froth usually means a lung hit. If you find it centered in the track (vs. alongside the tracks), it means that the animal is hemorrhaging from the mouth or nose and is not likely to travel far. Darker blood with green browse fragments indicates a stomach hit. Fecal matter in blood signals an intestinal wound. Darker blood free of debris can be either from the liver or the right side of the heart (the left side yields much brighter red blood). Because of its location well up in the gut cavity, blood from the liver doesn't escape readily, so a lot of darker blood may well mean a wound in the right side of the heart.

Medium-red blood without any lung-air bubbles may mean only a non-serious flesh wound, although a lot of it indicates major arterial bleeding, which can eventually be fatal.

Location of blood sign sometimes tells a story. Blood smeared on tall grass or brush can reveal roughly how high or low the wound is. Very low blood stains probably mean a broken leg. I recall one long shot I took when I feared I had gut-shot a broadside whitetail from the way it humped, then ran. But careful looking showed small *intact* blood droplets that fell on *top* of compressed snow crystals in the tracks. That could only mean bleeding from the extreme rear of the animal and not much at that. A hit in the ham? No, because a lot of extra-long, white hair was cut off at the shot scene—the length of hair found only on rump and tail.

That told me I'd only creased or grazed the rump or tail underside enough to barely draw blood. No doubt it stung and made the deer flinch or hump. But trailing verified no serious wound because of the following evidence: minor bleeding stopped soon; the animal never bedded, as badly wounded deer do when not followed right away; the deer used all legs normally (according to tracks), meaning no broken leg; and the deer was able to bound over windfalls with ease and run at full speed up a steep ridge, indicating a fully vital, healthy animal.

Pay attention to the animal's tracks and line of travel. An animal with a bad leg or shoulder wound often shows stumbling or misplaced tracks. If not pursued right away, a wounded animal usually lies down. Typically, it will make a sharp turn off its line of travel and then bed in some cover where it can watch its backtrail.

Once, while tracking a buck wounded at daybreak by one of our party, I was hard put to be sure of the tracks. The buck had headed down a dew-wet runway loaded with all kinds of seemingly fresh tracks. He lost both upper body hair and some blood at the hit scene and bled heavily in his first bed before sneaking off when he heard me following later. Worse, the bleeding stopped. But I looked sharply for his departure from the main trail and found it. The buck had taken a 90° leap off the trail. I knew that those were his tracks because he had fallen—obviously in the soft forest floor—when he bounded. From there, the trail headed for a thick stand of young pine. Rather than try to single-handedly get him there, I retrieved two of our party to stage a drive. It worked, and we bagged him.

When you are unsure how seriously an animal is hit, study its travel route, which should tell you something. A gut-shot animal will often head for the near-

*Careful trailing from the target spot will often prevent a lost-game situation. Photograph by Norm Nelson*

est water. Knowing that led me to a wounded moose one of our party had paunched two hours earlier. A hard-hit animal avoids climbing steep grades or jumping over sizable obstacles. Partner Bob Nelson fired at a young bull in a small elk herd. All of the animals flashed through timber too thick for a second shot. The spitzer bullet cut no hair on entry and never exited. There was no blood sign. But Bob had faith in his shooting (which is important) and followed.

Typical of spooked elk, the herd fled uphill. Less than 50 yards up the slope, one set of tracks abruptly left the others and angled downhill toward heavy

cover. There Bob found his bull dead from a lung hit. (But again, a solid shoulder hit would have spilled that elk at least long enough for a second shot and spared the suspense.)

Every wounded-game situation must be played by ear. Circumstances vary, but here are some useful tips:
• If you have hours of daylight, there are few hunters around, and if sign indicates a deer or moose hit in the chest or paunch, it's usually best not to trail immediately. Chances are the animal will bed down if hit hard, giving you an opportunity to later quietly trail within close range. (Unfortunately, wounded elk may travel long distances before bedding.)
• If heavy rain or snow threatens, or if darkness or other hunters are close at hand, start tracking immediately. Time is not on your side.
• When tracking, watch carefully to the sides as well as ahead. Game often bed to one side to watch their backtrail, as already explained. Tracking here is best done by two hunters, one piecing out the trail, the other doing nothing but intently scanning cover.
• Two-man tracking also helps when blood sign is hard to follow. One hunter stays at each blood spot while the second tracker casts ahead for the next sign. That way, you don't lose the known trail if you make a false move or two.
• If tracking alone, leave a bit of toilet paper at the last known blood sign before looking ahead for the next or when just trying to follow tracks on difficult ground.
• Hard-hit or dying animals often dive into the thickest available cover. A running elk I once hit with a .340 Weatherby in the lungs didn't go far, but vanished. We had quite a time in dense cover until we spotted a patch of elk rump barely visible in similar-colored, yellow cottonwood leaves growing out of an old logging slash pile. In its terminal dive, the elk buried itself so thoroughly that we had to chain-saw brush and logs to more easily extract it.

A last tip—important and often ignored! A momentarily shot-deafened shooter usually doesn't hear his bullet hit game—but a distant companion may. Furthermore, he can often even tell where the bullet hit. A rather tympanic *plokk* often means a chest cavity hit. A paunch shot makes an unmistakably water-sounding *palump* noise. Hearing that sound convinced me of a partner's hit on a running moose he swore he missed completely. Following up, we found the moose bedded nearby. And it had been paunch-shot, all right.

Properly done, hunting kills are far more humane than the "natural-causes" death of a lot of wildlife. Typically, those can mean agonizingly slow starvation in a bad winter or from the debility of old age. In the final crunch, it's good to know the fundamentals of locating downed or wounded game. But for both ethical and practical, meat-in-pan reasons, never depend on those as a crutch for poor or irresponsible shooting.

# PART 3

# WESTERN DEER

# The Muley Lifestyle

*By Sam Fadala*

**H**unters think of deer in man's image. That's understandable; our usual point of reference is ourselves. One old hunter, for example, told me that mule deer don't like the wind because it makes them nervous. The first part is true. Mule deer often get out of the wind. We don't know, however, that wind makes them nervous, depressed, annoyed, or concerned because we have no idea how mule deer reason—we only know how we reason.

There's little practical value in hunters' worrying about the *motivation* behind muley behavior as long as they know what deer do and when they do it. Smart Western hunters understand mule deer ways: territory, feeding behavior, social organization, daily schedule, senses, escape mechanisms, and rut. These behavioral traits tied with the twine of sound hunting methods and good shooting equal a package marked "success." This episode deals with one of these criteria: mule deer territory.

Mule deer have their own home grounds, which is why looking for them along lowland waterways, such as creek bottoms in the Rockies, is mainly a waste of time. These are whitetail niches, not major mule deer habitat during fall hunting seasons.

Mule deer live in a vertical world of four zones: summer range, lower summer range, winter range, and critical winter range. Their migration patterns drive them up the mountain or down. Most hunting seasons normally occur when deer are on their lower

*Knowing how mule deer behave can help you get up close for a good shot. Here a 5-point buck. Photograph by Len Rue Jr.*

summer range. By the time the muleys reach wintering grounds, seasons are usually closed. The deer are far more accessible in winter. That's why winter hunting seasons are so rare. Many grand bucks taken in the past were tagged during the late season, a hunting time now generally abandoned.

"Oh, that one," the lady said. "My husband shot that old buck at Christmas time many years ago. Jim went out on a sled to cut a Christmas tree. He took his rifle with him and got the buck. It was standing in some trees off to the side of the road." These words were in response to my asking about a huge mule deer buck mount adorning the wall of a motel in western Wyoming.

Mule deer territory provides food, water, shelter, and a staging ground for the mating season. Deer know every bump in their own geography. I've hunted mule deer too long to believe otherwise. When you see a buck ambling across a hillside, he's not wandering aimlessly; he's going somewhere. He knows where and, *I presume*, why.

Remember that empirical knowledge is dangerous knowledge. Sometimes we aren't seeing what we think. "Oh, look, that deer is searching for his herd." Really? How do we know that? Maybe he's heading for a food patch or bedding site or to visit a territorial spot he hasn't seen for a while. We don't know. What we do know, however, is that mule deer move within their range, and it's safe to say they know where they are going and why. That premise leads to an important hunting tactic: Find out how mule deer use their territory where you hunt. Learn where the deer are under various conditions because the four zones are seasonal and dependent on time of year, weather, and food conditions.

I thought I learned something new about mule deer vertical movement a few seasons ago. Deer were all over a wintering area—as they should have been in late November in the high Rockies. As far as I knew, though, not one flake of snow had fallen. "At last," I said to myself, "I've got evidence that it's timing, not weather, that forces this particular mule deer herd down from the high country." I always believed that weather, more than a seasonal clock, motivated that herd to descend the alpine heights in November. We were enjoying an "open winter." Yet, here were the deer on their wintering grounds. I told my son about my theory. "Sorry, Pop," he said. "There was a huge storm up top a week ago." I returned to my original premise: Mule deer come down when the weather tells them to, not when the clock strikes November 15.

Rocky Mountain mule deer are generally migrational, even in the badlands. That generalization stated, be hesitant about making others; all deer herds in a region do not behave alike. Nor do

*Mule deer leave high country when the weather tells them to, not when the clock strikes November 15. Photograph by Bill Kinney*

members of one herd all use the habitat in the same way. Bucks, does, and youngsters use territory differently. Sometimes they range together. Often they do not. A perfect example of this is a particular deer-filled area near Arvada, Wyoming. If you take an evening drive along the Housetop Route out of Arvada, you can see a couple of hundred mule deer in a few hours of touring, no matter the time of year. So there are always mule deer in that badlands area of the Powder River. But where are the nice bucks along the Powder?

"I don't know about you guys as hunters," Maurice Neville used to say to us. "Last winter I saw 10 big bucks in the canyons you're hunting now, and you fellows can't find even one of them." Neville, then foreman of a ranch along the Powder, had about given up on us as mule deer hunters. He'd sighted fine bucks in the area and his neighbor had four big busters hanging on the wall as proof of what lived in the area. We, however, never took any trophies.

One day I spoke with the neighbor who owned the big mule deer mounts. "Oh, those old bucks. I got them years ago when we had a November hunt in here. Bucks like those are way up there when you folks hunt." He pointed to the northeast, assuring me that the big boys stayed in the high range until storms drove them down. That year I dropped into the area during mid-November and brought along my son John and my hunting partner Gene Thompson. We saw what we had never seen in that place before: big bucks, heavy-antlered mule deer that had no like in the area during the October hunting season. So, you have to know where the bucks are and when. And, if you're talking about Rocky Mountain mule deer, you're dealing with migrational creatures. An astute hunter who studies a specific mule deer herd will learn where to look for the bucks during the hunting season—it's not a matter of territory alone, but of what piece of real estate is used under what conditions.

Mule deer patterns are complex. After scouting western Wyoming one year, my two sons said, "Dad, you've got to get a look at the big boys we found in the high country." The area had an early season and the bucks stayed in the high country until snow. But we found none of the big bucks that year, nor the next. We were correct in believing that they remained in the highlands during the early fall; but we were wrong about their exact location.

That's another aspect of mule deer territory: the buck stomp. Bucks have favorite pockets. I scouted an area with a wildlife biologist who assured me that the food and water supply in a buckless part of the territory was just as good as the food and water supply in the buck stomp. But in one spot, you'd be hard-pressed to find any antlers walking around. In another niche one-half mile away, a hunter would have to be blindfolded not to see a buck. The smart hunter scouts for and locates the buck stomp—that special piece of territory that the males like for whatever reason. If the hunter hits the timing just right, he and the mule deer occupy the same turf simultaneously.

Where did our high-country bucks go? The third hunting voyage into big-buck land prompted a wider search. For reasons only mule deer could understand, our bucks were down-country and to the north of where we had seen them only two weeks earlier. We recognized three of the eight big bucks we had seen before. Unfortunately, they were not the biggest of the big, and only one of us filled a tag. The key to success is prediction. When you can accurately predict what part of the range the mule deer will roam at a particular time of year under particular weather conditions, then your chances of a rendezvous with a big buck increase dramatically.

It is my philosophy that a deer that should be harvested is harvested. Only mature bucks are trophies. Bank on it. When you don't get the big boy, the elements do. Rarely will a trophy buck wear his crown for more than a few years. A life span of 10 winters is a long one, and a buck will be antler-prime only during the latter part of his tenure. Biologists who age big bucks will tell you that trophy heads are not juveniles.

When thinking of deer, territory, and movement, don't think only of migration—think, too, of how a deer uses an area each day. If you don't know how a buck uses his homeland on a daily basis, you're handicapped as a hunter. Mule deer—as a rule—are most active early and late in the day. I kept track of a mule deer herd on its lower winter range one year and found activity reduced to a couple of hours in the morning followed by a long period of day-bedding, and another couple of hours of activity in the late afternoon/evening followed by night-bedding.

At night—I know, because I spent several nights watching—the animals got up, walked around a little, and foraged briefly. During the hunting season—mid-October for this particular herd—the deer rose a few times during the day for brief feeding sessions. But the twilight pattern continued. So, if you want to find a feeding mule deer, look for him in the morning and afternoon, not midday. During the day you're going to have to find his bed.

I've jumped bedded mule deer bucks from timbered clefts in the high country that took me two hours of hard labor to negotiate. The odds of finding a bedded buck are directly proportional to the difficulty of the landscape. Man goes on two legs, and he goes well, considering this handicap. Compared with the four-legged masters of the mountain, man is a snail. A mule deer can pop up and over a steep mountain ridge before a two-legged hunter can cover 50 paces. We have to work with what we have, though, so the dedicated mule deer hunter burns shoe leather during midday and wears out his pant's bottoms in the early morning and late afternoon. I call it boot and binocular hunting: boots over the ground during bedding hours and glassing over the territory during the rest of the day. Not that I ever stop glassing. I have found bedded bucks by using my binoculars. But chances of doing so are slim.

Instead of hunting a bedded buck, you may prefer

*Mule deer are most active early and late in the day; at other times, they bed down. Photograph by Len Rue Jr.*

to pursue the bothered buck. Where does he go? This is another territory question. Based on the premise that mule deer are aware of the geography of their habitat better than we know our own houses, the buck knows exactly where to go to get away from a disturbance. Sure, that theory is couched in human terms applied to mule deer behavior. I'd want to hide if I thought something were after me. So I figure the deer does, too. But the statement comes from years of observation. I've seen many mountain bucks pushed out of their beds by hunters, bucks I had no interest in tagging. I only watched them. All of them dropped quickly into a black hole in the landscape. These bucks went up and over; down and around—but seldom out into the bright open of day.

One season I watched a buck pushed from his bed on the side of a steep hill. My glasses followed his movement through the trees—up, up, up until he topped the rise. I thought he was gone from view, but he popped out again on the next hill. He went two-thirds of the way up that hill, made a sharp right turn and re-bedded in an outcropping of boulders. I think a hunter who knows the location of probable mule deer hideouts in the area has an advantage.

Mule deer use their territory as mule deer, not as people. It's difficult, though, to refrain from thinking in human terms on matters of cervine behavior. I glass-searched a snowy hill a couple of seasons ago, looking into every patch of sunlight. It was colder than the inside of an ice-cream truck. Early bad weather had set in, and I figured that the storm might have triggered a premature down-mountain run for a big mule deer buck. Across the way there was a long, partially wooded ridge. Maybe my glasses could op-

tically lift a bedded buck out of the place. The sunny spots seemed inviting. The shady spots looked dismal. You guessed it. I found a buck, not the one of my dreams, but a mature animal, bedded not only in the shade, but on top of a sheet of ice. No human being with a brain larger than a walnut would have chosen that frigid bed, but the buck appeared as content as a cat by the fireplace. He used his micro-territory as a deer, not a person.

The general territory of the Rocky Mountain mule deer is vast; the deer does not, however, live in all of it at once. He selects certain niches from his habitat and uses each in its own time. Why he chooses one area over another, we cannot say. What makes one bit of micro-habitat a buck stomp and another a doe, fawn, and juvenile ground we don't know. Over a long period of hunting, each experience becomes a piece of a puzzle. Matching pieces make a picture. The picture is never absolutely clear. It's hazy and bordered in doubt, but it provides a look at mule deer life, if only a dim view. And that's better than a blank canvas.

Most mule deer hunting is based on wandering and hope—wander as far as your legs can carry you and hope for the best. Many fine bucks are taken that way. The largest specimens each season are usually claimed by hunters who bump into a big one. The mule deer hunter who fills his tag every season with a mature buck has more going for him than luck. He knows something about mule deer. He knows the territory of mule deer and how bucks habitually use their homeland.

# Six Methods for Mule Deer

*By Walter L. Prothero*

S ome hunters, or even guides, may be good at only one or two kinds of hunting—standing or driving for instance—and never try anything else. That would be all right if those methods always worked, but sooner or later, they're going to fail.

A good example of this kind of inflexibility occurred during a recent season when I was hunting whitetails with an outfitter in western Saskatchewan. The outfitter relied mainly on stand-hunting and driving to collect bucks. On my six-day hunt, I was able to rattle in two small bucks from my tree stand, but I saw no adults. The other three hunters had even less luck. We quite frequently found big tracks after a fresh snow, but the guides just didn't think tracking would be fruitful. They'd apparently never tried it, or if they had, it hadn't worked. I'd had great luck at tracking, not only for whitetails, but also for elk, moose, and especially mule deer. I'm still convinced that if I'd been left to my own devices, I'd have tracked down a good whitetail.

Year after year, a friend of mine uses a good stand overlooking a major escape trail that runs from a canyon, through a saddle, and into a very rough gorge where big mule deer apparently hide during hunting season. He's more often than not successful, and he's taken some good bucks from that place. But if he doesn't get a buck on opening day, his chances drop about 90 percent. If he hasn't taken one by the second day of the season, odds are he won't at all, because the majority of the bucks that are going to be pushed through that trail have already been pushed. Before

*Leon Parson American Painter*

long, he simply gives up. If he felt more comfortable with stillhunting and tracking, for example, he could hunt into that gorge and have a good chance of getting a buck.

On the other hand, the hunter who is adaptable and who can use all mule deer hunting methods with nearly equal facility is the guy who always brings home an animal with good antlers. If you're caught in a hunting rut and have had only mediocre success, try the following mule deer methods. You'll become a "complete" mule deer hunter, and you'll probably be happy with the results.

## STANDING

Stand-hunting for mule deer, though not quite as popular as stand-hunting for whitetails, is the most popular method of hunting in many places. However, most mule deer stand-hunters aren't as sophisticated as their whitetail counterparts and understand little about the art of stand selection.

The most common error muley stand-hunters make in selecting a site is finding one that looks good to them, not necessarily to the deer. The trick is to select a stand that will afford you a high probability of seeing deer, not one that's out of the wind or against a sunny warm stump. Trails between bedding and feeding areas are very good bets, but first a hunter has to find one. Typically, big mule deer bucks bed in thick timber or brush and feed in open areas not far from bedding sites. They use one to four trails to go to and from feeding areas, and even if there is more than one trail, more often than not, one will be more heavily used than the others. It's a good idea to determine when a given trail is used—often a big buck will leave the timber on one trail in the evening to feed and return to it on a different path in the morning to bed. So you'll need to wait along different trails in the morning and at dusk.

Always situate your stand downwind of the feeding or bedding trail you're watching, of course. When the air is cold, it typically drifts downhill, so, if you're watching in the cool evening near sundown or in the dawn before sunup, hide downhill of the trail. There are enough variations to that rule, especially in the mountains, to make doing some research on your own prudent.

As my opening weekend buddy has found out, standing along escape trails can at times provide exceptional action. Escape trails, obviously, are trails deer use to run from danger. They usually, though not always, lead to places where deer will be relatively safe, such as a vast and thick stand of timber or brush, inaccessible gorges, or swamps. One advantage of ambushing along escape trails is that bucks are often so intent on escaping that they're less alert to danger ahead. Select a stand that is downwind and out of sight. Logically, these escape-trail stands are only useful when other hunters are in the vicinity and moving deer.

I've got a favorite place on the rim of a large canyon in northern Utah where I like to just sit and stare out over a vast chunk of wild, spectacular country, especially after things have begun to settle down after the opening weekend melee. By midweek, most hunters have left the hills, deer are starting to get back into at least some of their routines again, and often deer have been pushed into the canyon by crowds in other places. I've seen more than 40 deer at a time from the boulder where I usually sit, and I've made a number of stalks after I've found a good buck.

Several seasons ago, I spotted a fair buck probably three-quarters of a mile away. I eased down through the thick Douglas fir timber below me, stalked quietly through the willows and chokecherries and across a beaver dam in the bottom, and then made my way up and into an open, sagebrush-covered slope. The buck was browsing just over the ridge, across the ravine. I stalked carefully, across the crest hidden by some big fir trees and then down into the timber. I spotted the buck from an opening.

He was just across the small creek, browsing in a thicket of wild rose, and oblivious to anything but sweet rose hips. The light was fading quickly, and I could just barely make out the crosshairs as I settled them behind his shoulder. I pressed the trigger and the muzzle flash blinded me momentarily. When I could see again in the near-darkness, the buck was gone, but I'd noted a single spruce near where the buck had been browsing. It was fully dark by the time I made it to the tree, and when I walked in the direction where I'd last seen the buck, I tripped over him. He hadn't moved a step.

## STILLHUNTING

My favorite method of big-buck hunting is stillhunting. When you're stillhunting you drift through woods and openings, looking ahead and listening carefully, searching for something that doesn't quite belong. You move slowly and try not to miss what's there. The idea is to find a good buck before he sees you and runs.

It's best to stillhunt into the wind, of course, but it's also possible to do it when the wind is from the side, or even when it's behind you. Strong wind directions aren't as critical because any scent is scattered far and wide. Hunting in a strong or moderate wind is also good because it masks any sounds you might make, and it's often possible to get quite close to bucks. However, one disadvantage of stillhunting in strong winds is that it makes big bucks even more spooky.

Stillhunting in thick timber is an exciting proposition. Any game you find is going to be close, so you must shoot quickly. Chances are that about the time you make out a bedded or hiding buck, he'll see you and run for it.

Actually, stillhunting in timber is often a combination not only of stillhunting but also of tracking and stalking as well. In timber, it's important to stillhunt more slowly and quietly than you would in the open. When you encounter the deer, they are apt to be close. Mule deer not only have incredibly keen hearing (witness the large ears), they also have a sense of smell

*A nontypical mule buck. Photograph by Leonard Lee Rue III*

that under the right conditions can pick up a man at a mile and eyes nearly as acute as those of pronghorns.

Once, in western Wyoming some years back, I spent much of one cold November chasing a buck off and on around and through an extensive, two-mile-long stand of lodgepole pines. One morning I was moving along a well-used game trail through the timber; there were elk, moose, and deer tracks on it. I knew from previous observations that the big boy I'd been hunting used it to travel to one of his favorite feeding areas.

It had become almost second nature for me to watch on the downwind side of any trail, because typically that's where big bucks will bed and where they can get a good scent and watch their backtrail. I had much more than the normal amount of anticipation that morning as I stillhunted. I was sure that something would happen. I'd been easing along the path for more than an hour, watching, listening, and even smelling. With the wind in my face, twice I'd caught the heavy, musky scent of bull elk. Twice I thought I heard the "roar" of a rutting muley buck, but the sound was so faint I couldn't be sure.

As I eased around the curve of the slope, I caught a faint movement out of the corner of my eye. Then I saw antlers above a deadfall, but they weren't big enough to belong to the buck I'd been after. I heard a roaring grunt from just up the slope, and a big buck rushed down at the smaller one. My .270 was up as he trotted and bounded down the loose, pine-needle duff hill, leaving big dark slashes in the soil. As he cleared a thick growth of saplings, I pressed the trigger quickly before he could disappear in timber. The monster buck skidded down the slope on his nose. Two does I hadn't seen and the smaller buck crashed off through the forest.

## DRIVING

Driving, or pushing, is a common tactic of whitetail hunters. It's not quite as common in mule deer country, but it is used and it can be effective. Basically, driving mule deer, like driving any other species, involves pushing game past the hunters in your party who are posted ahead of the drive near likely escape routes. Good places to post hunters in mule deer habitat include canyon or ravine heads, river-bottom

*An adaptable hunter who uses different techniques will increase his chances of bringing down a mule buck. Photograph by Leonard Lee Rue III*

goosenecks, and river or brush "islands." Driving can be good in any weather, though unfortunately, a drive may frighten an old buck right out of the area for the duration of the hunting season.

A good tactic is to post hunters at the head of a canyon, forming a half-circle around it, with hunters stationed down the side slopes a few hundred yards. Then, drivers, whether on horseback or afoot, push up-canyon.

For years, a troop of horseback hunters drove a big canyon that I frequently hunted. Hunters were posted at the head of the canyon and in the saddle that led into another canyon. The horsebackers started a mile or so below and pushed up the canyon bottom and side slopes toward the shooters waiting above. There was always a good deal of shooting, but most of the bucks they collected were small. There was a side ravine thick with brush and timber partway up the canyon, and I often posted myself along it during the drive. I must have done it at least five times, unknown to the drivers, and I collected two good bucks there.

Another good place to drive is on river-bottom goosenecks or peninsulas. Rivers in the West turn frequently on themselves and create small or large peninsulas up and down a river bottom. The best way to drive these peninsulas is to position "sitters" across the river from the peninsula tip and then to drive from the base of the peninsula toward the top. Deer will often break from the sides of the peninsula and cross the river, but drivers can usually hear them splashing and make it to the riverbank as the buck climbs out on the other side. Or, the deer will bound out of cover at the peninsula tip and hesitate before entering the water, and this provides the hunters on the riverbanks an excellent shot.

A third good place to employ driving is on river or brush islands. The techniques used are similar for either. Quite frequently, there are stands of timber or brush surrounded by relatively open country. Often, these islands contain bucks. This is a fairly simple drive—the island is surrounded by hunters and a driver or two is sent into the tangle to push deer into the open.

## BRUSHING

"Brushing," at least how we define it where I come from, is similar to driving, except it's not necessary to post sitters. In other words, one person can do it, and the object is to move deer to a place where you can get a shot, such as an open slope of a canyon or ravine.

One brushing method I use is what I call the stop-pause-start technique. A hunter works up a likely canyon or ravine, preferably above timber or brush, or on the open slope, finds a likely looking place to stop (to perhaps eat lunch), and after 20 or 30 minutes, starts out again. Often, if there's a buck in the vicinity, he gets pretty nervous while you're just sitting there. When you start out again, he's about convinced himself he's been spotted, and he'll flush.

A few seasons back, I'd picked a large south-facing slope of a plateau to brush later in the hunt, perhaps after bucks from other places had been pushed into it. There were a number of ravines running off the plateau. The southwest-facing slopes were pretty open, covered with only a few stands of short, twisted oak scrub, chokecherry, or maples. The southeast-facing slopes had more brush, mostly stands of big-tooth maple and some larger stands of oak. I hiked up one steep ravine on the brushy southeast-facing slope, hoping to flush a buck from the brush below me onto the opposite open slope where I could get a shot.

But it didn't exactly work that way. I sat down directly across a ravine from a big, short tangle of oak brush. It was a nice day, so I had lunch and enjoyed the sun beating down on me. I lingered a bit as my mind wandered here and there. Probably a half-hour later, I stood up, fumbled around for a few moments, and started off up-canyon again. At that moment, a good buck bolted from the oak brush just across the ravine and started bounding up the open slope. I was so startled I missed with the first shot, but then I cooled out and drilled him between the shoulder blades. He was a good, fat four-point buck (10-point, Eastern count).

Another method used frequently in the West is what I call platoon brushing. As the name hints, it's used by platoons of horseback hunters. They simply ride through brush and hope to flush deer onto the opposite slope of the canyon where they can get some shooting. Too often, though, the shooting is hurried and deer are wounded; and it spoils the day for other foot hunters in the area. I don't encourage this type of brushing.

One of the simplest and most effective methods of brushing out muleys is to move up a canyon on the timbered or brushy north or east-facing slope, with the hope of flushing bucks from the timber below to the open opposite slope. This has been an effective technique for me for years, though now it's less effective for really big bucks. The trophies that survive today's crowds are smarter and less apt to run from the brush until they're absolutely certain they've been detected.

## TRACKING

Tracking is one of the most satisfying methods of collecting a trophy. It requires patience, finesse, intelligence, and a certain single-mindedness. You have to always be aware of wind direction, where you put your feet, and the habits of big bucks (which are quite different from those of younger bucks).

Several years ago, I spent the better part of three days tracking a huge buck I'd spotted the day before the season opened. His trail led in and out of canyons, through stands of timber and brush, across creeks and boulder slides, over ridges and plateaus, and into a completely different major river drainage.

I learned a lot on that trail, among which were what a big buck's hoofprint looks like (a good fore track measures about 3½ inches long); where bucks bed (most often where they can see and smell their backtrail); what they feed on (there, at the season, it was on bitterbrush, wild rose, cliff rose, and a variety of dried forbs); what times of day they tend to move during hunting season (mostly at night); and how to find a track again after I'd lost it on hard clay or rocky ground (by making ever-widening circles, until I found the print again on soft soil). In the end, the tracks moved into a steep, rough canyon, and the droppings were

fresh again. As I moved in, I spooked him from a chokecherry thicket below, and three days of tension were suddenly released. I was astounded by his size, and I cleanly missed with the first shot. Again, I settled down, and I hit him twice with fatal shots.

A common tracking technique is the loop method. It's been used for millennia by primitive hunters, not only on this continent, but anyplace where man has hunted big game. When using this method, the hunter finds a set of tracks he wants to follow and follows them directly for a short distance. When he's got an idea where the buck is going, he loops on the downwind side of the trail, returning to it every few hundred yards if it's in the open, or every 50 or so yards if it's in heavy brush. Because big bucks habitually bed downwind of their backtrail, chances are the buck won't scent the hunter using the loop method because he's downwind of the trail most of the time, too. If the hunter passes the end of the trail, he makes smaller loops back in the direction where he last saw the tracks. The shooting is often done quickly because the buck is apt to be surprised at close range.

## RATTLING

Rattling for whitetails has been written about for at least a century, and recently it's been refined almost to the point of being a science. Mule deer rattling, because it's not nearly as successful or as well-known, has received almost no press. Granted, it's not as fruitful a method as it is for whitetails, moose, or even elk (yes, I've rattled in all of those species), but it can be useful during the rut, when a number of does are in estrus in a given area at a given time. It may also work very near the center area of a big buck's home range, especially just before the rut. If other methods aren't working for you at these times, try rattling. It may just put the venison in the freezer, as it's done for me.

When I took my first mule deer using this method, rattling was just a novelty for me. Earlier that morning I had found a buck that had died earlier in the autumn. I broke his antlers from the skull and put them into my daypack. Toward evening I stillhunted through a stand of spruce and found several big rubs in proximity to several beds (which indicated I was in the muley center, or core, area). What the heck, I thought, and quietly took the antlers out of the pack. I clattered them together, waited a few minutes, and clattered them again. I heard the unmistakable grunting roar of an irate, dominant buck just upslope, and a moment later he crashed down through the trees. If I hadn't shot him when I did, I think he may very well have run over me. And I got him because when other, more common hunting methods failed, I was able to reach into my bag of hunting tricks for one last technique.

The most complete mule deer trophy hunter, and the most successful one, is going to be the guy who can use all methods, and whatever else is necessary, when combing muley country. To be successful, he's got to be as adaptable as his cagey prey.

# Farm-Fed Muleys

*By Michael Pearce*

The last half hour had been rough on me. I'd sprinted myself to exhaustion, slid on my hindquarters down a rocky slope, plopped myself down on a cactus cluster, and slithered on my belly back and forth over a rugged trail enough times to have paved it with skin.

Yet, as I sat there, with cactus thorns in my legs and hands and with my clothing drenched in sweat, I felt no pain. Having a herd of gargantuan-racked mule deer bucks within 200 yards will do that to you.

My host, Kent Rains, and I had found the herd at first light. Silhouetted against a crimson sunrise, their racks were visible to the naked eye from more than 500 yards away. Through binoculars and a spotting scope, the seven bucks looked breathtaking.

Any of the bucks would have easily made the record book for the muzzleloader I was carrying. Three were particularly big. One sported a gently rising rack that appeared to be wider than a yardstick. His two buddies carried headgear not quite as wide, but both racks were impressively high.

We'd kept our distance for close to two hours. As the deer moved, so had we. Eventually we had ended up within the confines of an old corral, watching and

*Mule deer, like flatland whitetails, will wait until late in the day to move out of draws and other cover to feed on exposed crops. Photograph by Michael H. Francis*

waiting for the bucks to bed down or settle into a pattern that would allow a stalk.

One major problem was the openness of the field that surrounded the muleys. The big boys weren't alone. Though the rut was still weeks away, the bucks were mingling with does that shared a common interest in the feeding area.

The ladies eventually laid down where they had eaten, and the bucks had finally decided to head for more rugged country. That's when my bout with nature's obstacle course had begun. It had looked like it would be an easy run to cut off the bucks where I assumed they would leave the plateau.

I was still 200 yards away from my chosen spot when the muleys had suddenly appeared. Caught in the open, I flopped myself down among the cactus until the deer had ambled from sight. More running and crawling had brought me to where I now lay curled up behind a small clump of brush at the base of the canyon.

Easing up to my knees, I could see that the group, which now numbered five bucks and one doe, was grazing along in my direction. I sat in the late September heat, waiting for the deer to play right into my plan of ambush.

It was a classic situation in a not-so-classic location. There wasn't an honest-to-gosh mountain for several hundred miles. I was in western Kansas—farm country of the finest kind.

But I could have been in any of the farm-belt areas across the West. To those who are used to traveling to the high, pine country, the farm ground below might seem a barren hunting ground for mule deer. But just as whitetails can thrive in the Eastern and Midwestern farm belts, so can Western muleys.

Food obviously is no problem. Scattered pockets of irrigation produce lush crops of corn and maize where there was once only sagebrush and grass. Farmland mule deer can also thrive on alfalfa, clover, winter wheat, and grassy pastures.

And though it may look a far cry from the forests in the Rockies, there is also good cover. Mule deer will thrive in the same vast pastures and canyons that support pronghorns and Herefords. A long, overgrown, meandering creek or river bottom can also be all the shelter that a big mule deer buck needs. Brushy draws and overgrown, abandoned homesites may hold more than pheasants.

The Conservation Reserve Program (CRP) is adding millions of acres of good mule deer habitat. This federally funded program, which is being implemented in several Western states, attempts to return marginally producing cropland back into natural grass. In the first year of transition, the land is planted with a cover of

tall cane plants, which give mule deer an abundant amount of food as well as a dense, junglelike place to hide. These areas are private and are not open to the general public; but landowners often will grant permission to hunt these areas.

Mule deer in such thick cover as standing CRP fields can still be taken by hunters who know how to get in there with them. In 1988, Kansas bowhunter Phil Kirkland waded into a huge field of standing CRP cane that he knew was holding several trophy-class muleys.

Kirkland entered before first light and moved as quietly as possible. Every time he felt he'd made an unusual amount of noise, he'd use a call to give a few soft grunts, mimicking a rival buck moving about. Several times he even got responses to his calls.

Not long after light, he came upon a big buck courting a doe. The pair passed within range, and Kirkland took a new state-record muley that scored 182⅛ Pope and Young Club points.

Being opportunists, mule deer will stay in areas where they can find cover and food near each other. The afternoon before we found the herd of monster bucks, hunting partner George Stanley and I spotted a trio of does and a small 4×4 buck standing in tall cover near a vast field of overgrown wheat stubble.

While Stanley crawled through weeds and stickers, I kept my distance and watched the herd alternate between bedding and feeding. My partner eventually stalked to within 60 yards. When the buck stood and started to nibble, exposing himself above the tall wheat stalks, my partner made a perfect heart shot with a .50 Hatfield.

Like whitetails, farm-country mule deer often fall into a pattern of moving from bedding to feeding areas. Late in the day, they will head out to the exposed croplands for a night of feeding and then vice versa the next morning. Though most of the feeding activity occurs at night, hunters can sometimes find muleys at the edge of crop fields at dawn and dusk.

The first mule deer buck I ever shot was first spotted coming from a series of draws up into a field of green winter wheat a half-hour before sunset on a cold, snowy December day. Having spotted me, the buck ducked back down into the canyons. A friend and I paralleled the slow-moving buck, occasionally stopping to peek down into the deep draws.

Getting within range of the chunky 5×5 was no problem, but getting a clear shot was. The buck seemed to pick up a following as he traveled, and eventually he was among a herd that numbered close to 30 deer, including some other good bucks. At one time, I could see six 3×3 or better bucks through my scope.

Patience paid off and the big buck eventually stepped to the edge of the herd, offering an easy shot. One shot from a .270 put the buck down at 235 yards just as the sun was touching the horizon.

A good place to begin morning hunts is on a hill or canyon top overlooking potential feed fields. An early arrival and a good set of binoculars are a must to locate muleys as they move from feeding to bedding areas. Hunters can either try to sneak ahead and set up an ambush, or they can watch the deer until they bed down for the day and then plan a stalk.

At midday, I will often spend time glassing known bedding areas. In this situation, hunters should take their time and thoroughly look over an area, keeping an eye out for such subtle things as ears or antler tips.

There are, however, times when the bedding cover will be too thick for distant spotting and stalking. Muleys, especially big experienced bucks, spend much of their time in thick cover. And when that's the case, you have to get right in there with them—and I do mean *in* there.

Several years ago, a group of pheasant hunters flushed a wide-racked mule deer from a thick draw that lay surrounded by grainfields. Word of the big buck spread, and on opening day of the deer hunting season, group after group glassed the draw and some walked its edge.

The next morning was a repeat. But, as a group of hunters walked the edge of the weed patch, an experienced local hunter arrived on the scene. As soon as the first group was gone, he loaded his rifle and waded into the draw. The trophy of a lifetime flushed like a pheasant and fell to a well-placed shot.

Always remember, too, that big muleys can sneak ahead of you in thick cover. Many hunters will work a draw or other cover as they would drive for whitetails, with several blockers being sneaked into place on potential escape routes and several drivers pushing through the thick stuff. Blockers will want to keep a sharp eye on both open country and cover alike, as a really big muley can sneak through amazingly sparse cover.

As with all big-game hunting, a few days of preseason scouting can make the difference between success and failure. Some bucks develop patterns so predictable you could set your watch to them as the same herd appears in the same field, at the same time, day after day for weeks on end.

There are places, however, where all of that will change on opening morning, when the influx of hunters arrives. One way around the problem is to have your buck so well patterned before opening day that he's on the ground before he's pressured by others. Another way is to wait until the opening day madness is over and the deer have settled. This usually takes only a few days unless the area continues to receive pressure. You can also try to find obscure pastures and fields that are far from the well-traveled roads.

Or, you can let the opening day hunters make your task a lot easier. The really big muleys aren't bothered that much by hunters who aren't willing to move off the beaten path. Some deer will go and flatten out in a

*Photograph by Michael H. Francis*

broad pasture or stubble field and not move a muscle from dawn to dusk. Others will quickly head to little pockets of terrain where they're virtually inaccessible—except for those who are willing to walk and stalk.

Those who are after a truly quality experience may want to opt for bow or muzzleloader hunting. There's far less pressure during those seasons, and it's generally much easier to get permission to hunt private ground.

Don't let the limited range of a bow or muzzleloader keep you from the open spaces of farm country. Success rates for some counties are often 50 percent or better. Those who know how to use a pair of binoculars to spot game and how to patiently work to within range stand an excellent chance of getting a shot.

Time dragged on as I waited in ambush at the mouth of the canyon that held my dream herd of muleys. I peered through the stiff leaves of a yucca and waited for the bucks and lone doe to come into sight.

They finally did, but a good 150 yards from where I expected them. The deer were slowly grazing and milling on the pasture grass at the bottom of the canyon. Doing my best snake imitation, I belly-crawled to a nearby game trail and then slithered to the last bit of cover near the bottom.

When I peeked up, I found the bucks to be a little more than 100 yards away, spread out perfectly. The two largest muleys were almost nose to nose, while the other bucks were scattered over a 30-yard area. I eased my binoculars to my eyes and studied the racks until my patience could take no more.

I eased my Hatfield muzzleloader up and started to cock the hammer, but good sense stopped me. Though it was true that the rifle could put shot after shot into a business card at 100 yards, it would be better to let animals as large as these come as close as

*Author with the 7 × 6 buck he took in western Kansas with a .50 Hatfield. The buck weighed 245 pounds full-dressed. Photograph by Michael Pearce*

possible. I slowly ducked my head and rifle down out of sight and started the waiting process all over again.

I checked a few minutes later, and the herd was slowly drifting in my direction—just a few more yards and I'd take my shot. But the next time I peeked, the canyon floor was empty.

Fearing that the deer might be exiting above me, I did my best duck-walk sprint to the lip of the canyon. I

*Photograph by Michael H. Francis*

*Photograph by Michael H. Francis*

looked up on the little plateau above the canyon and saw nothing. Suddenly my heart was firing like a car engine and my lungs were working triple-time. The deer had to be coming my way through a little pocket not 40 yards away from me.

The wind had shifted around and would be blowing from me to the deer. I eased the Hatfield's hammer to full cock and got ready for a quick shot.

But there wasn't time to panic. The head of the doe came into sight and behind her I could see the tops of four or five wide-spread racks.

The doe had bolted a short distance when she caught my scent and saw the movement of the rifle being shouldered. Raising to my knees, I could see the racks of the two big bucks bounding from sight.

The only buck that was in the open started to turn, but my bleating fawn call froze him for the split-second that I needed. At 30 yards, the .495-inch round ball drove through one shoulder and buried in the other. The buck dropped and didn't move.

Though far from the largest in the herd, the muley was still huge. His rack was massive from bases to tine tip. A 7×6, the deer still had dried velvet hanging from the uppermost tines and sported a decent 24-inch spread. Three days later, the field-dressed buck weighed in at 245 pounds at the meat-packing house.

I sat by the buck for 10 to 15 minutes before I started the chore of field dressing. Then, for a reason known only to them, the herd appeared at the top of the canyon again. They gazed down upon us for several seconds before trotting by within 100 yards. The two big giants brought up the rear and stopped broadside for close to a minute before continuing over the hill and out of sight.

A rifle hunter lucked into one of the bucks during the December season. The deer was a perfect 5×5 with a 32-inch spread. A few weeks after the deer seasons had closed, Rains spotted the other of the pair. As far as we know, no one got the exceptionally wide-racked buck—reason enough to stay in the farmlands next time I go mule deer hunting.

But I know that there are many more reasons to hunt these fertile plains. With all of the available food, many of the bucks grow fat and carry wide racks. Their daily patterns are often predictable, and their bedding areas are thick but often obvious. Next time you hunt mule deer, don't overlook the farmlands. You may harvest a trophy.

# Buck 'N Bull Bow

*By Rick N. Hinton*

I had been on the road for seven hours, driving toward the camp that would be home to me for the next few weeks. As I bounced over the bumps in the heavily rutted mountain road, I thought of both the good and the bad parts of last year's bowhunt, mentally preparing myself for opening day, which was now only one short night's sleep away. Glancing in the rearview mirror, I could see only a billowing cloud of white dust that threatened to engulf my old, faded Chevy if I slowed down in the least.

Cresting the top of the final hill, I could at last see the convergence of the two canyons below me where I planned to park my truck and begin the long hike back to my campsite. Vivid memories of a previous hunt came back easily now as I recalled one particular bull that I had bugled in not far from there. He was not the largest bull that I had ever seen, but he was definitely the biggest that I had ever called in to shooting distance. I had called him in to within 40 yards twice in less than an hour, but I had been unable to shoot through the thick, frost-laden brush covering the hillside.

Miraculously, the bull came in a third time but was now very cautious, making alarm barks like a spooked cow. Still he kept walking closer. At 60 yards out, he stood broadside in a small sunlit clearing, looking downhill, trying to locate me while barking nervously. (I hadn't made a sound in the last four or five minutes, and he was unsure of my location.) Crouching downwind from him, I was amazed at how strong he smelled. I have been in on a lot of bulls, but I have never smelled one whose scent was that overpowering.

He was an incredible animal with extremely long eye guards. I drew 85 pounds of bow and lowered the 60-yard pin until it was right behind his shoulder. I held the pin steady for about five seconds as I concentrated on a smooth, fluid release, and then I let the string slip from my fingers.

The arrow arced perfectly, but in the blink of an eye, it hit an unseen twig about 50 yards out and clattered noisily into the trees 10 yards in front of the bull. The elk decided that it was high time to get the heck out of there and exploded down the hillside and out of sight through the lodgepole, dirt clods flying in the air behind him as he ran. My last glimpse was of long, white eye guards and even longer back points racing through the trees before he disappeared into the shadows.

Those old memories suddenly evaporated into reality as I rounded the bend and saw what for me was a terrible sight. Several shiny new trucks and horse trailers were parked at the head of the trail, my trail. I didn't want to believe what my eyes were seeing, which was a truly terrible turn of events! After parking the truck, I got out to talk with a few of the guys standing around the horse trailers and discovered to my dismay that an outfitter was taking nine hunters right into my favorite hunting spot.

Crestfallen, I walked back to my truck and sat there

on the seat with the door open, staring at the ground and trying to figure out just what to do. It was already 5 P.M., the day before opening morning, and my favorite hunting spot in the area was about to be overrun with nine other hunters. Two or three other guys in the area would have been bad enough, but nine was intolerable. I had to make a major decision and make it fast. I grabbed several maps and quickly spread them out on the hood of my truck.

In my opinion, nothing ruins elk hunting faster than hunting pressure, and I knew that I had to change plans if I was going to have a good hunt on the first day of the season. I had scouted two other places during the summer, but the closest one was six hours away.

"Well," I thought to myself, "it's either move now and drive all night, or stay here and stumble over nine other hunters for the next few weeks. Which is it going to be?" My decision didn't take long to make. I was off.

About 6½ hours later, I was almost to my second choice camp. I had been driving on narrow, bumpy dirt roads for the last 50 miles, and I was beginning to wonder whether I had made a serious error by changing hunting areas instead of staying with my first choice. It was almost midnight, and I was only about 10 minutes from where I planned to camp when I saw movement in the darkness up in front of my rig. That something materialized in my headlights as a large 5 × 5 bull elk running down the narrow dirt road in front of me. He ran down the center of the road in front of my truck for about 40 yards, then bailed off the right side of the road, and vanished into the dark of the night.

I let out a whoop of joy and pounded my fist on the steering wheel in excitement. All doubts about my decision to change hunting areas were now gone, replaced with the excitement of seeing a nice bull only 10 minutes from where I planned to camp. My spirits were soaring, as I was sure that the bull I had just seen was out searching for cows, which meant that the rut was definitely under way. I could barely contain my excitement as I anticipated hearing the first bugle of the season.

I did not even bother setting up camp that night. I just laid out my sleeping bag in the back of my truck under the camper shell and waited for sleep to come. It never did. I lay there thinking about past hunts, missed shots, triumphant moments, and all kinds of other elk-related things until the eastern sky began to show a slight trace of light. I curled up on my right side and enjoyed a few more precious moments of warmth before I finally forced myself to get up.

"Let the hunt begin," I said to myself with a smile as I unzipped the sleeping bag and pulled on my favorite pair of old worn camouflage pants. It was almost shooting light as I slid my canteen inside the old, beat-up daypack and zipped it closed. Shining a flashlight into the mirror on the door of my truck, I hurriedly darkened my face with paint and then slung the daypack onto my shoulders and walked to the edge of the ridge, only 20 yards from my truck.

Exhilaration coursed through my veins as I surveyed the rugged scenery that unfolded in front of me. This was perfect elk country, steep and deep. Just out of curiosity, I decided to try to bugle from that spot before I started hiking. I took a deep breath and then let out the first bugle of the season. The long, high-pitched bugle pierced the silence of the cool morning and echoed off the far canyon. Then, with eager anticipation, I listened.

As if in a dream, I heard a bull answer about 10 seconds later. You could have pushed me over with a feather! There I was on opening morning, and my first bugle not 20 yards from my sleeping bag gets an answer. I couldn't believe it. I waited in silence for about two minutes and then let out a loud, angry bugle followed by six or seven grunts. He literally screamed back, and I could tell that he was fired up. I heard two other bulls way off in the distance answer, and then the first bull bugled again.

Clutching my bow in my left hand, I took off, running through the trees toward the first bull. He was in a saddle on the other side of a small finger ridge, about a half-mile to my left. The slope was very steep, and the trees were so close together that it made running difficult and totally impossible in some places where I had to climb over numerous deadfalls. Finally, slowing to a fast walk, I crept around the small finger ridge and bugled. About 20 seconds later, he let me have it, and I could literally feel the anger in his deep, guttural answer. He was about 125 yards in front of me and at about the same elevation.

The lodgepole grew very close together, so I began weaving around the trees in a low crouch, stepping over seemingly endless deadfalls that looked like a giant version of a child's game of jackstraws. I snuck up to a small knob and noticed that the trees were not quite as close together and that there were several places between the trees where I would be able to shoot out to about 30 yards. I knew that this was about the best place that I was going to find to set up, so I knelt down on my right knee in front of two trees, nocked a green and yellow fletched arrow on the string, and listened.

Dull, thudding smacks resonated through the woods; he was tearing up a tree a scant 100 yards away. I was a little bit below him, and the morning's slope winds were traveling downhill. So far, everything was perfect. Cupping my hand over my mouth, I let out a half-hearted, wimpy-sounding bugle. The tree-raking stopped for a few seconds and then began again. He didn't answer. Waiting was difficult, but I knew that I had to. Finally, after waiting in silence for about three minutes, I screamed a bugle at him with all of the vehemence and anger that I could muster up. This time, he really started tearing up that poor tree. Then, an even larger-sounding bull let out a huge bellow about 300 yards below me. What a way to start the season.

I bugled twice now at close range, but I had only persuaded the first bull to rake some trees. I couldn't get him to bugle back or come closer. The bull below

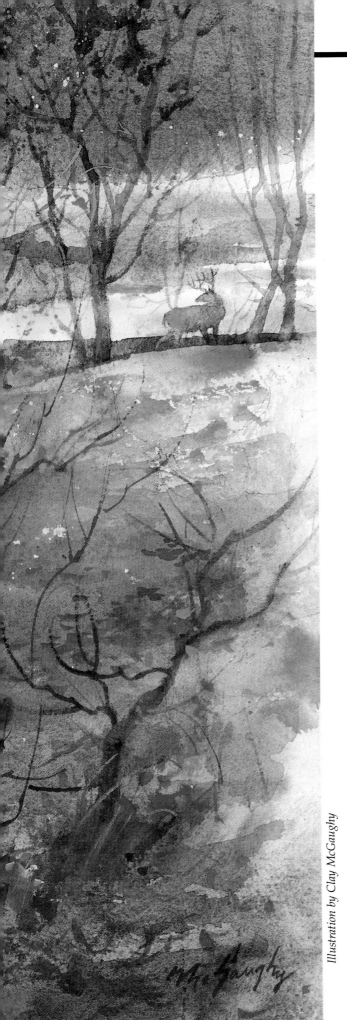

Illustration by Clay McGaughy

me sounded bigger, so I decided to try to get some rivalry going—stir things up a bit and maybe get a shot at one of them. I let out two plaintive-sounding cow calls and got an instant reaction. The tree-raking stopped instantly, and the first bull was suddenly crashing through the forest straight toward me. The tinder-dry forest floor snapped and cracked louder and louder as he ran toward me. He slowed down to a regal strut at about 40 yards, and then I saw him.

"Oh man," was all I could say to myself as he kept getting closer. This was definitely a big bull. He was walking very slowly now, and 15 yards away, he laid his antlers back and, while still walking defiantly, he double-bugled. This bull was not intimidated in the least. I have called in a lot of bulls, but never have I seen one do what this one was doing: he snorted loudly through his nose with each angry step like a bull moose. He was big and bad, and he knew it.

He was slightly above me, moving toward my left when he walked behind a group of three narrow trees just 12 yards away. As soon as his head went behind the first tree, I drew my 90-pound Cougar Magnum and, in my kneeling position, followed him through the trees at full draw.

He stepped out broadside 10 yards away and stopped. His flanks were still behind the trees, but he was quartering slightly toward me. Then I watched those huge, wide, white-tipped antlers rotate slowly as he swung his head to the left and stared right at me, long eye guards rising straight up toward the sky. I held my aim right behind his shoulder, waiting for him to look away. He didn't—he had me pinned and seemed to be looking right into my eyes.

*Thwump!* The arrow buried itself to the fletching, right behind his shoulder, and all hell broke loose. He swapped ends and exploded back to my right, crashing through everything in his path. I immediately bugled with the diaphragm in my mouth, and he skidded to a stop only 25 yards away. I could see him standing between the trees, but his body was partially hidden behind two of them. He just stood there for about 30 seconds, antlers back, nostrils flared, trying to detect danger. He took two steps and stopped again, testing the wind.

He didn't even know that he was hit. He probably would have fallen, but I wanted to be sure. I quickly pulled back the string, came to full draw again, and slowly lowered my sight pin right behind his shoulder. He was beautiful, that creamy white body contrasting boldly against his dark mane and legs. I could see clearly now that he was carrying one heck of a rack. I held the 20-yard pin as steady as I could behind his shoulder and then let the string slip from my fingers. I heard a loud crack, and the bull tore off at full speed, smashing through enough brush and deadfalls to kill a horse. Suddenly, the noise stopped.

I knew that I had my bull. I marked my position with orange surveyor's tape and then paced off the distance to the first shot: 10 yards. I could see a good blood trail leading down to where I had shot at him the second time, so I sat down and pulled out some homemade granola and started munching. I knew that he was down, but I wanted to wait awhile just to be sure. I stopped in mid-chew. Just 200 yards below me was another bull, raking his antlers against a tree, completely unaware of the drama that had just unfolded. The bigger bull had arrived. I had completely forgotten about him.

"That's all I need," I thought to myself. "This bull is going to come up here, jump the wounded bull out of his bed, and make me lose the blood trail."

Luckily, after tearing up the tree for a few anxiety-filled minutes, he finally seemed to lose interest and eventually walked away. I slowly, quietly walked down to where I had shot at the bull the second time. He left a heavy blood trail.

I had followed the blood trail only 30 yards, when I heard something walking toward me on my left. I figured that it was just a lonely cow looking for the bull that I had just arrowed, so I froze and waited to see what would happen. My jaw just about hit the ground when I saw what walked out. Twenty yards away, a mule deer buck in full velvet was walking straight toward me. He kept walking until he was only 15 yards away. Then he suddenly saw me and froze. We both just stared at each other.

The whole situation suddenly struck me as being very funny. Here it is, opening morning of the season, and I am minding my own business, trying to follow the blood trail of a rather huge 6 × 6 bull with two arrows in him; another bull is only a couple hundred yards away threatening to come in and screw everything up; and now, as if I don't have enough to worry about, I have a buck standing there within easy bow range.

I mewed like a cow elk once and then very casually turned my back on the buck as if I wasn't interested in him in the least (which I can assure you is just the opposite of how I really felt). With my back turned, I very carefully pulled a razor-tipped arrow out of my bow quiver, put it on the string, and very, very slowly came to full draw, facing completely in the opposite direction from the buck.

With my bow at full draw, I swung back around to the buck, fully expecting him to instantly bound off out of sight. Believe it or not, he began feeding only 15 yards from me. (The area that I was in was hunted very little, if at all, so apparently this buck had never seen a human. Otherwise, he would have been long gone.) As I swung around, his head jerked up and he bunched up as if to jump, but it was too late. My arrow took him through both lungs, passed completely through him, and skidded into a log 20 yards away. He took two steps backward and bumped into a tree. Then, with head hung low and on unsteady legs, he started to walk away. I pulled out another arrow, aimed, released, and I shot about two feet in front of him. The buck took two bounces and then disappeared from sight over a small bluff right behind the spot where I had been kneeling when I had arrowed the bull only 20 minutes earlier.

As I watched his velvet-covered antlers disappear

from sight over the bluff, it suddenly dawned on me that I now had not one, but two, blood trails to follow. Then, I realized what I had just done: I had filled both my elk and deer tag within 20 minutes of each other, and it wasn't yet 7:30 A.M. on the first morning of the season. I suddenly had a very strong urge to sit down—this was just too much for my feeble brain to absorb all at once. I just sat there on that log, shaking my head and grinning stupidly for several minutes until a strong whiff of elk came to my nose. It was coming from right where I had heard the bull hit the ground. That brought me back to my senses in a hurry, and about 40 yards away, I could just barely see a glimpse of tan lying between two trees.

I slowly and cautiously walked over to the trees. There he lay, one very impressive animal, even bigger than I had first thought. As bulls go, this one's body would definitely stand out from the crowd—it was every bit as massive as his tremendous rack (his antlers later scored 326 Pope and Young Club points), and I was going to have to pack him out all by myself. I pushed my body to its limit. But believe me, it was worth it a thousand times over.

Wanting to give the muley some time to stiffen up, I grabbed my camera, took a whole roll of photos of the bull, and began what was going to be a long, hard day of work. After several minutes of straining, tugging, and pulling, I managed to get the elk rolled over onto his back, where I finally got a look at his left side. I was surprised to see that I had indeed hit him with the second arrow, and only four inches behind where the first arrow struck. The loud crack that I had heard was the second arrow breaking a rib.

Upon closer inspection, I discovered that the first arrow hit about one-quarter inch behind the shoulder, went completely through one lung, and was almost poking through his heart—and it still had enough energy to curl the broadhead back upon itself upon impact with the far shoulder bone. Getting penetration like that on a bull elk of that size is the main reason why I shoot a 90-pound bow.

I quickly took care of the bull. Then, with much curiosity, I went back and began following the buck's blood trail up to the small bluff. I carefully backed down the vertical face of the bluff, walked about 50 yards, and found him lying on his left side in the shade at the base of a small tree. Admiring the beautiful velvet covering his antlers, I laid my hand on his shoulder, feeling the warm texture of his fur on my open hand, and said a silent prayer of thanks. This was a day I would not soon forget.

After taking care of the buck, I hiked back to camp to get my packboard. I packed the buck out whole and then brought the bull out in four quarters. I was a sweat-soaked sore-muscled bowhunter before it was over, but I finally managed to get the last load of meat out just before dark. I saved the antlers for the last trip, knowing that it would give me added incentive to get everything out in one day. I took a deep breath and went in for that last load just as the sun was touching the mountains to the west, turning the sky to a beautiful shade of streaked orange.

# Death Came Calling

*By Marguerite Reiss and*
*Larry Mueller*

L ess than a city block up the heavily timbered slope, a man-eating bear was defending its kill. The bear had already roared its challenge. It had threatened with an eruption of short, brush-breaking false charges. But the man-eater couldn't be seen because it was up a slope of old growth spruce and western hemlock that stood 80 or 90 feet above an understory thick with blueberry bushes and saplings.

It was a doubly tense moment for Don Kluting and his six-man search-and-rescue team. Besides facing a killer bear ready to kill again, Kluting was with a team he hadn't asked for—and the team hadn't asked for him. The six men were untrained and poorly armed friends, as well as friends of friends, of the bear's victim. Kluting was a total stranger—and at 22, a very young stranger at that—trying to take charge of a job that the rest of the group was pretty sure they could do better by themselves.

Kluting asked three of the six men to stay on the vantage point of a ridge. The other three would go up the slope with him. Kluting and his group had gone only 15 feet when two of the three with him declined. In fact, they said, they would go farther back down the slope a safe distance. They felt that their rifles weren't heavy enough to be of value in a close encounter with an Alaska bear.

The third man, Jim Lange, who was the best armed of the three, not only volunteered, but he was determined to go—right now! He was carrying a .338/06, a necked up version of the .30/06. Kluting had a .338 Winchester Magnum. The pair started up the hill slowly, quietly, hoping to get a clear shot at the bear before it saw them. An unidentified noise stopped the two before they got 10 feet. Was the bear circling? They listened and then moved on another few feet. At this point, they were less than 30 feet from the three men who remained on the ridge.

*A Sitka blacktail buck may present a good shot in the Alaskan muskeg regions. Photograph by Leonard Lee Rue III*

Suddenly, the bear stood on its hind legs and grunted. Its head poked above the bushes for just a moment at about 70 yards, and then all hell broke loose. Crashing through the undergrowth, knocking over 2-inch-diameter saplings as easily as a running man might stomp down weeds, the giant bear charged all five men.

At first, Kluting and Lange could only see bushes whip and saplings fall. Then the bear became flashing brown blurs among the blueberries. At 50 yards, both men fired, each confident that he had hit the man-eater. But the bear charged on. It was like throwing rocks at a freight train, Kluting thought, as he desperately chambered another cartridge.

Two of the three men on the ridge then fired their rifles. The third stepped backward, tumbled, and found himself hanging over a 15-foot drop-off. One rifle jammed after the first shot. The man with the .30/30 fired again.

The charging bear glanced toward Kluting and Lange as if intending to attack them first but then at 20 yards he swerved toward the group on the ridge, probably because the .30/30 had stung the killer in the foot.

Kluting's rifle was set up for deer and goat hunting with a Leupold 3×-to-9× variable scope. There hadn't been time to remove the eyepiece, and Kluting had difficulty keeping the bear in his sights. Every-thing was too magnified, even though the power had been adjusted down to 3×. Kluting picked up the bear's head in the scope and then swung to the front to establish a lead, keeping part of the head in the left edge of the glass. Both Kluting and Lange were trying for shoulder shots that would break the bear down and put it on the ground where it could be finished off. Only a brain or spine shot would have killed him instantly, and both men knew that those are terribly small targets to hit on a bear running broadside. A heart or lung shot would have been useless. The bear would have had time to kill all of them before it died. A bear can run another 100 yards after a heart shot, farther after a lung shot.

Lange fired. Kluting saw the bear flinch. Kluting then fired again, just as he could see the orange muzzle blast of the .30/30 flash in the right-hand edge of his scope. It wasn't that he fired quickly, because there was no more room to continue leading the bear. Pulling the trigger and seeing the flash in his scope were simply simultaneous events. But the horror of the situation drained through his body. The bear was perhaps a yard off the end of the .30/30 barrel—a fraction of a jump from the three men. Although Kluting automatically began chambering another cartridge, he knew that there was no way that either he or Lange could get off another shot before the bear killed or badly mauled all three men. Furthermore, he and

ILLUSTRATION BY JOE GARCIA

Lange were only 20 feet from the bear themselves. If they couldn't break the bear's shoulders or hit the brain or spine, they'd be the killer's next victims.

**A**ll of this started very pleasantly. Harley Sievenpiper Jr., 40, of Juneau, Alaska, was engaged in one of life's greatest pleasures—his 10th annual deer hunt with old friends. Sievenpiper joined Jim Hendricks and Dave Traygo, residents of Port Alexander on Baranof Island, and the trio motored a fishing boat down the coast to a bay called Port Conclusion. It was only a 45-minute tip, so the three planned to hunt the day, then return to the anchored boat, and sail back to Port Alexander for the night.

Sievenpiper told his friends that he planned to use a deer call that sounded like the bleat of a distressed fawn. He would hunt the edges of muskegs where visibility would be better than among the blueberries and tall evergreens. A few bull pines and cedars grow in these areas, but muskegs are mostly open, with thick moss and potholes up to 15 feet deep spotted here and there. A Sitka blacktail deer coming to a call in a muskeg would make for a relatively easy shot. The three hunters then scattered about 200 yards apart.

Around 1:30 P.M., Jim Hendricks heard a bear roar, followed by Sievenpiper's scream. Hendricks fired three shots to call Dave Traygo, and the two immediately went to investigate. Walking in the direction from which the sounds had come, the two found the attack site within 10 minutes, but the hopelessness of the situation was all too evident. Being experienced hunters, Hendricks and Traygo recognized that Sievenpiper couldn't have survived losing the amount of blood that covered much of the terribly torn-up area. The body had been taken, and this made the situation even more dangerous, with the possibility of encountering the bear trying to defend its kill. The men were also quite uncertain whether they could handle the sight of what had happened to their close friend. They decided to go for professional help.

**B**ack in Port Alexander, Hendricks called Ketchikan. No, they told him, they couldn't handle it, but he might try calling Petersburg or Wrangell. Neither of those towns would provide help either, so Hendricks called Juneau. No, they said, call Sitka. Hendricks finally reached fish and wildlife protection officer Roland Young; and yes, indeed, Young told him, jurisdiction and responsibility did rest in Sitka. By that time, however, all the residents of the tiny fishing village of Port Alexander were highly agitated by what they perceived as a run-around. They concluded that, one way or another, they'd have to take care of the matter themselves.

Back in Sitka, officer Young called Don Kluting for assistance. Kluting helped Young in cases of wildlife violations, so Young trusted Kluting's professionalism. Kluting worked for the city of Sitka, was a volunteer EMT (emergency medical technician) on the ambulance, belonged to the volunteer fire department, had been trained in both tracking and search-and-rescue field management, and had already demonstrated his abilities in a number of search-and-rescue operations.

As the Bel-Air floatplane slowed and lost altitude to land them at Port Conclusion about 8 A.M. the next day, Young and Kluting glanced at each other with concern. Two fishing boats at anchor in the bay below had only one man watching over both. As feared, a dozen Port Alexander residents, resentful of what they had thought was bureaucratic indifference and unnecessary delay, had taken off on their own. And 12 men milling around on a trail can obliterate a whole lot of evidence in moments.

"Can the group be reached by marine radio?" Young asked. The watchman then affirmed that the group had a portable unit with them. "OK," Young said, "let's call and tell them to stay put until we catch up."

Harley Sievenpiper's day-old footprints in the mud of a worn, well-traveled trail then led Young and Kluting to the second muskeg, about 200 yards from the beach. Kluting spotted a blue fannypack. It was the attack site. Sievenpiper's glasses, gloves, hat, lighter, watch, and pack were scattered about on the bloody, torn-up vegetation. Apparently, Sievenpiper had been positioned behind an old stump, blowing his deer call and watching the muskeg. His Ruger .300 Winchester Magnum rifle had been driven at a 45° angle through the deep moss and into the stump by the impact of the bear. Only inches of the shoulder stock remained visible above the moss. The muzzle was embedded so deeply in the partially rotted stump that it required both hands of both men to pull it free.

Fortunately, the search party hadn't found the site and stomped out the signs. Kluting was then able to read that the bear had come running (the prints in crushed moss and in the dirt below were far apart) down a 15-foot high hump of ground directly behind its victim. Sievenpiper had probably never known of the bear's presence until it hit him. His rifle had remained on safety, the scope covers had been removed, and a cartridge had been in the chamber, with three more in the magazine.

The drag trail going away from the site and up the slope was then easy for Kluting and Young to follow. It was evident that for a time the bear had dragged Sievenpiper by the shirt. When a piece of the shirt had torn off, the bear had spit it out and taken a new grip.

Within 100 yards, Kluting and Young caught up with the search party. The group's tone was openly hostile. Four-letter words flew freely, as the more vocal members made it clear that they weren't out there to take orders from anybody. They had missed the first 75 yards of the drag but had followed the trail another 25 yards after discovering a boot and bits of cloth.

**T**railing is slow, tedious work, and Young immediately recognized that it couldn't be done by 14 men. While Kluting would be patiently searching for minute clues, the others would, no doubt, be impatiently walking ahead of him, blotting out the signs. In addition, the extra 12 men were armed—most not well enough to challenge a grizzly, but all well enough to do each other harm. Young then cut the problem in half by asking six men to go with Kluting and the other six to accompany him. He would stay behind 100 yards or more to be out of the way while Kluting tracked.

Nevertheless, Kluting had problems. Six men are still too many to control when you're concentrating on tracking, especially when those men don't believe that you know what to look for, anyhow. To compound the problem, unknown to Young, two of the men he had sent with Kluting had been drinking.

Finally, Kluting found a splinter of bone, and some of his team began to exhibit more confidence in his ability. He radioed Young, who then caught up to photograph and collect the sliver. Trust continued to build as Kluting found other bits of flesh and bone, but the sight of these parts also made everyone increasingly nervous.

Each time thereafter that a squirrel darted or a bird flew, safeties clicked and three or four rifles jumped to shoulders. "OK, guys, calm down a bit." Kluting had to give his speech over and over. "Think straight. Don't try to shoot at everything that moves, or we'll get someone shot out here."

Bits of evidence were scattered for more than a mile. The longer the group trailed, the more serious and

*Illustration by Joe Garcia*

dangerous the situation became. Many bears leave their victims at the attack sites, and 70 percent of these people survive. If a bear claims its kill, it'll usually drag the body 200 or 300 yards at most and cover the remains with brush and other vegetation. Some victims have survived being covered and left behind. Seldom is the bear seen by searchers who arrive on the scene, and Young and Kluting didn't expect to see this one. Kluting had brought along his rifle, just to be sure, but Young carried only the medical supplies to stabilize Sievenpiper if he was found alive—and a body bag if he wasn't.

On and on the team trailed until they were 1,700 feet above the bay and 1½-miles from the attack site, an incredible distance for a bear to drag its kill. Kluting gave his stay-calm speech one last time, and he then began to have his own strange feelings. "Guys, it's just something in my guts, but I think we're close."

Somebody laughed. "Now who's nervous!"

No more pieces of flesh or bone were found for 200 yards, but the team was controlled, staying behind as Kluting slowly searched his way from one little piece of overturned moss to the next. About 100 yards beyond where he had his gut feeling, Kluting thought that he heard something and stopped the team. Nothing more. Kluting then whistled, and that was when the silence was shattered with the enormity of the unseen giant's roar, huffing challenge, and brush-breaking short false charges.

Kluting then radioed Young. "The bear is close. We can't see it, but it's just up the slope. And it's threatening. What do you want us to do?"

"If you get a good shot, put it down," Young came back. "The main thing is concentrate on getting that good shot. A wounded bear could be a disaster."

Kluting had never before killed a bear. He had hunted with his father since age 8 and had hunted deer by himself since 14. He had gotten bear tags for six years to avoid having to surrender the hide to the state in case he had *had* to kill a bear. But shooting a bear wasn't a desire of his, and so far he had been successful in chasing off curious bears by shooting close to them.

Nevertheless, Kluting then split his team, as mentioned in the beginning of the story, and confidently started up the slope with Lange. Rifle handling was practiced second nature, and adrenalin was perhaps making both men steadier and more sure of themselves than they had a right to be.

This bear's behavior had already proved to be bizarre when the animal had attacked Sievenpiper, who didn't have a deer to steal and who wasn't exposing the odors of meat and blood to the air (which is usually what attracts a grizzly to a hunter). The bear had continued to act strangely when it had dragged its victim 1½ miles instead of the usual couple of hundred yards. And the bear had compounded the unexpected when it had raged down the slope to attack five men—seven, if it had known about the other two 30 or 40 yards below.

The charging bear showed no response to the shots by Kluting and Lange at 50 yards. Lange's next shot caused a flinch, and Kluting triggered his second shot just as the bear was in the faces of the three men on the ridge. Kluting then reached for the bolt on his Ruger M-77 with the full knowledge that there was no more that he could do to protect his team. Even if the bear died at that instant, its momentum alone would carry it into those men with the impact of a car going 35 mph. And bears—assuming that this one was hit at all—do not die instantly from shoulder wounds.

At the precise moment that Kluting reached for his bolt, the bear, in its most unpredictable move of all, changed his mind about killing the three men just a step away. Kluting saw the bear's head swing toward him and Lange with its teeth bared and an unmistakable message issuing from the raging hate in its eyes: "You are the ones hurting me; you will die."

Kluting was seeing and registering every little detail as if things were happening in slow motion. The bear pivoted on its right leg. The left leg came around the right one as the bear executed its sudden 90° turn. Kluting's bolt had not yet quite ejected the empty case. The bear was now two jumps away, when once again, this time not through choice, it did the unexpected. Its right front leg was collapsing. Downhill momentum rolled the bear's front end onto its left shoulder while its rear end twisted until both hind legs were straight up—for just a moment. Then the hind legs flopped down, too, leaving the whole bear on its left side. But through it all, the bear's head remained level, angry eyes fixed on Kluting and Lange.

Movement 40 feet up the slope caught Kluting's eye. Everything had happened so fast that a skinny, dead sapling 30 feet tall and 5 inches in diameter was still in the process of falling after the bear was down.

The man with the .30/30—psychologically frozen into a split-second-earlier time—was still firing up the hill. The bear had been just off the end of his rifle barrel. Someone shouted, and he stopped.

Kluting finished chambering a live cartridge and quickly moved to his right to take the three men on the ridge more safely out of the line of fire. Stepping on a log to gain better elevation for a more effective head shot, Kluting extinguished the rage from the bear's eyes.

"What's going on? Is everyone all right?" officer Young was radioing urgently. "We heard shooting."

"All OK," Kluting radioed back. "The bear is dead. But now that it's over, I'm shaking so badly I can't stand up. The bear was so close to three of our men that I'm amazed they aren't dead from heart attacks."

The two men down the slope had only seen bushes whip and heard gunfire, so they weren't as shaken as everyone else. They had been close friends of Sievenpiper, and both immediately hurried up the hill to see if he was there and possibly alive. One of them yelled to say that they'd found him, but everyone knew from the tone of their voices that Sievenpiper was dead and worse.

"Come back down," Kluting yelled back. "Don't touch anything."

When the second group caught up, Young got the Port Alexander people started skinning the bear. Then he and Kluting went up to get the body. The details of the badly eaten remains are in the official reports, where they shall remain. Young rolled the body into the bag using peripheral vision. Kluting made the mistake of looking directly at the remains.

Today, although the mind protects itself with forgetfulness, the details of the body are still etched in Kluting's memory with the same slow-motion, fine-grained accuracy with which he recalls the bear's charge. One more detail emerges with that kind of clarity. "We had just gotten back to Port Alexander in the fishing boats," Kluting said. "I remember seeing a little girl, maybe bordering on or just into her teens, walking away down the only road in town—out past the end of the houses and into the woods along the beach. Someone said, 'That's Harley's daughter,' and they went to be with her."

Harley Sievenpiper was the 17th person to be eaten by a bear this century. He was the first in 12 years. The bear took six bullets. A .30/30 bullet had hit one of its feet as the bear charged directly at the shooter. One of either Kluting's or Lange's first shots at 50 yards had struck the chest cavity, possibly hitting the heart. The other had hit just behind the rib cage. Lange's second shot had broken the bear's right shoulder and gone halfway through its body. Lead from Kluting's .338 Magnum further shattered the bear's right shoulder, broke the left shoulder, and was later found emerging from the hide and hung up in the hair. The head shot was the sixth.

Although Young and Kluting offered with some trepidation, Mrs. Sievenpiper declined to hear any more of the details. She requested and would have cherished her husband's wedding ring, but it was never recovered. Neither were the deer call, Sievenpiper's wallet, and perhaps other unknown personal items.

Don Kluting was subsequently presented with the State of Alaska's Medal of Bravery, plus a $600 bonus from the city of Sitka's honor board, for risking his life in the service of others.

Considerable controversy continues to divide both Alaska's hunters and its biologists over what prompts bears to attack hunters. Some claim that all bears are programmed to function as all bears function, and that they are motivated to attack only by smelling or seeing what they consider to be food. This group denies that bears are called to dinner by reports of firearms or that they would be attracted by deer calls. Others believe that it is naive to think that individuals of a species as intelligent as the grizzly would be unable to learn new clues to finding easy meals. This group not only believes that some bears learn to respond to hunter sounds but also that sows, in turn, pass on this knowledge to their cubs.

"It has become a definite problem in my area," Kluting said. "The salmon runs have been poor the last

*A big—and dangerous—grizzly may sometimes answer a deer call. Photograph by Len Clifford/Leonard Lee Rue Enterprises*

couple of years during August and September, when the bears should be laying on fat. Maybe the bears are forced to hunt deer instead. Drew Mathews, a member of our search-and-rescue team, was hunting along a hiking trail with a partner when a sow with cubs came running to his deer call. The two men yelled, and the bears stopped, but the bears wouldn't go away. They circled the hunters for an hour. Every time the men tried to leave, the sow would head them off. Finally, the men tried to run. The sow was right behind them. Drew's buddy fired a warning shot, and the bear took off. The men ran another quarter-mile, looked around and there was the bear again. This time, another warning shot chased it off for good."

In October 1988, one month before Harley Sievenpiper was attacked, Kluting was hunting mountain goats above Katlian Bay and had killed his animal at about 3,100 feet. Ten minutes later, just as he had gotten to his goat, Kluting had seen a bear coming from a half-mile away. The bear had kept coming, so Kluting had fired a warning shot. Several shots later, the bear had finally stopped at a small group of trees 400 yards below. All the while Kluting had boned meat off the skeleton, the bear had paced back and forth in the trees, occasionally stepping out tentatively, but going back when the hunter had yelled.

When he had finished packing the meat, Kluting had thrown the goat remains over a drop-off and walked up the slope away from the bear. Although bears are supposed to have poor eyesight, this one obviously knew what Kluting had done and had immediately trotted toward the carcass. Kluting had slipped off the safety and raised the rifle in case the bear had run past the goat, but it hadn't.

"This bear came to the sound of my rifle shot," Kluting said. "Even if it could have smelled blood over a half-mile away, air currents couldn't have conveyed the message that quickly. In fact, any air movement that day was in the wrong direction. There was no wind, and it was hot. Heat causes updrafts, and this bear was down the slope.

"That bear was hungry. And the bear that killed Harley Sievenpiper was hungry, as it had very little fat for a bear in early November. I'll let the experts argue whether certain individual bears have learned to correlate gunfire and deer calls with free lunch. But I've seen and heard enough to conclude that it's wise to hunt in pairs and to watch each other's backsides when calling deer or when field-dressing any kind of animal in grizzly country."

# PART 4

# BIGGER GAME: ELK, MOOSE, CARIBOU

# Snow-Trek Trophies

*By Jim Zumbo*

Gary Duffy rode his horse through the timber ahead of me, moving at a good clip. Our horses walked along a trail etched in the Montana forest, headed for an area that Gary figured would hold trophy elk.

Darkness was just 20 minutes away when Gary dismounted and tied his horse to a tree. I did likewise and quickly pulled my rifle from the scabbard. We wasted no time walking through the timber toward the place Gary wanted to hunt.

I saw an opening ahead, a windswept ridge bordered by a three-foot snowbank. We eased through the soft powder deposited by strong winds and crept to the top.

Moments later we spotted animals on the slope below us. A dozen elk had their heads down, hungrily feeding on the frozen yellow grass exposed by the wind. Among the herd were two bulls, neither of them very interesting.

"We can do a whole lot better," Gary said. "Let's watch the edge of the timber until shooting light is over. There are some big bulls in here."

Our vigil was unrewarding. A few bighorn sheep appeared, but the bull I was looking for didn't show.

It was well past dark when Gary and I arrived at the corral. We made plans to meet before dawn the next day.

I was confident about the hunt's outcome for several reasons. Gary is a competent outfitter working in superb country for big bulls, and there was a blanket of snow on the ground. Snow, in my estimation,

*Zumbo took this bull after it emerged from the timber looking for graze. Photograph by Jim Zumbo*

is an ingredient that works magic for elk hunters. Snow inundates feed in high country, forcing the elk to lower elevations. Because elk must migrate to survive when snow piles high, they place themselves in a vulnerable position when they're forced from the upper contours into areas more accessible to hunters. Snow allows elk to be seen more readily at long distances, and it also offers better tracking opportunities.

Gary's hunt area is close to Yellowstone National Park, which gave me even more reason to be confident. Not only do resident elk herds in his territory have big bulls, but there is always a good chance that Yellowstone's bulls would move down into his hunting area.

The hunt began with my good pal, Jack Atcheson Sr., a resident of Butte, Montana, and one of the best big-game hunters I know. Atcheson is a hunting consultant and accompanied the late, great Jack O'Connor on several hunts. Atcheson and I were hunting on our own, hiking through the deep snow. The spot we hunted was just a few miles from Gary's ranch.

One evening, Gary drove up and invited us to hunt with him. He had horses, as well as some good spots to hunt. Atcheson and Gary have been good friends for years, and Jack wasted no time accepting Gary's invitation. The outfitter is an affable man with a wide grin and a firm handshake. He had a fine reputation for producing big elk, and I was delighted at the opportunity to hunt with him.

The next morning, Gary, Jack, and I hiked up a mountain long before daybreak. The trees cast eerie shadows in the moonlight, and we found our way without flashlights. After walking for 45 minutes in freezing temperatures, Gary pointed to an open knoll in the timber, which offered a good look at much of the country below.

"Stand right there and keep your eyes peeled," Gary advised. "This is a great elk crossing, and that opening offers a good look at some excellent country."

Jack agreed, having killed a big bull in the same general area a few years ago. I made my way to the knoll while Jack headed off for a vantage point across the ridge. Gary left to do some scouting, checking tracks in the snow.

The temperature was not much above zero, which is typical for the middle of November in Montana. I wasn't uncomfortable during the vigil, but I can't say that I was toasty warm when I walked down off the mountain several hours later after an uneventful watch. I'd learned a long time ago that a bit of suffering was involved during late-season elk hunts.

It was just as cold the next morning when we walked back up the same windswept ridge where we had seen the elk and the bighorn sheep. I had just settled myself and adjusted my heavy mittens when three big bulls appeared from the timber. They stopped momentarily in a small area of sparse brush, looked at me, and suddenly bolted into the trees.

I pulled my mittens off, fired at the biggest bull, and in a few minutes, Gary and I admired the elk. He was one of my best, scoring 343 Boone and Crockett points.

Gary hiked back to the ranch to get horses to pack out the bull, while Jack tracked the other two bulls. Jack was unsuccessful, but he returned a couple of days later to kill a bull nearly as big as the one I had killed.

Late-season elk hunting often ends on a happy note such as ours. Most of the best bulls I have taken came at the tag end of the season when many hunters have oiled their guns and put them away. There are a couple of simple, but important, prerequisites to hunting elk during the late season. One is being in an area where big bulls live. That might sound academic, but there are plenty of places in the West where there are no six-point bulls. To attain massive antlers, elk must be able to survive at least five or six years. On public lands where there is good access throughout, elk are often harvested too consistently. They simply don't live long enough to grow large antlers.

Gary's area not only has big resident bulls, but it also encompasses a prime migration route out of Yellowstone Park. Those two factors make his territory a prime spot for giant bulls. Rocky Mountain National Park in Colorado offers similar opportunity, and there are special hunts in and around Teton National Park and the National Elk Refuge near Jackson, Wyoming. In Alberta, Banff National Park holds huge elk. In 1977, Clarence Brown killed the biggest bull of the century just outside Banff. Brown hunted in November, camping a few miles from the park. The temperature dropped to 40° below zero when Brown killed the giant bull.

It doesn't take much research to learn about the land you intend to hunt. Places that produce outsized elk are usually well documented. If you're looking for a record-book candidate, or a brute that will score better than 325, you obviously need to select areas that support exceptional bulls.

To find one of these areas, contact the state wildlife departments and talk to biologists. They'll be able to give you a general picture of elk hunting in their respective states.

The Boone and Crockett Club record book is a good reference if you're seeking a record-book trophy, but you need to check on the most recent entries. States that produced big bulls in the distant past might be poor for trophy-elk hunting today because of changes in habitat and wildlife management.

Practically every state holds the general rifle elk hunt well after the September rut. Middle to late October openers are the norm; and only a few states offer hunting until the end of November. The later the hunt, the better the chances of heavy snow. During some years, however, snow falls earlier than usual, offering late conditions.

Though elk are somewhat oblivious to the cold, they rely on grass for a major part of their diet—so they have no choice but to migrate to lower elevations when deep snow covers their feed in the high country. Those migrations don't necessarily have to be long journeys of 50 miles of more, such as the distance elk travel each year to the famous elk refuge in Jackson, Wyoming. There, 8,000 to 10,000 or more animals show up each year, coming from Teton and Yellowstone national parks and several national forests. In places like Gary's area, resident elk may move only a mile or two, or much less, to obtain feed. It's not uncommon for snow to vary considerably within a half-mile or so.

I recall a wintry November Montana hunt with OUTDOOR LIFE's Senior Editor Ralph Stuart in 1988. Ralph took a nice bull after elk herds moved out of snowy, timbered mountain slopes each day to a large ranch in a valley bottom. More than 20 mature bulls were taken in the area that season; the hunters intercepted the animals as the elk traveled back to the mountains in the morning after feeding all night. Biologists said that it was one of the best harvests of big bulls in years, due exclusively to feeding habits altered by snow.

Big bulls don't necessarily migrate all of the way out of mountainous regions. Ralph and I hiked through waist-deep snow to get to the high, grassy windswept ridges, just as Gary and I had done. As long as sufficient grass remains to satisfy the elk's large appetites, animals will linger until the feed is either consumed or covered by deep snow.

I've often been perplexed by the amount of feed that will hold an elk in one spot. Some animals will remain in an area that seems to offer nothing, but if you scrape away the snow with your boot, you find a thick carpet of grass. Virtually all grass species will keep elk happy. If you see yellow bunch grass six inches to a foot above the snow, you're probably looking at a superb feeding area. If elk tracks are in the vicinity, you can expect animals to return.

It's interesting to note that wind patterns are usually identical each year. Except under extremely unusual weather conditions, a windswept slope that yields elk feed one year will do so every year. Those feeding spots become hot spots, known to outfitters or hunters who take the time to look for them.

Hunters often make the mistake of looking for elk on sunny southern exposures because it's warmer there than on northern exposures. It's important to remember that elk are quite well-suited to extremely cold temperatures. Biologists say that elk originated in Asia and crossed into North America via the ancient land bridge between Alaska and Russia. Today's ancestors of those elk are just as hardy. They thrive in snow and cold, having thick skin and dense fur to protect them from the bitter arctic weather. Look for them on northern exposed slopes, in bitterly cold places that seem inhospitable. That's precisely where elk will be. They'll also be in pockets of dense timber on steep slopes. My rule of thumb is to seek elk in the nastiest timber I can find, preferably a spruce/fir blowdown forest. And if the timber is on a steep slope exposed to the north, so much the better. It is in these isolated pockets that elk feel most safe.

Many elk hunters believe that the bugle season is the best time to hunt for big bulls. Though I prefer to be in elk country in September, when the aspens are yellow and the wonderful music of elk echoes in the forests, many of those big bulls are almost impossible to find then. They can roam anywhere in their enormous landscape, and they're more apt to hide and move into rugged places when confronted by challenging bulls interested in stealing their harems.

That all changes when the mountains are covered with snow. The extensive summer and early fall habitat become sterile. Elk concentrate in small winter ranges, and big bulls suddenly seem to appear for the first time of the season.

The bottom line to hunting migrating elk is doing it late. Some states offer options. Colorado, for example, has three seasons—the first starting in mid-October, the third starting in November. I'd hunt the last season, even though I know that other hunters would have worked elk over the first two hunts. It's possible the hunters missed seeing many of the bulls in the high country. Those animals will be more accessible if you hold out until after the winter has pushed them to lower elevations.

In Montana, another top elk state, the season runs five weeks. Many savvy hunters don't bother hunting until the last week, which is in late November or early December. I recall an area in Montana that yielded nothing for me, though I hunted it hard on and off the first two weeks. I returned the last week and saw a half-dozen bulls within a mile of my pickup truck. I claimed one of the bulls after a short stalk through two feet of snow.

Once you locate an area that you believe is a migration route, set up a vantage point where you can see a considerable distance. Be there before daylight and prepare to suffer. You'll likely encounter sub-zero temperatures. Use a spotting scope to look for animals in and around distant timber patches. It's also a good idea to survey the snowy landscape with a spotting scope to look for trails made by elk.

Don't look for elk on the move in the open country. Although it's always possible that elk will move through open areas during the day, migration is often done at night. When they're moving, they'll travel along the edges of timber or through draws. In the daytime, the animals are usually feeding or bedding. During the late season, hunters again have an advantage. When snow is on the ground, elk will frequently bed in the open in the snow, which is rare under other conditions.

Though I hunt elk with fervor anytime during the season, I'm much more enthusiastic and confident when the days are short, the air is bitterly cold, and there's a generous blanket of snow on the forest floor. Pain is often a requirement for a successful elk hunt. In my opinion, a certain amount of discomfort makes the quarry seem more earned. There are easy elk hunts and tough elk hunts. If you'll prepare yourself for the tough ones when conditions are hostile, you might very well tag the biggest bull of your life. Many hunters willing to take on nature's worst do it every year.

# Lower 48 Moose

*By Fred Bouwman*

"I was originally looking for a moose that was a legend in the area. The locals called him the 'plywood bull' because of the tremendous palms on his antlers—they looked like a couple of sheets of plywood," said Dr. Hugh Hogle, a Salt Lake City physician as he described a recent, rainy September hunt. "I went out and glassed that morning and didn't see anything. I was headed back to camp about 9 A.M. when I spotted two bulls from the road, but the 'plywood bull' wasn't one of them.

"The two bulls left the area, moving from one basin to another. As I headed out in my vehicle, I saw them again. This time the larger bull was standing looking straight away from me, and I saw that his entire rear end was covered with blood.

"I decided to go for him, not only because he looked better than I had originally thought, but because he was wounded. It was still raining as I got out my bow. I could hear them both thrashing their antlers on the brush, as I followed their tracks around the hillside.

"He took about four steps after I shot him and then went down. We found that the blood was a result of being gored by another bull."

Though this moose wasn't the "plywood bull," it carried a Pope and Young rack. And Hogle didn't have to cross part of the continent for a Canadian or Alaskan moose hunt or mortgage his home to pay

*At least 11 states now distribute moose permits. Nonresidents can hunt in seven of these. Photograph by Leonard Lee Rue III*

for it. This trophy moose was taken in his home state of Utah.

The sight of a moose brings visions of the far reaches of Canada or fly-in Alaskan camps nestled along wild rivers. But more than 5,000 hunters stayed in the Lower 48 states to hunt moose in 1989; and with healthy, huntable, expanding moose populations in much of the Lower 48, that number will continue to grow.

Hunters in 11 states can currently apply for resident permits. Nonresidents can apply in seven states. Most of these states guarantee a designated percentage of permits to out-of-state hunters.

## MAINE—FOR A PREMIER HUNT

The state of Maine, home to a herd numbering 20,000 to 25,000 animals, offers the premier lower 48 moose hunt. One thousand permits are issued yearly, 10 percent of which are reserved for nonresidents. There is a two-year waiting period before a successful permit holder can apply again. Maine's system allows the permit holder (the permittee) to designate a subpermittee. Either one can take the one moose allowed on the permit. This system is shared by some other moose hunting states and stretches the available permits twice as far.

"I'm big on the moose hunt. I think it's the greatest thing that ever came down the road," explained guide Jerry Packard, who runs moose hunts from his camp on Lobster Lake in central Maine. To date, Packard has a 100 percent success rate with moose for his clients. "We've taken some nice ones. Sixty inches is the biggest, one 59-incher and several others in the 50s. Forty-inch racks are real common."

Packard hunts from canoes and boats. "We try to move around in the boats a lot—put on a lot of miles," he said. "You see more moose that way."

Sybil Brock Scheilhagen of Cyprus, Texas, hunted from one of Packard's boats in the fall of 1989. She had hunted deer, elk, and turkeys in Texas and farther west, but this moose hunt was her first. "I saw moose every day feeding in the bogs and along the streams. We saw most of them the first day, and then a storm went through, and they went back into the woods. I was getting desperate. I wasn't looking for a trophy, just a fairly good rack."

At the end of the fourth 12-hour day spent paddling the bogs in the snow and freezing rain, Sybil and her guide had just finished loading the boat into the truck at the landing when a large bull walked into sight. She took it with a 180-grain bullet from her .30/06.

"I made it convenient for the guides. They dressed it out right by the truck, instead of having to pack it out in the boat," she said.

Sybil got a permit on her fifth try, one of the 82,824 applicants for the 1,000 either-sex permits. Her moose was one of 922 taken during the 1989–90 season. The permittee forks over the cash for the $200 permit, while the subpermittee only needs to purchase a Maine hunting license.

The number of hunters applying for Maine's fixed number of 1,000 permits has climbed from 60,150 in 1982 to 82,824 for the 1989 hunt. Bills presented to the legislature in 1988 and 1989 to increase the number of permits failed to pass.

"We've supported several bills over several years to raise the number of permits to 1,500, and we can defend that biologically, but it's a pretty emotional issue," explained Tom Shoener, director of information and education for the Maine Department of Inland Fisheries and Wildlife. Shoener notes that it is not only the antihunting crowd that is holding back a harvest increase. "There is a surprising amount of resistance to changing it on the part of hunters," he said. "There seems to be a pervasive feeling that the hunt is going very well right now, and if it ain't broke, don't fix it."

According to Shoener, the moose hunt has not interfered with nonhunting users of the moose herd. "Moose watching is such a popular thing to do here that no one—including us—wants to do anything to jeopardize that. There was concern when we started shooting 1,000 animals, and now, when we start talking about 1,500, there are even stronger fears. But it is still easy to go out and see moose."

## SMALL HERDS IN NEIGHBORING NEW HAMPSHIRE AND VERMONT

The northern third of New Hampshire is home to about 4,100 moose, according to Howard Nowell of the state's fish and game department. The either-sex hunts began in 1988 with 57 moose taken that year and 59 in 1989. Seventy-five permits are currently issued per year, with between 10 percent and 13 percent reserved for nonresidents. There were about 6,000 applicants for the 1989 hunt, but a three-year waiting period for successful permittees and a subpermittee system similar to that in Maine spreads the opportunities around.

Nonresident New Hampshire moose permits cost $300. Both permittees and subpermittees are required to attend a prehunt seminar, which could be difficult for nonresident hunters.

The Vermont legislature passed a bill authorizing a moose hunt for the fall of 1991. That herd is between 400 and 800 animals, and the fish and wildlife department estimates that 30 to 50 permits will be issued at $200 each, with 10 percent of the permits set aside for nonresidents.

## MINNESOTA AND NORTH DAKOTA— FOR RESIDENTS ONLY

Minnesota is home to approximately 10,000 moose, which are concentrated in the northeastern and northwestern corners of the state. The state's resident-only moose hunt resulted in a harvest of 882 animals from 994 permits in 1989. The subpermittee system allows four hunters to share a permit, spreading out the chances for a hunt among the more than 16,000 applicants for the every-other-year hunt.

*Check with local game departments. In many areas, moose hunters have a 85–100% success rate—and may get a large bull like this one. Photograph by Len Rue Jr.*

Minnesota's moose country can be compared to Maine's with its northern aspen and pine forests and numerous lakes and rivers. A particularly challenging hunt takes place in the Boundary Waters Canoe Area Wilderness, a federal wilderness area where vehicles and most machines, including outboard motors or any devices with wheels, are banned. Travel—and hauling out your moose—is by canoe.

For the time being, at least, Minnesota plans to keep its moose to itself. The state has a herd the size of those in Montana and Wyoming, both of which offer nonresident moose hunting. But Minnesota doesn't have the pressure from guides' or outfitters' associations such as those found in the Western states.

"One of the concerns we have is criticism from resident hunters," explained Jay Janacek of the Minnesota Department of Natural Resources. "When you hear things like, 'I've been applying since 1971 and haven't got a permit yet,' it is pretty hard to promote a nonresident hunt. I think that until a major share of the resident hunters here are satisfied, it will be hard to do anything." Janacek doesn't foresee any major growth of the state's moose population in the future. "I would guess that we are at the optimum number now. A major change in vegetation type, like from a big, sweeping fire, could help."

North Dakota's herd of approximately 300 moose is "small but expanding," according to Roger Johnson of the game and fish department. The 9,900 North Dakotans who applied for 119 permits took 116 moose during the 1989 resident-only hunt. Most North Dakota moose hunting takes place in the timber country in the northeastern part of the state, with a few permits designated for the Red River bottomland where residents have experienced depredation problems.

## WYOMING AND MONTANA— TWO DIFFERENT APPROACHES

Wyoming's moose harvest has steadily increased, from 190 in 1943 to the 1,434 taken on 1,635 permits during the 1989 season. The moose population is estimated at 10,000. The $305 nonresident-permit fee carries a five-year waiting period between successful draws. A generous 20 percent of bull permits are set aside for nonresidents.

Wyoming moose are mostly confined to the western and northwestern portions of the state, although there are a lot of moose in the Green River area, according to guide and outfitter Jim Allen of Lander. "I have taken two myself, one which scored 145. We have one 44-inch rack listed in the Safari Club book."

Bud Weaver, another Wyoming guide and outfitter, says that though getting a permit can be difficult, the successful permit holder is practically guaranteed a moose.

"Your chances of getting a moose are almost 90 percent once you get a permit," he said. "Our success for taking moose with nonresident hunters is 100 percent."

The choice of management district applied for can affect the chances of drawing a permit. "In the real good moose country, like around Jackson, the odds for drawing a permit can go as high as 120 to 1," Weaver added. "Statewide, you're looking at about 1 in 23, but in other areas the odds drop to 3 or 4 to 1."

Western Montana is home to around 10,000 Shiras moose. Around 20,000 applicants applied for a little more than 700 permits in 1989. The department of fish, wildlife, and parks estimated the 1989 harvest at slightly more than 600, with a hunter-success rate of 87 percent. The department reserves up to 10 percent of the tags per district for nonresident hunters, who pay $322 per tag.

Although the Montana moose population is almost identical to that of Wyoming, the latter state issues approximately twice as many permits and harvests close to twice as many moose each year. This is due to Montana's conservative approach toward the number of moose that can be taken from the herd each season. Moose are difficult to census, and the Western states tend to spend less time counting their herds than the Midwestern and Eastern states.

## COLORADO AND UTAH— NEW POPULATIONS AND STRICT LIMITS

Colorado's resident-only, one-moose-per-lifetime hunt was established in 1985. With a population of only 250 moose in 1989, there were only five permits to be divided among the 450 applicants. Though moose have been sighted in Colorado for more than 100 years, there has only been a documented resident population since 1978. In that year, 12 moose from Idaho were released, and the following year 12 more from Wyoming were released. One theory states that the Shiras moose is moving its range southward and will eventually reach Colorado anyway, which explains the relatively recent establishment of populations in southern Wyoming and northern Utah.

Colorado's program is considered a success by Gene Schoenfeld at the division of wildlife, "There were no great racks this year, but a year ago someone took a 41-incher." Schoenfeld's comments on a nonresident hunt mirror Minnesota's, "It will be quite a few years in the future. When you have 450 residents in line, it's hard to have a nonresident hunt."

"Moose wandered into Utah in the early part of the century from Wyoming and have gotten distributed around the state in the last few years by us moving them," said Grant Jense, assistant chief of big-game management for the Utah Division of Wildlife Resources. Utah's herd numbers about 3,000 animals, for which 274 permits were issued for the 1990 season. One tag per lifetime is allowed.

Utah's bulls-only nonresident hunt is a little pricey at $1,002 plus license fee, but this is tempered by the excellent chances of drawing a permit in some management zones and the 100 percent hunter-success rate. Some areas have very few nonresidents applying for those permits.

"Ogden River is our trophy area," Jense said. "We have consistently taken what could be Boone and Crockett heads out of there."

Only four nonresidents applied for the one tag available in that area last season, and there were three applicants for four permits in another. Total odds for nonresidents drawing a permit in 1989 were 1 in 6.

## INCREASES IN IDAHO AND WASHINGTON

"We are in the process of writing a new five-year management plan for moose, and nonresident hunting is one of the issues that people in Idaho have identified," explained John Beecham, species plan coordinator for the Idaho Department of Fish and Game. "Over the last five or 10 years, our moose population has been growing out of sight. We have no idea of the total number, but we know we are seeing a lot of moose and that permit levels have gone up considerably."

Idaho's moose range encompasses most of the state with the exception of the southwestern corner. Part of the growth of the "rapidly expanding" herd is due to relocation of "problem" moose by fish and game personnel. Sixteen moose have been successfully moved since 1983.

Both permit and harvest numbers in Idaho have risen steadily over the years, from 118 moose taken on 140 permits during the 1980 season to the 400 taken on 472 permits in 1989. The requirement that a successful moose-permit holder wait two years before applying again, and a regulation that restricts hunters to applying for only a bighorn sheep, mountain goat, or moose controlled-hunt permit, and not a combination of two or three in the same year, has cut moose applicants from a high of more than 25,000 in 1980 to 3,635 in 1989.

As in Utah, some hunts offer better odds than others. "Ten years ago, the odds of drawing a moose permit were something like 1 in 128—just horrible," Beecham said. "Now they are down to around 1 in 20, but some hunts are 1 in 2 or 3. If you throw nonresidents into the pot, the odds get worse. The consensus among the department people is that the fair thing to do is allow nonresidents 10 percent of the permits for hunts with more than 10 permits, similar to what we now do with sheep and goats. In fact, our odds on moose now are better than they are on mountain goats, and those are nonresident hunts."

Idaho is looking at increased permit numbers for the immediate future, which can only help the chances of a nonresident hunt. "Our habitat is changing to favor moose," Beecham said. "Each year we will raise the number of permits a little until we see hunter success drop or the size of the bulls decrease."

"We're not really a moose state," explained John Riech of the Washington Department of Wildlife. The Shiras moose population is estimated at somewhere between 100 and 300. The hunt is open to nonresidents and 1,029 applicants contended for six once-in-a-lifetime permits in 1989.

"The herd is expanding," Riech added. "They are working their way south and west. It's kind of an oddball situation in our moose range. There is a lot of arid, desert-type land east of the Cascades. When you get to the northeast corner, you start running into more rainfall. It's kind of a mixed-up area, with a lot of willow growth. The moose are doing best in recently logged areas."

## PROTECTION IN MICHIGAN

The Upper Peninsula of Michigan is native moose range. A combination of habitat change, unrestricted hunting—including a severe population drop during the years of World War II meat rationing—and an increase in the whitetail deer population reduced the moose population to the point that complete protection was given.

A successful reintroduction of moose took place in 1985 and 1987, when Michigan wild turkeys were traded to the province of Ontario for 61 moose. The 1989 population stood at about 220 animals. Rob Aho, a Michigan Department of Natural Resources wildlife habitat biologist, notes that though the program is not committed to providing a hunting opportunity, "Moose hunting is a possibility. I'd like to think the moose population would be so successful that we can hunt them," he added.

Aho says that a population of around 1,000—a possibility by the year 2000—would be necessary for a hunt to take place.

## HABITAT AND DISEASE FACTORS

As moose populations increase nationwide, wildlife managers will face some conflicts. Moose do not commonly cause crop depredation, though North Dakota issues permits in agricultural areas because of complaints from farmers. Cattlemen's associations in Colorado initially opposed the introduction of moose into agricultural areas of the state due to fears that the animals would damage hay crops or compete with cattle for forage. In the Northeast, it has not been uncommon over the past few years for confused bull moose to get a glint in their eye for dairy cows, but the only significant property damage seems to be caused by crowds of human onlookers rather than the moose. Moose have been shot by authorities on numerous occasions when they wandered into cities or along major highways and posed a hazard to human life.

In the Midwest and East, some choices may have to be made during the early stages of reintroducing moose populations, when numbers are still low. Besides habitat considerations that would favor moose over whitetail (moose thrive in deep snow conditions, for instance), a parasitic worm that causes no apparent damage to whitetail is often fatal to moose. *Parelaphostrongylus tenius*, a brain worm, infects whitetail and moose alike. It causes no visible damage to the smaller deer species, but affects moose with "moose sickness," the symptoms of which include weakness, apparent blindness and deafness, and running into trees and walking in circles. The disease is invariably fatal. The only known treatment is a vaccine used when transplanting moose, which is only effective for 30 days.

Though the brain worm can devastate a small moose population, large populations, such as that in Maine, seem to be able to survive by strength of numbers.

"It is not a big cause of moose mortality in Maine," explained Tom Shoener. "We have deer and moose range overlap in a big part of the state. Moose are still found sick and dying from the disease, but it doesn't seem to be as common as it used to be."

The brain worm is apparently not a problem in Western states with Shiras moose populations, according to Glenn Erickson of the Montana Fish, Wildlife and Parks Department. "There are lots of whitetails in Montana, and their range and moose range overlap. We have not noticed any problems."

## THE MOOSE/CLEAR-CUT CONNECTION

"They cut massive areas—looks like the Russians nuked the place," is how fourth-generation Maine guide Jerry Packard describes some of the clear-cuts made in his moose hunting country in northern Maine. Although some habitat types serve both moose and whitetail, logging practices can have an effect on which species becomes dominant.

Modern industrial timber harvesting often creates larger clear-cuts, which can favor moose over whitetails because the larger deer can feed in these unsheltered areas under deep-snow conditions.

"One of the reasons we have such an increase in our moose population here is because timber harvesting techniques are different than they used to be," Packard said. "They clear cut up to several hundred acres in the northern sections of Maine, and this creates excellent moose habitat."

Jay Janacek of the Minnesota Department of Natural Resources notes a similar relationship in his part of the country.

"In line with our other management objectives, we tend to approve larger clear-cuts up here in the northern part of the state than we would in country that is more whitetail range," he said. "In strictly whitetail range, a 40-acre clear-cut like we make in some northern areas would be considered awfully big. For whitetail range you are talking more like a 10 or 20-acre cut."

## DIFFERENT HUNTING METHODS

Methods of moose hunting change from the East Coast to the Rocky Mountain states. "We go in by four-wheel drive and hunt from boats," said Maine guide Jerry Packard. "We like to call moose, but that has been a problem the last few years because the hunt has been right at the end of the rut. We move along the bogs, rivers, and lakes. They lie down in these big bogs. If you stand up high in the boat you can see the antlers sticking up out of the bushes. If you make a little noise, they will stand up to look, and you have your shot. If there is a really big bull around, we will make a blind and wait."

A 1,000-pound moose will leave the lucky hunter and subpermittee with 500 pounds or so of moose meat. Getting the animal out of the woods deserves some forethought on the part of the hunter used to dragging 150-pound whitetails out of the woods. A hand winch or come-along is a wise accompaniment for the hunter, if only used to move the animal out of the water for field-dressing.

"You usually have to quarter them out in the field," Packard added. "You can haul an 800-pound moose out in a 17-foot canoe in one trip with calm water, but it's safer to do it in two trips."

Shiras moose hunting in the West compares to elk hunting.

"We hunt from horse tent camps," said guide Jim Allen, "with a lot of glassing and horseback riding. We feel the hunting is best with snow, both for tracking and because it bunches the animals up."

Dr. Hogle, in Utah, finds the hunt more challenging with a bow.

"Moose are highly visible, particularly during the rut because they are out there running around and because of their dark coloration," Hogle said. "You can close to within 100 yards without bothering them, but as you stalk within bow range and invade what the moose perceives as his 'survival zone,' they become extremely cautious. When alarmed, they have a warning bark—not like an elk, but almost a short, staccato roar. Every deer, elk and anything else in the country takes note of that."

Hogle was certainly pleased with his lower 48 moose. "I had taken moose in Alaska before with a rifle, but this was my first Shiras moose. The rack scored 161 and a fraction. It will be in the top 10 to 15 Pope and Young heads, and it will rank around the middle of Boone and Crockett. It missed being a new state-record moose by about two points—the Utah state record is 163." And though Utah's once-in-a-lifetime permit system means the end of hunting moose in his home state, there are book trophies waiting for other Utah residents or out-of-staters.

"The year before, I also saw a bull in the area that would have easily eclipsed the current world record," Hogle said. "An incredible animal."

The challenge of obtaining a moose permit in the Lower 48 makes every hunt a trophy hunt. And it doesn't get any better by heading farther north, according to Jerry Packard, Maine guide.

"I'm spoiled when it comes to moose. I'm the fourth generation of guides here," he said. "We've been here a hundred years. I've hunted them in Canada, and I've hunted them in Alaska. I've never seen any place where there is moose like here. Lots of moose."

---

### IF YOU GO

Colorado Division of Wildlife
Department of Natural Resources
6060 Broadway
Denver, CO 80216
Hunter Success: 100 percent
Nonresident Hunt? No

Idaho Department of Fish and Game
600 South Walnut
Box 25
Boise, ID 83707
Hunter Success: 85 percent
Nonresident Hunt? No

Maine Department of Inland Fisheries and Wildlife
284 State St.
Station 41
Augusta, ME 04333
Hunter Success: 92 percent
Nonresident Hunt? Yes

Minnesota Department of Natural Resources
500 Lafayette Rd.
St. Paul, MN 55155
Hunter Success: 85 percent
Nonresident Hunt? No

Montana Department of Fish, Wildlife and Parks
1420 East Sixth Ave.
Helena, MT 59620
Hunter Success: 87 percent
Nonresident Hunt? Yes

New Hampshire Fish and Game Department
2 Hazen Drive
Concord, NH 03301
Hunter success: 79 percent
Nonresident Hunt? Yes

North Dakota Game and Fish Department
100 North Bismarck Expressway
Bismarck, ND 58501
Hunter Success: 97 percent
Nonresident Hunt? No

Utah Division of Wildlife Resources
1596 West North Temple
Salt Lake City, UT 84116
Hunter Success: 100 percent
Nonresident Hunt? Yes

Washington Department of Wildlife
600 Capital Way North
Olympia, WA 98501
Hunter Success: 100 percent
Nonresident Hunt? Yes

Wyoming Game and Fish Department
5400 Bishop Blvd.
Cheyenne, WY 82006
Hunter Success: 89 percent
Nonresident Hunt? Yes

# Jinx of the Bad Luck Bulls

*By Valerius Geist*

The late September snowstorm that had swept over northwestern British Columbia was just what I had been waiting for. The cold would keep any meat from spoiling (a good thing in our cabin with no refrigeration, hundreds of miles from civilization), and the snow would reveal every moose track. I was actually almost looking forward to tracking; almost, that is, because tracking in tall, wet, snow-covered dwarf birch and alpine fir is no pleasure.

I reached for my old 7mm Mauser, a fine custom-built rifle made long ago by master craftsman Tom Burgess, but at the last second I hesitated. A steep climb awaited me, as I was heading for timberline, where rutting moose tend to concentrate, and I knew that the Mauser would be a heavy load. Why not take a lighter rifle, I thought, such as the small Husqvarna in the same caliber topped off with the tiny Boone scope—a prismatic-type riflescope now long out of production? With this little rifle I had grouped 10 shots into an inch at 100 yards, and I had used it to take deer, bears, mountain goats, and caribou. Not only that but I had also collapsed several moose with just a single shot using handloads that I had developed for the gun. So with all of this in mind, I shouldered the little rifle with confidence and headed out the door with it and the moose jinx in tow.

Within two miles of the cabin, I found a fine bull moose guarding a cow. The cow browsed below me in the willows that grew along an avalanche gorge. The bull stood behind her in low alpine fir, his body and fine, spreading rack fully exposed. It was as fine an opportunity as I have ever had in hunting. A dead fir that had been up-rooted by an avalanche allowed me to place the rifle across my cap into a steady rest. At something less than 200 yards, I figured that I couldn't miss. The crosshairs settled just behind the bull's shoulders, where the aorta sweeps up from the heart, and I concentrated on slowly squeezing off my first shot.

*Bang*—the moose never flinched. Must be a tough one, I thought. I remembered having read somewhere that a moose can have its heart shot out and not even know it. I decided that a second shot would be good insurance.

*Bang*—again the bull didn't budge. The cow looked my way this time and listened. I knew that both animals had to have heard the reports. A third shot would surely clinch it.

*Bang*—a response at last. The bull wiggled an ear! The cow turned back to feeding. Good old German hunting tradition requires shooting until the game falls over!

*Bang*—were these moose hard of hearing? The bull must be dead on his feet by now, I thought. Maybe he'd require a push to fall over. Perhaps I could accomplish this with another shot.

*Bang*—the bull and cow took off, disappearing in a split second among the trees. The mountain stood empty, and I was left sitting with a long face, wondering if I had been dreaming.

Two shells remained in my pocket, so I loaded them into the rifle and headed down to where the moose had been. There, in six inches of fresh snow, were the

*A great opportunity—or will you be jinxed? Photograph by Leonard Lee Rue III*

tracks of the bull where he had stood while I shot. I could find neither a drop of blood nor a single bullet-clipped hair—nothing betrayed an injury. I followed the evenly spaced tracks for a mile, through avalanche gorges, fir forests, and birch scrub. The tracks betrayed unflinching steadiness. This was no wounded dying bull! This was a perfectly healthy bull. I had missed five well-aimed shots.

I know that I missed, because I found the same bull two days later tending to his ladylove. By then, however, a friend of mine had flown in and brought along the haunches of both a record-class bull moose and a caribou bull that his clients had taken. For this reason, I simply watched the courting pair for a while, and then cautiously, so as not to disturb the two, climbed back down to my cabin.

What had happened with my shooting?

A close inspection of my rifle showed that the scope's reticle had broken and was rattling around inside the scope housing. The jinx had struck, and it was to strike again—and again on moose!

How often have you been hit by lightning? How often have you had a reticle break? Well, it happened to me a second time, again while I was hunting moose. It was the last day of the big-game season in southwestern Alberta. I was in the middle of conducting a deer study and had squeezed out a couple of days of hunting from a busy schedule. A pan-size mule deer buck had fallen to my rifle earlier in the season, but I still had a moose and a whitetail deer tag remaining.

The day before I had come down with a grim cold, and as I walked about in the throat-scouring frigid air, I coughed convulsively every few minutes. Try as I might, I couldn't suppress the hack. My plans to sit on a well-used deer trail thus came to nought. I knew that no deer or moose would stand for the racket that I was making, and so I decided to head for the hills and look down into draws. I thought that I might be able to spot some game at a distance.

Then, I remembered that I had just reinstalled the scope and that I should try a test shot—just in case. I flopped on a big snowdrift into a comfortable prone position and aimed at a black knot in a dead, peeled poplar some 100 yards away. The bullet splintered white wood about a foot below my aiming point. How curious! A second bullet splintered wood about a foot above my aiming point. Well, what do you know!

Before going to the tree, I turned the rifle this way and that way, looking for a clue. Nothing. Then I shouldered the rifle, and holy cow! The crosshairs stood at an angle—the reticle was loose.

When in trouble, sit down five minutes and think. That was the advice that an old bushman had given me years before—and I was in trouble all right. It was the last day of hunting season, I had a nagging cough, and I was out with a useless rifle. I wondered if I would have to call it a day before the day had even begun—or would I? The crosshairs in this particular scope were mounted on a lens, and it was the lens that was rotat-

ing. I knew that I would still have been able to hit a pie plate with the rifle at 50 yards and that was good enough to hit a buck in the shoulder at close range in the bush.

I felt distinctly better for having thought. Besides, I love sneaking about in thickets, anyway. My spirits continued to rise after that, and my cough got better, so I dove into the thickest aspen bluff I could find.

Within 20 minutes I had a whitetail buck out in front of me, but try as I might, I could not get a clear shot, and the little fellow faded away in the willows and aspen.

Suddenly there was a crash to my right. Spinning around, I saw a moose's black rear end disappearing down a trail and heard the distinct clanking of antlers against branches. Instantly, I ran after the bull, knowing that this can be a most useful trick if several moose spook at the same time. Within 50 yards, I ran past another bull who stood craning his neck behind a big clump of willows five paces away. He took off immediately, and I heard him running parallel to me, following the first bull.

All three of us were making an awful racket, which was just fine by me, because in such a situation, moose will sometimes get confused about who exactly is running and will stop. For the most part, both moose were out of sight, only occasionally giving me a tantalizing glimpse of black or leaving a waving branch in their wake. My legs were giving it all they had and then some. As I sprinted around a bend in the trail, I came upon one of the bulls standing 10 yards away, broadside, looking at me. In a jiffy, I had the rifle up as I skidded to a halt, and that was that!

A moment later I saw the other bull behind me, watching, taking it all in. Then the innocent dodo walked toward me, utterly consumed by curiosity and glancing from me to his fallen buddy and back again. He ignored my shouting, waving, and clapping, but eventually became uneasy and consented to walking away—slowly. Both moose had become thoroughly confused by the noise of all three of us running. And as I had hoped would happen, my bull had stopped to investigate.

The bull was a poorly developed four-year-old with small short-tined, light palms. Moose in the aspen parklands of southern Alberta rarely grow large, but this one was a runt even for the Alberta foothills. I had gotten the better of the jinx that time, but it had taken some revenge. The ebony forend tip of my prize rifle had come off during the run, and it cost me a pretty penny to replace it. Have you ever had a forend tip come off your rifle? It was certainly a first for me.

The jinx continued.

It was a glorious, sunny September morning, all glittering dew drops, lemon-yellow aspen leaves, and blue skies. The smell of Indian summer was in the air. I was sitting on a cut-line, watching a ruffled grouse that was pecking clover leaves close by. A stick snapped to my left, and a yearling bull moose cautiously stepped out into the cut paces from my stand. My rifle was raised in anticipation; I was prepared. The crosshairs settled just behind the bull's front leg, searching for his heart.

*Bang!* Something hit me smartly over the head, brushed down my face and chest, and fell on my toes—my riflescope. It had spun loose. The young gunsmith had installed much too short a tension spring in the Bausch & Lomb top mount, and the recoil had shaken it free. Because windage and elevation are in the mount, I quickly picked up the scope, hand-held it in place, and fired two more shots. I doubt that they were needed, however, as the moose was well hit the first time and collapsed on the cut-line within seconds.

On my next moose hunt, a fall in the mud plugged up my rifle barrel. I hadn't brought along a cleaning kit, but a friend generously loaned me a second rifle that he had brought along. It was a beautiful scope-sighted Sako .30/06. Before I had a chance to test fire the rifle, a young bull showed up and I fired two shots at very short range. A third shot by a friend dispatched the bull, and that was the only bullet wound we found. I had missed twice. Now I religiously carry a cleaning kit—and a spare rifle.

The jinx worked on!

My oldest son, Karl, was the proud owner of his first hunting license. He carried a single-shot .22 and that September day he had given the rifle a good tryout, collecting several nice ruffed grouse. The moose were in rut, but the day was warm and I had seen neither hide nor hair of a bull. I had, however, repeatedly flushed flocks of grouse. In my hands was a fine Remington Model 700 in 7mm Remington Magnum, but the 175-grain Core-Lokt bullets were hardly the appropriate loads for grouse.

Well, this time I had brought with me a spare gun. It was a Browning over/under combination gun in 12 gauge and 7mm Mauser. Toward evening I swapped guns in the happy anticipation of shooting a grouse or two before calling it a day. In addition, I knew that I

had a sufficient load in the 7mm should I happen to see a moose.

Karl joined me and we had a good hunt, taking several more grouse. And after a long day, we walked briskly back to the Jeep to get started on the drive home. Moose were no longer on our minds. Well, you guessed it. As we entered a cut-line, there, barely 75 paces away, stood a bull moose looking at us. We could clearly see a crooked left antler. Karl made eyes as big as saucers. He knew that things were about to happen, and they sure did! I figured that the bull was as good as venison.

With great cool, I raised the gun, put the aiming point of the crystal-clear Zeiss scope on the bull's neck where I figured the fourth neck vertebra ought to be, exhaled by half, and squeezed the trigger.

*Bang!* The bull gave us one long, dirty look and hurled himself off the cut-line. And as he faded into the undergrowth, I could still hear the No. 7½ birdshot raining down into the trees. I had pulled the wrong trigger. What was worse was that I then had to explain my performance to my son.

The next year I hunted hard. On opening day, I saw seven moose, but they were all cows, and only bulls were legal. The following day I saw more cows, and more still the day after that. This continued on into November, as I tracked down cow after monotonous cow. Finally, the last day of the season arrived, and I proceeded to track down moose No. 25. It took me nearly a day of going through snow-covered thickets and none-too-solidly frozen muskeg, but I finally caught up with the moose that had been making the impression. It was another cow.

At dusk I was bone weary, when I cut a really fresh track. This one was big! My adrenalin surged back. I felt reborn, fresh, alert, and eager. Cow or bull? That was the question! But with a moose track in a foot of loose snow, that question isn't very easy to answer. The strides were long and the tracks spaced well off the center line of travel. And though this did not make for positive identification, it was encouraging. With

*Careful tracking may let you surprise a huge bull in rut. Photo by Leonard Lee Rue III*

a half-hour of daylight left on the last day of the season, I simply had to try. I figured that it could be a young bull.

Tracking down moose is not terribly difficult, but conditions do have to be right. Conditions such as soft falling snow, a thaw after a good snowstorm with lots of water dripping and snow plopping off branches, or a strong wind blowing are right because any sounds that the hunter makes are dampened or covered up. In addition, if you are dressed warmly in lots of soft wool, if you watch your steps to avoid stepping or scraping against branches, and if you do not mind getting soaked, you are some way toward success.

The trick is not to follow the moose directly, but indirectly. You must spend a minimum of time on the track. The most productive method is to swing out, downwind of the track. If a moose is hotfooting it through the country, there is, of course, no point in careful circling. But if you can determine where the moose has begun to meander and feed, it's a different matter, because then you can expect that the moose will be bedded downwind of its track, and you can circle downwind from there. I try to cut the track every 300 yards or so and move not more than about 150 yards from it.

This way of tracking moose is probably as old as moose hunting itself. There is no magic formula here, and there never was. Success comes from looking with some knowledge and understanding at the land and judging its acceptability to moose either as escape terrain, cover, or a feeding site. Developing an eye for this comes only with experience—and my moose jinx saw to it that I got plenty of that.

Moose No. 26 was heading down the pine-covered ridge toward a flat expanse of spruce forest mixed with stretches of low dwarf birch and islands of tall willows. Upon cutting the track a second time, I noticed that the moose was meandering—a good sign. I never completed the next semicircle. A small island of aging, tall willows within a stand of old spruce caught my attention. It looked like a typical moose bedding site. It was. There followed a loud rumble and for a second a huge moose looked down on me. You guessed it: it was a cow. And, in an instant, she whirled and vanished.

We were having Indian summer when the moose season opened the following year. Karl was a husky lad now, an avid fisherman and hunter. Dawn one particular day found us on a large moose meadow without moose. Karl, eager for grouse, took the combination gun and headed off. I remained at my stand enjoying the splendor of the morning. Then a young bull moose trotted across the meadow. I had a single-shot along in 7mm Remington Magnum with 160-grain Nosler handloads that grouped in a dime at 100 yards. Moose hunting for the year was over in seconds, and Karl and I had a time of it getting the bull skinned, cut up, and transported back to the car.

What had happened to the jinx? I knew that some-

thing bad just had to happen! I was worried stiff all day. I drove home being extra cautious, double-checked the guns and licenses, looked to see whether I had lost anything, wondered what I had forgotten, and expected the Jeep to break down—but all went well. Nothing noteworthy at all happened. The only thing that I can figure is that the jinx must have been sleeping that day, because it returned with a vengeance the next year, and the year after that. I guess that I would miss the jinx if it left, because it's been around for such a long time.

For years I'd tried getting a really fine trophy bull. I'd lived in fine moose country, and I don't know how many bulls I'd passed up. For one reason or another, the really good ones I could never go after. For weeks one season, I hunted about a lake where I'd found exceptionally large shed antlers. I never saw a large bull. Yet, as I was departing in the aircraft, I looked down, and there, right where I had been the day before, stood the largest bull moose I have ever seen, with wonderfully symmetrical antlers.

One November day, I saw across a lake a huge bull moose in the company of two others. We were a half-mile apart, but the old fellow had heard my snow-shoes and stood alert, watching my way. In the spotting scope, I saw a wavy, uneven set of huge, ragged antlers, typical of a very old bull. Like other old bulls that I'd inadvertently alerted, this one did not hang around, but turned and headed off into the willow fields, his mighty rack thrown back as he trotted. He was a great bull, but not one that I wanted because of his asymmetrical, ragged rack.

But the jinx put me to the test on that one!

A week later, I again bumped into the big bull. He, who had previously been so wary, hadn't noticed my approach this time, despite the fact that it hadn't exactly been a silent one. The bull browsed in some low willows barely 100 paces away. He was huge! The ragged, wavy antlers were as ugly as they were large. Their spread was immense, as was their mass.

"Should I, or shouldn't I?" I wondered. I did need winter meat, and I needed it soon. The bull was only a mile from my cabin, and hauling him across the frozen lake would have been easy. Moose were not common within a day's walk of my cabin. However, I'd had past experience trying to eat gaunt, old bulls that I'd killed late in the season. And looking over the huge bony frame, the caved-in haunches, and the sinewy shoulders, I shuddered. Eat him all winter? I decided that he was just a tough old veteran of many winters in the harsh mountain valleys, and that whatever he was, food he was not!

I don't know how long I stood and just watched that bull as he fed along, snipping off willow twig after willow twig, turning each around in his mouth before crunching it down, thick end first. Then I slunk away so as not to disturb the old boy, and I never saw him again. I guess the jinx knew me too well in my resolve, or maybe it didn't want me to wear out my natural dentures. Had the old bull carried symmetrical, broad-palmed antlers of equal spread, I might have had to figure out how to eat him after all!

# King of the Mountain

*By Ernie Peacock*

"The San Francisco area has been rocked by an earthquake that measured 7.0 on the Richter scale," the TV blared in the lonesome cafe along northern British Columbia's Alaska Highway.

"Must have been a doozer," drawled our guide, tall, rawboned Ted Cobbett, as he washed down his last cup of coffee. "C'mon Buds, we gotta make tracks to the ranch."

Somehow, even news of that magnitude seemed insignificant in the vastness of the country we were in, as I and my hunting companion, Jon Alvin, climbed into Cobbett's beat-up truck.

Cobbett had picked us up from the airport in Fort Nelson, British Columbia, five hours earlier, and after leaving the cafe, we drove one last brief stretch on the highway before taking a hard right off the asphalt and into the bush. From there, it was just a seven-mile drive to the ranch, from which we would be flown to our ultimate destination—Cobbett's spike camp in the rugged foothills of the Liard River Valley, several miles from the Yukon border.

This was my first hunt for trophy moose, and the thrill and anticipation that had gripped me on the flights from my home in Minneapolis, Minnesota, to Edmonton, Alberta, and then on to Fort Nelson had only intensified. On the plane, I had read about the shock that a hunter in Alaska had experienced when he was confronted by a 72-inch bull moose as he rounded the corner trail he was riding on a horse. Now, on the bumpy truck ride, I wondered how I would react if faced with a similar situation.

We arrived at the ranch by nightfall, and I noticed a definite chill in the mid-October air. A few days earlier, I had watched my sons' final high-school football games in just a sweater, but at the ranch, there were six feet of snow on the ground. "Winter comes early up here," Cobbett commented.

Alvin and I stashed our gear in a small guest cabin, met Cobbett's family for dinner, and then settled in for a night of dreaming about trophy moose.

The next morning we were up at first light and hustled up to the main lodge for a welcome breakfast cooked by Cobbett's wife, Maggie. Their three little girls were attentive onlookers as we ate.

After breakfast, Cobbett decided that Alvin would be the first to fly in with him to the spike camp in the two-seat Super Cub. I checked my gear at the makeshift airstrip while they were gone, and when Cobbett returned, loaded my cased Ruger 7mm Magnum and large duffel into the plane. I noticed that Cobbett threw in a guitar case. "Good," I thought to myself, "we'll have a little entertainment at night around the fire."

It was barely a 45-minute flight to the spike camp, which consisted of two small 8 × 8-foot log cabins and a slightly larger cook shack and storehouse. Our first job upon arrival at the camp was to entice the horses into the corral with a bucketful of oats and then latch the rail door behind them.

After that, we ate dinner and listened as Cobbett reminisced about his experiences as an outfitter and guide—experiences that included one of his hunters taking the current Boone and Crockett Club world-

*Ernie Peacock's huge Canada bull should rank as one of the best in the Boone and Crockett records. Photograph by Jeff Murray*

record Canada moose back in 1980. He told us that his Scatter River Outfitters operation has exclusive hunting rights in an area approximately 120 miles long and 70 miles wide. The range includes beautiful boglike tundra, foothills, and mountains, with a variety of freshwater creeks and glacial lakes. Moose, caribou, elk, black bears, grizzlies, and timber wolves are plentiful.

The next morning, we ate breakfast at first light, and then went to the corral, saddled up the horses, and loaded our gear for the day's ride. Neither Alvin nor I had ridden much since we were kids, so thoughts of long rugged horseback trips into the wilderness didn't have great appeal.

Though the horses at first appeared to be on the wild side, they were easy to ride, trail-smart and sure-footed. (They had to be to negotiate the numerous half-frozen creeks, spongy tundra, and rocky trails that we encountered.)

The snow was only about three inches deep on the ground in the valley, but it was already waist-deep in some areas of the upper mountains. Along the way, it was a treat to drink cold water right from the creeks.

After leaving the ranch, we rode steadily until 3 P.M., traveling around bogs, through creeks, up hillsides, and through brush that was 10 feet high. Finally, we stopped just below the crest of a small mountain and secured the horses.

We then started cautiously up the remainder of the incline, and upon reaching the crest of the ridge, we peeked carefully over the opposite side into a brush-covered basin. Cobbett said that he had seen a lot of sign in the area.

We spent 10 or 15 minutes glassing the cover, but there were no signs of life. Cobbett commented that the wind was bad and that he didn't want to proceed farther because our scent would go directly into the bowl. But it was too late.

"There!" Cobbett whispered. "Over there in that opening." As we scanned to the area where the guide was pointing, we could see the antler palms of a large bull that was standing and looking directly at us. It was obvious that the bull had winded us and was nervously getting ready to retreat. The large gray antler palms looked to be about 350 yards away.

Because it had been agreed that Alvin would take the first moose, I readied myself to watch the action.

"You'd better take your shot now, Buds," Cobbett warned, " 'cuz he's moving off."

Alvin took a quick rest and touched off three shots from his .30/06. I heard a couple of the shots hit; but Cobbett motioned for me to shoot, too, when the bull began to move off. I was able to fire twice before the moose disappeared. Cobbett confirmed that the bull was hit, as he said that he had seen the animal go down.

Farther back in the basin, we saw another bull linger and then move into a thicket before I could shoot. The second was a big bull also, definitely trophy material.

Cobbett signaled for us to mount up and get over to the fallen moose, which we found dead where the guide had seen him go down. Alvin's bull was a real trophy, and Cobbett said that the antlers should make the Boone and Crockett record book. We discovered then that Alvin had hit the bull clean with two shots and that only one of my shots had connected, clipping the moose low in the leg. My immediate thoughts were that something might have happened to my rifle, and I decided that I would recheck the sights when we returned to camp.

We butchered the bull, enjoyed a Spam sandwich and a cup of field-made coffee, and then loaded the meat, rack, and cape onto the horses for the ride back to camp. Needless to say, Alvin's spirits were at an all-time high.

I don't believe that I've ever seen a more welcome sight than the light that was on in the cook shack when we returned to the spike camp later that night. An Indian guide, who we came to know only as Roy A., had arrived, and he greeted us warmly.

After dinner, Cobbett pulled out his guitar. "Whaddya wanna hear, Buds?" he cackled and then broke into some twangy Country Western songs. I admired this guide for his hardy, carefree attitude in the wild.

Cobbett is a real study. I judged him to be in his mid-30s, and at 6 feet 2 inches tall and 180 pounds, he looks as lean and hard as they come. He is an accomplished bush pilot, hunter, guide, outfitter, woodsman, and guitarist, and he has an opinion on just about every topic. I got the feeling that he could be dropped anywhere in the world, and he'd be entirely self-sufficient. He also seemed to have a sixth sense about where game would move each day. And that was one of his qualities that I liked best.

That night, we went to sleep feeling pretty good. There was already one trophy moose in camp, and I hoped that I'd have a chance to take another, perhaps even larger, bull.

The next day, after I re-sighted my rifle and confirmed my thoughts that the scope had been jarred a bit, we split up into two parties. Alvin had both black and grizzly bear permits, and he and Cobbett went off in pursuit of a 9½-foot grizzly that had been seen in the area a week before our arrival. Roy A. and I instead headed for Moose Mountain, a favorite resting spot for big bulls after the rutting season.

Roy and I proceeded up a long ridge, through some brush, some woods, and then across several creeks. As we neared a flat saddle in between two mountains, Roy stopped and looked to a nearby tree. There, on a branch, clung a defiant marten, apparently angry because we had invaded its territory. Roy looked longingly at the animal and said, "Fur's worth $190." He shook his head, obviously thinking that had I not been along, he could have taken the animal and been $190 richer.

We moved on through the saddle and started up the other side of the mountain. At one point, I noticed that the horses were cocking their ears and looking into some timber to the right of us. "It must be some sort of an animal," I thought, but I couldn't see anything.

Halfway up the side of the ridge, we stopped to rest the horses, and lo and behold, out walked a nice-size bull moose down below. He started to follow our tracks up the ridge and came toward us for about 50 yards, before turning and proceeding to eat his way through the brush on the saddle that we had just crossed. Roy tried to encourage me to go back and stalk the bull, but I told him that I wanted a trophy bull or no bull at all. Again, the guide shook his head.

We continued on and topped Moose Mountain, but when we scanned the valley below, we spotted only one cow and a calf. It was a bust.

We took a slightly different trail back to camp, and again it was long after dark before we saw the warm glow of the cabin light off in the distance. Cobbett and Alvin had blanked that day, too, but we were all in good spirits, and it wasn't long after dinner before I fell into bed for the night.

The next morning, it was my turn to hunt with Cobbett. "You up to a hard ride?" the guide asked.

"Sure!" I replied.

"See that range of mountains way over there?" he asked, pointing to a long ridge covered with snow in the distance. I saw it and swallowed hard, knowing that it wouldn't be easy to get there. "Let's go, Buds."

Cobbett wasn't kidding about the hard ride. We crossed hills, creeks, and half-frozen bogs before beginning to work our way up into the mountain range. At about 1 P.M., we stopped at one of Cobbett's many small spike camps, which are nothing more than a couple of boards nailed to a tree to mark spots where he's left supplies.

Over a cup of thermos coffee, Cobbett said, "We're

going up on the tundra where it'll be windy and cold, so button up 'cuz it'll be rough when we get there."

Again, the guide spoke the truth. Up in the high tundra we encountered blinding snow and quartering winds that approached 60 mph. We moved along the frigid ridge for a couple of hours before Cobbett stopped to rest the horses.

By the time we started up again, conditions had worsened. I could make out only a faint gray outline of Cobbett and his mount ahead of me, and the left side of my face felt like it was starting to freeze. I cupped my left hand over my cheek every 100 feet or so to keep it warm.

After what seemed an eternity, Cobbett led us off the crest of the mountain to the side of a valley. We secured the horses to some rocks, and Cobbett motioned for me to grab my gun and follow. We scrambled down the valley side until we reached the treeline. Then we started glassing the area below.

The snow was still blowing, but the wind had slowed, which made things somewhat more comfortable. Glassing conditions, however, remained anything but good, and though we glassed and glassed, we saw nothing. It was 3 P.M., and I was figuring that it was another bust.

Suddenly, Cobbett jerked his right thumb upward. He had seen a moose! Sure enough, I panned along his sight line and caught a pair of giant antler palms against the snowy backdrop. It was a big bull, and he appeared to be looking right at us from the far side of the valley.

Cobbett motioned for me to follow him. He crept farther down the valley side through the trees. There was a crosswind between the bull and us, and there was a chance that the moose would catch our scent. When we had crept to within 450 yards of the bull, Cobbett turned to me.

"Can you get him from here, Buds?"

"You gotta be kidding!" I said. "I don't have confi-

*The trip out from camp was mild compared to the return struggle in the dark and freezing cold. Photograph by Jim Zumbo*

dence in this shot." The moose was in a small thicket of pines and still at a steep angle from us on the opposite side of the valley. I wanted to get closer and have a more level shot, but I could see that Cobbett was concerned about the moose bolting.

We moved farther down the valley wall, and again the guide paused.

"You're going to have to take your shot from here," he said.

I found a fallen tree and rested my rifle across it for support.

"Where should I hold?" I asked.

"High on his shoulder. When you come down with the scope, you'll have plenty of time to squeeze your shots off."

I lined up the crosshairs of the Leupold $3\times-9\times$ on the top of the bull's back, then took a deep breath, and released it slowly. I estimated that I was 350 yards from the target. I slowly squeezed off the first round—my best shot, I thought—but nothing happened.

The moose stood rigid.

I fired again, but the bull still didn't stir. One more shot. Nothing. I turned to Cobbett in disbelief.

"What happened?"

"You hit him twice," he whispered, as the bull walked slowly behind a clump of pines. "You missed the first shot. But you hit him with the next two."

I nervously fumbled in my pockets for more shells. I wanted to catch the bull when he came out from the other side of the pine, but nothing happened.

Cobbett pondered the situation for a few minutes. "I think he's down, but I can't be sure," the guide said. "One of us has to go up after the horses and the other has to go after the bull."

"Guess who's going after the horses?" I laughed nervously.

"Take my .30/30," Cobbett whispered, "'cuz that scoped gun of yours won't do you a bit of good at close range. He's somewhere close to that stand of pines, so use that as a reference point and make a circle downwind, so he can't smell you.

We parted company, and I started sneaking to the valley floor. Once down there, though, everything seemed to change. The brush was 10 feet high, making it impossible to see the stand of pines. As I moved cautiously in a semicircle around where I guessed the pines were, I began thinking of a giant wounded bull charging me. I made sure that there was a shell chambered in Cobbett's rifle.

Eventually, I reached the far side of the valley, and I hadn't cut any fresh tracks. I knew that the bull was still in the area, but where? I located the stand of pines and slowly worked my way to where I thought I had last seen the moose. I then spotted the unmistakable form of the huge fallen bull.

I approached the animal slowly, and when a prod in the haunches produced no reaction, I moved forward.

It was at that point that I realized how truly huge the moose was, and I spent the next few moments admiring the magnificent animal. What a great feeling it was to know that he was mine!

I pulled off my red vest and tied it high in a pine tree so that Cobbett could spot me in the blowing snow. I then started skinning the animal.

Soon the guide rode up, tied the horses to some trees, and came over and looked down at the moose.

"You know what you've got there, Buds?" he asked, after a brief silence.

"Yeah, I've got myself a big bull," I grinned.

"You've got yourself a world record," he announced. "You just shot the King of the Mountain."

**M**y first thought was that Cobbett was simply trying to make me feel good. I didn't think it was possible for a guy to simply look at a moose in the field and make an accurate judgment about something like that. But the guide was grinning from ear to ear, and that wasn't like him.

It was hard work skinning the bull. The hide was so tough that I had to stop and put a new edge on my knife every few minutes. I looked up and noticed that the weather had gotten worse again, and we both began working furiously to get the job done.

After finishing, we packed the rack, cape, and meat on the horses and began the climb back to the high tundra. Visibility was terrible, and Cobbett guessed that the temperature had dropped to about minus 10°. It took almost three hours to get back to the small spike camp where we had stopped for coffee earlier, and we still had a considerable distance left to the cabins.

It was 1 A.M. by the time we finally rode into camp. But, despite the time, Alvin and Ray were up like a flash to greet us. After reliving the story with them and helping to unload the horses, I grabbed a cup of soup and collapsed into bed.

The next morning, Cobbett was holding forth in the cook shack. He had pulled out his Boone and Crockett book and had already measured the bull's rack three times.

"Yup, it's a world record all right," he proclaimed. The bull had a 63½-inch spread and green-scored 244 points—exceeding by two points the score of the 1980 record bull taken by Cobbett's client. Only then did the idea start sinking in. Cobbett was so excited that he suggested we tie the rack to his plane and fly to the ranch and then go directly on to Fort Nelson.

Alvin and Roy decided to keep trying for bears while they brought the stock out of the mountains for the winter. So, it was agreed that they would hunt their way out with the string of horses.

Cobbett and I closed up the camp, flew to the ranch for a short stop, and then on to Fort Nelson, where our reception was something to remember. At a local watering hole, friends and fellow outfitters celebrated with us for quite some time. And though Cobbett suggested that I stay another day to continue the party, I had had just about all the celebrating that my weary bones could handle.

Besides, I had already gotten what I had come for. The King of the Mountain would be flying home with me.

# Ungava Bulls

*By Tim Jones*

"**S**hould I take him?" I whispered.

"I don't know," replied my ever-helpful hunting partner.

"Those top points are great, and he's got good bezzes."

"But not much in the way of shovels."

"Yeah, but look at those tops! Should I take him?"

"It's up to you."

"He's big enough for me."

While we had been debating, however, the big bull caribou had made up his own mind. He'd watched us warily, as we'd beached the big freighter canoe and jumped out to hunker down behind a rock with our binoculars. Two hundred yards, he'd decided, was too close. So he'd just started walking away toward the ridgetop.

You can't believe how fast a caribou covers rough ground. By the time I'd decided the bull was big enough, he was 300 yards out. And when I had fumbled a shell into the magazine and another into the chamber, he was 400 yards and still moving.

Then he stopped and looked back.

"Too far," I decided. "Let's let him go over the ridge and stalk closer."

The caribou obligingly disappeared over the ridge.

At most Quebec caribou camps, missing a chance at an exceptional bull might be a tragedy. Most herds of Quebec/Labrador caribou, including the giant George River and Leaf River herds, are migratory: here today, gone tomorrow. The caribou may or may not be there when you are. And if you do miss an opportunity at a particular bull, it's likely that the animal will be miles away in no time.

My partner, OUTDOOR LIFE Senior Editor Ralph Stuart, and I weren't worried, though. We were hunting out of Akuliak Camp on the northeastern shore of northern Quebec's Ungava Bay. Around Akuliak, the caribou are of the Korok herd, which is nonmigratory. The caribou stay in the area year-round. Also, because they are freed from the rigors of migration, Korok bulls grow huge antlers each fall.

Ralph and I were sure that we'd find this big bull somewhere in the next valley, so I took a moment to open the action of my Ruger M-77 and put two more 7mm Remington Magnum shells in the magazine. Then, Ralph and I left the Inuit guides behind and set out.

After huffing and puffing our way over several hundred vertical feet of boulders and blueberry bushes, we topped the ridge over which the bull had disappeared. We eased over without skylining ourselves, fully expecting to find the big caribou feeding somewhere in the glacier-scoured valley beyond.

But no such luck. He had disappeared. The lower rim of the valley was covered with a forest of the scrawny spruce trees that characteristically grow wherever there's shelter from the area's harsh north

*Author had tough time getting into smokepole range of this big bull. Photograph by Ralph P. Stuart*

A herd of caribou crossing barrens. Photograph by Leonard Lee Rue III

winds. We proceeded to glass every inch of that valley, spotting several cows, calves, and small bulls, but never again saw the trophy.

Never again, that is, until we decided to circle above the stunted spruces and back to the bay from where we had started. Moving quietly into the wind, we managed to get very close to two smaller bulls, and as we neared the beach, we looked back over our shoulders in time to see the big bull bolt from a thicket 600 yards out and head for the safety of another valley. We watched until the bull was out of sight, marveling at the whitetail trick he'd pulled on us. Who says caribou are pushovers?

Ralph's and my adventure had begun about a month earlier, with a call from Steve Ashton, a Quebec booking agent. After having heard Steve describe the hunting at Akuliak, it had taken me about three minutes to decide to make the trip. After that, it had taken me only about a minute to convince Ralph to come along on the trip.

The month before our trip had been a rat race of choosing clothing and equipment. We had both debated taking bowhunting gear, but with this being the first-ever caribou hunt for either of us, we had finally settled on centerfire rifles for the first of our two-caribou limit and muzzleloaders for the second.

On August 28, Ralph drove to Montreal from his home in New York, while I drove up from New Hampshire. We rendezvoused and overnighted in Montreal before catching a flight from Dorval Airport to Kuujjuaq (formerly Fort Chimo) on the lower tip of Ungava Bay. When boarding the plane at Dorval, we met fellow hunters who would share the camp with us— Doug Bisballe, Tony Jaecques, and Neil Godbey, all from Texas; Paul Cerwinka from Pennsylvania; and Danny Foote from Nova Scotia.

At Kuujjuaq, we were then shepherded aboard a Twin Otter for the flight to Akuliak. The Otter flew low along the edge of Ungava Bay, giving us a view of the magnificent, empty landscape. Northern Quebec,

like Africa, is miles and miles of nothing but miles and miles. In one hour and 20 minutes of flying, we saw one outpost cabin—the only sign of "civilization," in the area.

A bumpy landing on a crude runway brought us to Akuliak, where we were greeted by about 30 Inuits— our guides, camp staff, and their families. Akuliak is located in Inuit Native Reserve Lands. It's owned and operated by Arctic Adventures, a native-owned corporation. Because they are working for themselves, the Inuits work doubly hard to ensure the comfort and success of the hunters.

Greeting us, too, were the eight departing hunters, all of whom had taken beautiful caribou. "The food is great!" said one.

"Super guides," said another.

"Don't take the first bull you see!" was the last shot of advice from all of them. As we listened, shivering a little in the bright sun and brisk arctic wind, our hopes soared.

Dinner that night was sumptuous steaks, perfectly prepared by camp chef Gerard Huegeney. (Calling Gerard a cook would be like calling a Rolls-Royce a jalopy.) Naturally, the main topic of conversation was caribou; and most of us decided we'd look a day or two before pulling the trigger.

The next morning, we began our hunt. At Akuliak, 24-foot freighter canoes powered by 30-hp outboard motors are used to reach distant hunting areas. Two hunters pair up with two guides in each canoe. To a great extent, the hunting is controlled by the tides, as Ungava Bay has daily tidal variations of up to 50 feet. It's amazing to watch the inlets and fiords fill and drain with the comings and goings of the ocean, and water roars like river rapids as it flows around the rocks of the bay.

Before we got into the canoes to go hunting the first morning, I carefully stowed my ammo in the bottom of my wool hunting pack, under my hat, gloves and

raingear. That way, I couldn't kill a bull without first making a conscious decision to dig out the ammo, load the rifle, and shoot. Ralph did the same.

It was a wise decision. Motoring along the coastline, only 20 minutes into the hunt, we spotted a couple of *huge* bulls standing on a ridgetop. The mass, height, and spread of their antlers was enough to give any confirmed whitetail hunter heart failure. Ralph and I got excited, to say the least.

Our two Inuit guides, both named Bobby Annanack (we quickly dubbed them Big Bobby and Little Bobby) had, of course, seen the bulls long before us. Both Bobbies spoke excellent English, and they gave us our first lesson in the Inuit language. These bulls, they said, were "mikiuk tuktuk"—little bulls—not the "amiuk tuktuk" we were looking for. Clearly our whitetail hunters' eyes needed adjusting.

Shortly afterward, we came ashore for a closer look at a different bull. With the 350-pound-plus animal feeding behind a small hummock, we stalked to within 50 yards and evaluated his antlers piece by piece. He had more than twice the spread and probably five times the antler mass of any whitetail we'd ever seen—and he, too, qualified as only average to our guides!

Unlike typical whitetails, with which trophy antlers are simply larger and heavier versions of uniform racks, caribou grow free-form antlers. No two racks look exactly alike. The basic element of the rack are the shovels (the palms rising vertically above the animal's nose), the bez palms (above the shovels along the main beams), the main beams (which define the spread), the back points (rearward-pointing tines halfway up the main beams), and the top (palms and points at the top of the main beams). Large size in one area of the antler may mean a deficit somewhere else. We found it helpful to judge racks out loud as we looked through binoculars. ("Single shovel, great bezzes, good spread, no back points, small tops. Too small.")

Late the first afternoon, we joined up with Paul and

Danny and their guides Stanley and Paul Annanack to cruise the shoreline back toward camp. All of the Inuit guides were adept at spotting game, but Stanley, who is more than 70 years old and who heads up the camp, had an uncanny knack for finding and evaluating trophy bulls with his naked eyes that the rest of us could barely see with binoculars. He picked up a couple of big bulls feeding in a basin, and we pulled ashore for closer inspection.

One of the bulls looked huge, even to our increasingly experienced eyes, and Danny, Ralph, and I enjoyed a grandstand seat watching through binoculars as Paul and Paul stalked, evaluated, and finally passed up the largest bull. None of us watching was sure we could have avoided pulling the trigger.

At camp the first night, Doug showed off his beautiful trophy, a bull with double shovels and antlers so perfectly symmetrical that the two sides of the rack looked like mirror images of one another. Doug had dropped the bull with one shot from his .300 Weatherby Magnum using 180-grain handloads.

The next morning, while Ralph and I were being made fools of by the big bull at the beginning of the story, we heard shots echoing. We later found out that Neil had been a couple of miles away taking his own trophy. He'd spotted the bull feeding out on an open flat, had come ashore, stalked to within 150 yards, and taken the trophy with his .300 Winchester Magnum.

After the big bull gave us the slip, we motored down an inlet to a fresh location. There, Ralph, Big Bobby, and I left Little Bobby with the canoe and climbed an 800-foot mountain to take a look around. Though it is possible to see caribou right along the shoreline, it sometimes pays to get a higher vantage point. And, believe me, climbing these small, steep mountains will tell you very quickly what kind of shape you're in.

Three-quarters of the way to the top, I decided to explore a nearby valley, and Ralph and Bobby elected to head for the summit. It was just after this that Ralph discovered how fast the deceptively slow walk of a caribou actually is.

What happened was that when Bobby and Ralph attained the uppermost reaches of the mountain, they spotted a group of four bulls walking straightaway from them over a series of finger ridges. The antlers of the last bull in line had a huge spread—larger than Ralph could resist—and the game of "tundra tag" was on. Trying to get closer, Ralph repeatedly ran after the bulls each time they dropped from view over one of the finger ridges, and then he hid each time they rose up into sight again. The unalarmed caribou continued to outdistance the hunter, however, and Ralph finally had to settle for a shot at more than 300 yards just before the last bull would have been gone for good. For some unknown reason, the big bull stopped broadside as he reached the last ridge, and Ralph capitalized with his Winchester Model 70 and 180-grain .300 Winchester Magnum handloads.

*The author and his companions were able to spot—and take—large caribou bulls like this in Quebec's Ungava Bay region in late August. Photograph by Leonard Lee Rue III*

According to Ralph, he had time to get down into a prone position, rest his rifle on his pack, steady the crosshairs of his Tasco variable high on the bull's shoulder, and fire. The bull fell and rolled to the edge of a 60-foot cliff, but Ralph was able to fire a coup-de-grace before the caribou could kick his way over the edge.

The bull's antlers, still in velvet, spread more than 50 inches. Ralph was ecstatic.

Then, of course, the work began, and by the time the rack, cape, and meat were ferried the mile or more to the canoe, we had to race the falling tide back to camp. Ralph was muttering about shooting the next bull close to the shoreline.

The next morning, our guides took Ralph and me back to the same area where the big bull had given me the slip the day before. We walked a mile inland toward the valley into which the big bull had disappeared. Stopping to glass the land ahead, Big Bobby spotted a large-racked bull bedded high on a hillside. The stalk was long—more than a half-mile—as we sidehilled across a slope covered with berry bushes, but we had no trouble staying out of sight.

As we eased into position behind a rock about 200 yards from where the bull was bedded, the caribou sensed that something was wrong and obligingly stood up. It took only seconds to judge the wide, heavy rack and decide that this bull was big enough for me. I leaned into the rock, steadied the Bushnell crosshairs behind the caribou's shoulder, and dropped the big animal in his tracks with a single 150-grain Sierra boattail.

Feeling confident about my one-shot kill, I lowered the Ruger and started to eject the empty. Then Ralph burst my smug bubble by exclaiming, "There he goes!" I looked up to see the bull stagger to his feet. Composure shattered, I fumbled home the bolt on a fresh shell. But before I could line up a shot, the bull wobbled and fell, never to move again.

When I finally walked up to the trophy, I was more than pleased. The antlers were, of course, important, and with almost 4 feet of spread and 37 scorable points, they certainly looked impressive. But even more important was the beauty of the country, the quality of the hunt, and the fact that I had made a successful stalk and a clean shot.

At Akuliak, the basic cost of the trip includes only one caribou, even though the Quebec license allows two. The second bull costs an extra fee for shipping and handling. This price structure allows hunters who want only one trophy to save money. As mentioned earlier, however, Ralph and I had each elected to go after a second bull.

Later that same afternoon, the tides prevented us from hunting by canoe, so Ralph and I grabbed our smokepoles and walked out along with Little Bobby to hunt. About two miles from camp, we climbed a mountain to glass from the top, and when Ralph spotted a bull in a valley another two miles away, we didn't need a spotting scope to tell that the caribou was huge. Unfortunately, he was out on an open isthmus that separated a large lake from the bay, and there was no cover for a stalk.

We thus decided to surround him, which may sound a little silly, considering the vastness of the terrain, but it seemed to be our only chance. While Ralph and Little Bobby tried to circle down to the strip of land behind the bull, I slipped around upwind to try to drive the bull to them. It didn't work. The bull disappeared into a little wrinkle in the landscape, and I was able to get within about 200 yards of him before the wind took my scent in his direction. Instead of moving off downwind toward Ralph and Bobby, however, the big bull hoofed it between me and the lakeshore, well out of muzzleloader range. I sat and watched him cross a ridge back in the direction we'd come from.

I started glassing the opposite side of the valley, trying to spot Ralph so that we could link up and formulate a new plan, when suddenly I saw a puff of white smoke blossom at the base of some cliffs. Several seconds passed before I heard the hollow boom of Ralph's .54-caliber custom caplock.

Hustling over, I found Ralph and Bobby standing beside a nice bull—not as big as the beast we had been stalking, but a trophy just the same. As Ralph told it, while he and Bobby had been maneuvering to get at the first bull, he had spotted this bull feeding at the base of the cliffs. By the time Bobby had lay down and pulled a camouflage coat over himself, and Ralph had weaved his way in and out of notches in the rock face to within 30 yards of the bull, the caribou had bedded down. The bull was in such a position, however, that he was angling toward Ralph with only half of his headgear and the lower three-quarters of his body visible behind a jutting ledge. But Ralph evaluated what he could see and decided to take the animal. The bull courteously stayed put through one misfire, then succumbed to a 425-grain Buffalo Bullet that entered just behind his shoulder.

I helped field-dress the animal, and as none of us really wanted to pack it the four miles back to camp, Ralph and Bobby decided to freighter the meat, cape, and rack a few hundred yards to the edge of the bay, where everything could be retrieved later.

I started back to camp to get Big Bobby and the canoe. About a mile into the journey, I spotted the big bull we had been stalking in the first place. I immediately lay flat in the ankle-high bushes, tried to look like a rock, and evaluated the situation. It didn't look good. The bull was feeding on the hill above me, and I was caught on an open flat with no cover for a quarter-mile.

I had nothing to lose, though, so I decided to try for him. Every time he'd lower his head to feed, I'd move closer, periodically belly-crawling in the damp bushes. Then, as the angle of the hill would hide me from the bull's lowered head, I'd dash forward in a crouch. I could only move a short distance at a time, and it took the better part of a half-hour to move the quarter-mile to cover.

Once I made it to the ledges below where the bull was feeding, I had rocks for cover, and it was comparatively easy to sneak to within 50 yards. After that stalk, I had no doubts about wanting the bull, but it took a minute or two for my heart to stop pounding both from the exertion and the excitement. Calm (well, sort of) again, I quietly cocked the hammer of the .50-caliber Thompson/Center Renegade, rested the rifle across my pack, set the hair trigger, lined up the big iron sights, and fired. The bull was quartering away when I shot, and the 340-grain Maxi-Ball did its job in the caribou's boiler room. The bull ran a few yards and dropped.

Ralph and Bobby showed up a while later, and we raced with the sun to take a few pictures as well as skin and butcher the trophy. It took us until well after dark to pack meat, antlers, and hide to a point where an all-terrain vehicle could haul them to camp. The rack spread 48 inches and had 32 scorable points. Some of the guides went back for Ralph's caribou the next morning.

And that, essentially, ended my first caribou hunt. All of the other guys had finished up, too, except Doug, who took a second bull on the fourth day of the hunt. Danny had taken a beautiful 50-inch-plus bull with his .30/06. Paul had used his Ruger .308 to drop a bull with magnificent, long top tines. Tony had used a Bell & Carlson-stocked .338 with 250-grain handloads to take another exceptional trophy. They were beautiful bulls, all, and we were one happy group of hunters.

We spent part of our fourth day fishing for five to 10-pound Arctic char. And on the way back to camp, we came across two large caribou bulls out for a pleasant swim in the 35° waters of the bay.

The fifth day, our last, we spent stormbound in camp with gale winds blowing sleet and snow across the landscape.

Fortunately, the storm stopped in time for us to fly out on schedule the sixth day, and the long route home was a typical anticlimax.

The first thing I did when I got home was show off my two magnificent trophies to my family and friends. My five-year-old twin boys were excited by antlers taller than they were.

The second thing I did was cut and wrap about 120 pounds of boneless steaks.

The third thing I did was pick up the phone, call Steve Ashton, and ask him to start looking for another caribou hunt for me—maybe at Akuliak. Once in a lifetime is just not enough.

## PART 5

# GUNS AND SHOOTING

# Best Guns for Deer

*By Jim Carmichel and Jack O'Connor*

J ack O'Connor's part of this article—"Deer and Deer Rifles" is a chapter from his famous book *The Hunting Rifle*, published in 1970. My "Coast to Coast Deer Rifles" was published in *Outdoor Life* in the early 1980s. No one spoke for O'Connor while he lived, and I will most certainly not attempt to speculate on what his view on deer rifles would be if he could have witnessed recent developments in equipment and ammunition. There is little likelihood that his philosophy on deer rifles would have ever changed. But, as rifles and cartridges become obsolete and are replaced by newer designs and developments, a conscientious gun writer not only must adjust to the new but also must guide his readers toward what he feels will be the most productive and satisfying equipment. For a gun writer, this is often a matter of dovetailing past experience with the guns and ammunition currently available. O'Connor was a great practitioner of this art: one who knew full well that no good

Editor's Note: This article includes two separate articles— one by Jack O'Connor, the other by Jim Carmichel—as well as a brief introduction by Carmichel. The advice of these famed shooting editors is timeless.

*Each hunter, including our famed authors, has his (or her) own favorite guns. Photograph by Stanley Trzoniec*

purpose is served by touting the "best ever" deer rifle if that particular rifle hasn't been manufactured for a half-century.

Though my thoughts on deer rifles were written 15 years after O'Connor's, I already see signs of obsolescence in my recommendations. Not obsolescence because the rifles and cartridges weren't good, but because today there is something better. For example, when I wrote my article, the 7mm/08 Remington was a recent introduction and ammunition of that time wasn't all that great. Now, it appears that the 7mm/08 is destined to become one of the all-time great deer rifles, especially when combined with today's compact and unbelievable light rifles. That's why if I wrote "Coast To Coast Deer Rifles" today, several of my recommendations of rifles and calibers would include rifles that didn't exist just a few years ago. What would not change, however, is my basic philosophy about hunting rifles, which is not just matching the rifle and cartridge to the game but also matching them to the hunter and the conditions of the hunt. There is nothing new or original about this philosophy; it was practiced by O'Connor before me and by the gentlemanly Townsend Whelen before him. If a gun writer is to be successful, it is necessary that his writing helps his readers be successful in their shooting and hunting. I can think of no writers who were more successful at this than Whelen and O'Connor.

A smart gun writer never argues with success, even if it doesn't mesh with his own ideas. O'Connor was primarily a bolt-action man, as I am, yet he graciously acknowledged the existence of lever and pump-action rifles and even gives the owners of such rifles a warm feeling by allowing that he would consider buying one himself. And, in doing so, he demonstrates smart politics by mentioning not one but several makes and models that he would find pleasing.

The areas where he and I would seem to be at odds are few and, with one exception, minor. If he were alive today, and still of the opinion that round-nosed slugs drill through brush better than pointed bullets, or that the .358 Winchester is the most deadly woods cartridge for deer and elk, we would have a cordial disagreement. O'Connor and I visited and talked a lot but, surprisingly perhaps, very seldom did we discuss guns or hunting. He loved to show off a new custom rifle, but once that was done, our conversation usually returned to gossiping about mutual acquaintances—especially women—whom he universally loved, or editors and book publishers—whom he almost universally detested.

If there is an item of deer hunting in his chapter that would cause either of us to challenge the other to step outside and fight it out man to man, it would be the choice of telescopic sights. Probably though, it is only me who is overreacting. O'Connor's ideas about telescopic sights on rifles were the products of the transition era between open sights and scopes. Today, we take scopes for granted—many hunters wouldn't dream of buying a rifle without a scope to go on it—but it wasn't always so. The transition was a difficult one, often painful, with O'Connor and other gun writers of the time bearing the brunt of the agony.

O'Connor was an advocate of scopes and had considerable influence on their acceptance; but at the same time, he was aware of the shortcomings of the scopes of his time. Back then scopes were much more difficult to use than those of today; they were less bright, with smaller fields of view, and shorter, more critical eye relief. These conditions were aggravated by awkward mounting systems and rifles designed to be used only with open sights. Thus, scopes tended to be rather slow to aim and a problem to use, a situation that is difficult for a modern hunter, accustomed to snapping a rifle to his shoulder and instantly seeing a bright world through the scope lens, to fully and completely comprehend.

Aware of the difficulties of using a scope in those days, O'Connor advised the sort of scopes that would cause the fewest problems for a first time scope user. As a rule of thumb, scopes with minimal magnification were easiest to use, so O'Connor became dogmatic in his recommendations of scopes in the $1\frac{1}{2}\times$ to $4\times$ power range, even for long-distance shooting. He was certainly correct in his conviction that a hunter would have a difficult time aiming a $10\times$ or $12\times$ scope, but that applied to scopes and hunters of the 1930s and 1940s.

By the end of the 1950s, scopes were being so rapidly improved that most of the original problems were all but eliminated, and by 1970 they were so highly developed that many of O'Connor's warnings were no longer valid. By then, the variable-$\times$ scopes were becoming the rage, and O'Connor was waging his famous battle to keep variable power scopes off the rifles of his readers. True, variable-$\times$ scopes of that time had some serious faults, and O'Connor was right to warn his readers of potential problems. But even after technical improvements overcame the problems, the warnings did not cease.

If O'Connor were alive today, he would be utterly astonished to discover that variable-power scopes have prevailed, and even more perplexed by the knowledge that today's mule deer or antelope hunter is at his best with his variable-$\times$ scope cranked up to its maximum magnification. I would not want to be the first to break the news.

Though comparisons of these two articles will intrigue deer hunters, perhaps even provide a modicum of titillation, the best service it provides, in my opinion, is the opportunity to read once again the rich prose of Jack O'Connor. There is a generation of new hunters who may never before have had the opportunity to discover the unique talent of this master storyteller. This is O'Connor at his best, his phrases as smooth as cream; beguiling, goading, tempting and challenging his readers. As you will see, he was more than a teacher. He reaches out to the reader, confronting him on comfortable ground. "Don't just do as I say," he tells his reader, "read on and we'll do it together." That's why he was the best.—*Jim Carmichel,* 1990.

## DEER AND DEER RIFLES
*By Jack O'Connor*

The scene was the Arizona desert, and the time was about two generations ago. One of the actors was a skinny, long-legged kid, a clumsy lout with big feet, green eyes, light hair, and a hide so browned by the sun that on the rare occasions when he wrote a hat, and his straw-colored hair could not be seen, he was often taken for a light-eyed Mexican.

The other was an equally skinny, three-year-old buck mule deer, slab-sided and probably beset with worms. The kid called the buck a blacktail because in those days everyone in Arizona called mule deer blacktails. The buck was not very well nourished, but it had a spindly four-point head, which in the East would be considered a 10-pointer.

Anyway, when he was hunting quail, the kid had found an area all tracked up by the desert mule deer. In addition, he had actually seen a doe and a fawn. In those lawless days, the sight of a deer was rare in the Arizona desert because the animals were hunted in season and out.

So, saying nothing to anyone about his plans, the kid had gone out the next day with a rifle instead of a shotgun. It was a .30/40 Krag with a 30-inch barrel. The kid had paid $1.50 for it. He had brought it from a bindle stiff (tramp) who had been camped down by the river beneath a wrecked railroad bridge. The bindle stiff had found himself in great need of a bottle of corn squeezings and in no particular need of a rifle

*Jack O'Connor*

just then. His asking price for the Krag was $3, and the lowest price he would accept was $1.50. By a curious coincidence, the price of a bottle of popskull was $1.50, and the kid happened to have that much scratch with him.

So, the bindle stiff got his jug and the kid got his rifle. Ammunition, as he now remembers it, cost about $1.25 a box. The cartridges were loaded with the long 220-grain bullet with a lot of lead exposed. The bindle stiff had evidently known a thing or two about a rifle, as he had put on a homemade front sight that lined up with the military rear sight so that the old musket shot at point of aim at about 150 yards.

So, that frosty winter morning, the kid was sneaking cautiously through that tracked-up desert forest looking for a deer. Generally he couldn't see more than 100 yards as this was a country of paloverde, and ironwood trees, saguaros (giant cactus), and cholla (jumping cactus). Then the kid became conscious of a movement on the other side of an ironwood tree about 50 yards away. He suspected it was a deer, and the shock was so violent that afterward he had a headache.

Next, he knew it was a deer, as the animal moved a bit and he could make out gray hide and dingy white rumps. Then he saw the deer's head as the animal reached up and delicately nipped off a delectable bit of browse.

After what seemed like an hour but was probably less than a minute, the buck was fairly well out in the open. The kid could see the gray-shiny antlers. It was time to shoot. Shaking, he lifted his rifle and tried to keep the homemade front bead in the middle of the deer.

He was trembling so violently that the front sight jerked off and on the buck. He tried to remember to squeeze the trigger. He tried to make himself quit shaking. He hated himself because he could not. He was desperately afraid the buck would see him and take off—forever losing a chance at the deer.

Finally, he yanked the trigger. The buck was gone, and the kid stood there, his heart pounding, his heart aching, his hands still trembling, his legs weak. After the roar of the shot, the desert seemed deathly still. He heard a quail call, and, far off in the quiet desert air, the sweet and melancholy whistle of a freight train. He had blown his chance, and he'd probably never get another.

Slowly he walked over toward the spot where the deer had been. There were the tracks all right; he could see how they had plunged through the soft, sandy soil as the deer had run. Desperately he tried to think of an alibi. It was that damned, long-barreled rifle, he decided. What he'd wanted was a real deer rifle, a .30/30 Winchester or Marlin carbine. But those cost $15 down at the hardware store, and as far as he was concerned, they might as well have cost $1,000.

Hopelessly he followed the tracks. He had gone about 50 yards when he got another violent shock. He saw blood. He could hardly believe it. At first, there were a few drops. Then, he found a big splash, then more. He followed the blood. Then he saw something gray and quiet beside a bush ahead of him. It was the buck—and the buck was dead. The old 220-grain softpoint had struck just forward of the flank and had come out behind the left shoulder.

Maybe the fact that the old Krag happened to wobble on just as the kid yanked the trigger had a lot to do with making him a hunter. Anyway, the kid grew up, became a father and grandfather, and almost every year of his life he has hunted deer—whitetails and mule deer, big deer and little deer, deer in brush and deer in open country, deer on the flat and deer in mountains almost rugged enough for sheep, deer far north in Alberta and British Columbia and deer south in tropical Sinaloa.

He has hunted deer with that old .30/40, with a .256 Newton, a .250/3000 Savage, a .30/30, a 7mm Mauser, several .30/06 and .270 rifles, a .35 Remington, a .257, a .348, a .35 Whelen, a .300 Weatherby. He has killed deer with a .22 Hornet, a wildcat 2-R Lovell, a .22/.250 and a .22 rimfire.

How many deer this chap has shot he does not remember, but it has been quite a few. He has done a little deer hunting in Pennsylvania and South Carolina and quite a bit of it in Texas, but most of the deer he has shot have been mule deer (of the desert and Rocky Mountain variety) and Arizona whitetails. He has heard of mule deer that have dressed out at 400 pounds and more, but he doesn't believe such an animal exists. The heaviest buck he ever weighed, field-dressed, was—as he remembers it—235 pounds, but he has shot two bucks that weighed about 175 in the quarters, and he thinks they might have gone 250 field dressed. The heaviest Arizona whitetail he ever shot weighed 118½. He once shot a whitetail buck with 19 points in all and has shot several mule deer with 13 and 14 points altogether. He once killed two deer with one shot. The mule deer antlers with the widest spread he ever shot went 37½ inches, but he has seen mule deer heads that went from 45 to 48 inches.

This hunter has missed more deer in the brush than anywhere else. The best shot he ever made on a deer was with a scope-sighted .30/06 at 330 paces. He could see only the buck's head and neck, took a rest over a log, held what looked like about nine inches over the top of the neck, and broke it. His worst shot was a clean miss—before two witnesses—at a standing buck broadside at not more than 125 yards. He was afraid the deer was about to jump, and he yanked the trigger. The deer did eventually jump.

A good deal of deer hunting has convinced this chap that deer are easy to kill if the bullets hit in the right place and behave properly. He also knows that if the bullets don't hit in the right place, deer are very hard to kill.

Almost always this deer hunter, if he has the opportunity, tries to place the bullet through the lungs back of the foreleg. If the deer is not broadside, he aims to drive the bullet up into this area. He likes the lung shot because it is a large target easy to hit, and because if a bullet placed there behaves properly, the deer seldom goes far and is generally dead within a few yards of where he is hit. Furthermore, the bullet that goes through the buck's rib cage from side to side destroys no edible meat.

This hunter thinks there are two very different kinds of deer rifles—one to be used in brush and forest and the other to be used in hilly, open country. For the kind of brush and forest hunting done for whitetail deer in the East, for blacktails west of the coast Range in northern California, Oregon and Washington, for mule deer early in the season in thick spruce and fir at high altitude, and for mule deer in the brushier parts of the Sonora desert, he likes a light, fast-operating rifle with a short barrel. He thinks such a firearm should be chambered for a reasonably heavy bullet at moderate velocity.

The reason for this is that the heavy, roundnose bullet that isn't traveling at breakneck speed gets through brush with less deflection than faster, lighter bullets with sharp points. But he also knows that any bullet can be deflected by brush. He remembers one time when he took a shot at one moose through heavy brush at what he remembers as being about 30 yards—and missed the whole moose. His next shot at the moose was in the clear and he killed it. He remembers also three shots at a whitetail buck that foolishly ran in a semi-circle around him through heavy brush. The first two shots, he afterward found out, did no damage except to nick the buck with some fragments of bullet jacket, but on the third shot the buck went through an opening and the 180-grain .30/06 bullet piled him up.

Unlike many hunters who look down their noses at the .30/30, he thinks it an excellent cartridge for this sort of thing. And he likewise regards the .32 Special as a good brush cartridge with adequate killing power, at moderate ranges and with well-placed shots, for any North American deer that ever walked. He also think that the light, fast-handling Winchester and Marlin lever-actions in such calibers are about right for deer.

Because there is always a possibility that the first shot at a deer in brushy country may hit a limb or a twig and deflect, he thinks that for hunting of this sort, a lever-action, a pump, or a semi-automatic is a good idea for the woods hunter. All of these are faster than the bolt-action. The Winchester Models 94 and 88, the Marlin Model 336, the Savage Model 99, the Remington Model 760 pump and the Remington Model 742, the Ruger carbine, and the Winchester Model 100 are all light, handy, fast-operating firearms.

This old deer hunter, as we have seen, has killed deer with a .22 rimfire. They were killed at a Mexican water hole at very short range. He has likewise killed a few deer with carefully placed shots with varmint calibers like the .22 Hornet, the 2-R Lovell, and the .22/250. However, he has seen the high-speed .22 bullets go to pieces on large bones (if a deer can be said to have large bones) and even on ribs; and he doesn't think deer should be shot with any bullet

*Former Shooting Editor Jack O'Connor probably used a .270 or .30/06 on this hunt. Photograph by Jack O'Connor*

weighing less than 90 grains. He thinks a minimum of 100 grains is better.

For short-range woods shooting, he thinks any fairly heavy bullet that opens up quickly is adequate for deer. The old .44/40 cartridge with its 200-grain bullet at a muzzle velocity of 1,310 fps (feet per second) has probably killed more whitetail deer than any other cartridge, with the possible exception of the .30/30. The .44 Magnum revolver cartridge shot in the Ruger carbine should be deadly.

But if he were going in hock for a new brush rifle, he thinks he'd acquire a Marlin lever-action or Remington pump for the .35 Remington cartridge or a Model 99 Savage in .308 Winchester.

He regards the neglected and obsolescent .358 Winchester cartridge with its 200-grain bullet at 2,530 or its 250-grain bullet at 2,250 as probably the most deadly woods cartridge in existence, not only for deer but also for elk and even moose. The .358 has the power and weight to drive deep on the rear-end shot, which the woods hunter all too often has to take.

Over the years, this deer hunter has had more trouble with bullets that didn't open up fast enough on deer than he has had with bullets that penetrated too deeply. He thinks that if the deer hunter has a choice he should take the fast-opening bullet.

For woods shooting, he hasn't got much use for open sights. Under the stress of excitement, it is easy to shoot over with them because the tendency is not to get the bead down into the notch. Receiver sights are

better, but the best iron sights were the peeps close to the eye—the old Lyman tang and cocking-piece sights. They were not the most accurate sights in the world, but they were adequately accurate for 50 to 100-yard shooting.

The best sight he ever used in the brush is a low-power scope (2½× or 3×) because of the wide field of view and because of the ability of the glass sight to resolve detail, to "look through" the brush, to tell deer from limbs and twigs.

For open-country deer hunting at longer ranges, this chap likes a flat-shooting cartridge giving a fairly light bullet a velocity of from 2,700 to 3,200 fps. Then, he likes to sight in for the longest range that will not give him midrange misses. The world is full of good, open-country deer cartridges—the .30/06 with the 150-grain bullet, the .270 with the 130-grain, the .280 with the 125-grain, the 7mm Remington Magnum with the 150-grain, the 7×57 Mauser with the 140-grain, the .300 Savage and the .308 with the 150-grain. He has never shot a deer with the .243, but he considers it entirely adequate with the 100-grain bullet. He bases this opinion on a good deal of use of the now-dying .257 Roberts on deer.

However, he has done more open-country shooting of mule and whitetail deer with .30/06 and .270 rifles than with anything else. The quickest-killing .30/06 bullet he has ever used was the old 150-grain Western hollowpoint. Bullets he likes for the .270 were the Remington 130-grain Bronze Point, the 130-grain

Super and Sierra, the Western Silvertip, the 120-grain Barnes. Some of the controlled expanding bullets don't open up quite fast enough, he thinks, and the kills aren't quite so quick. He remembers a buck he shot with his rifle rested on a rock at about 325 yards. Dust could be seen to fly above the deer's back as it stood on a hillside. "Over," his companion said. But before he could shoot again, the buck was down. If the bullet had opened faster the deer would have collapsed in its tracks.

For this open-country shooting at deer, this hunter now uses 4× scopes. They have sufficient field and they give a better picture of the deer and more precise aim. However, this hunter admits that probably a 2½× or 3× scope will do just about as well for any big game, even at ranges of 300 yards and more. Before World War II, he used 2½× scopes almost exclusively and never felt himself underpowered.

Flat-shooting, high velocity, bolt-action rifles, such as those described, are also excellent for those Eastern hunters who shoot from hillside to hillside at deer when the leaves are off the trees and bushes and for those who plan to shoot across pastures at deer coming out of the woods to feed.

But those rifles are by no means ideal for ordinary woods hunting. The fast bullets deflect badly in the brush, this deer hunter thinks. In addition, the 4× scopes are a bit shy of field for brush hunting, and the bolt-action is on the slow side for the fast second shot.

Few of the brush cartridges are much good for open-country shooting, where shots will often be taken at 300 to 350 yards. Used as it should be, the .30/30 is a good killer on deer. Shot wildly at deer 250 to 350 yards away, it isn't so hot. When this chap got out of college his pocketbook was thin and he had sold his rifles so he would have enough jack in his jeans to take pretty girls dancing. He ordered the then brand-new Model 54 Winchester rifle in .270 caliber, but until it came he tried to make do with an ancient Model 8 Remington automatic for the .35 Remington cartridge. He hunted in semi-open country of juniper, pinyon, and yellow pine, and the shots he got were long. It was a pretty frustrating experience.

But cartridges like the .308 Savage and the .30/06, when used with suitable roundnose 180-grain bullets, do pretty well for the brush as well as for open country. The .270 and .280 with the roundnose 150-grain bullets are usable in the brush and shoot flat enough for much open-country shooting. Once this chap hunted in the jungles of India, shot everything including hog deer, spotted axis deer, wild boar, and even peacocks with the 150-grain Core-Lokt and Hornady roundnose softpoint .270 bullets. He didn't have much to complain of.

The old deer hunter in this little piece is, of course, your correspondent. The piece is directed to the readers who have done little or no deer hunting but who hope to. The old deer hunter wishes them well and hopes they get a good bullet in the right spot. If they do, they'll find that almost any reasonably potent rifle will get them venison.

## COAST TO COAST DEER RIFLES
### *By Jim Carmichel*

The first explorers and colonists on the Atlantic shores of North America discovered a deer that offered them succulent venison, supple hides, and unequaled hunting pleasure. For a while, the whitetail was a mainstay of colonial life and commerce.

While the English, French, and Dutch settlers were reaching westward, a current of Spanish aristocrats and soldiers flowed north from Mexico into the fertile coastal valleys of California. They too found a shy deer that provided tasty venison, skins that were fashioned into ornate suits for Spanish grandees, and hunting that appealed to adventuresome spirits. The Spanish had loving names for these graceful deer but we call them blacktails.

The buckskin-clad adventurers who traveled beyond the awesome Mississippi found yet another deer. It was a lordly creature with such big ears that its resemblance to a mule was unmistakable. The nickname stuck, and these animals have been known as mule deer ever since.

These three races of deer can be further divided into a host of subspecies, and the sporting merits of each one can be debated until the crack of doom. The rifles and calibers deemed best for the taking of these deer have also been divided, subclassified, reclassified, de-

*Jim Carmichel*

bated, and re-debated until one could easily believe a battery of some 20 rifles is needed to take each sub-species of deer in its respective haunt. Of course, the makers of firearms love that notion and some gun writers are enthusiastic, too. But with a bit of logic, we come to the money-saving conclusion that we can hunt deer from the East Coast to the West Coast with only three or four rifles. With some compromises, a skilled hunter could actually do very well with only one rifle.

### Blacktails

The prim Pacific blacktail is almost unknown to most American hunters, but in Washington, Oregon, and northern California, they outnumber other deer by nearly two to one. In Oregon alone, the blacktail population is more than 500,000, and the annual harvest runs around 50,000. That's a lot of deer and it's not surprising that my hunting pals on the West Coast get excited when the season draws near. The August blacktail opening in California reminds me of the "Glorious Twelfth" grouse opener in Scotland. I haven't hunted blacktails enough to claim any special expertise, but because I have bagged a few in California and Oregon and have talked with many successful blacktail hunters, I have a fair notion of what's required in the way of rifles.

Like other deer, blacktails have a tendency to shade up in cover during the middle of the day and to show themselves on grassy hillsides early and late. This is especially true during the early part of California's season when midday temperatures often sizzle into the 90s. Hardy souls can get some short-range jump-shooting by busting through brushy valleys where blacktails hide out during midday, but the few times I've done it, I encountered more buzzworms (rattlers) than deer.

The most productive technique is to walk ridges and glass valleys and slopes. Because the coastal hills tend to be quite steep, slopes and ridgelines are often only a few hundred yards apart. This provides shots at deer that are interesting and productive, if the hunter has the right rifle. Most of the shots I've had at blacktails remind me of woodchuck hunting in the Tennessee hills where hunters belly down with a flat-shooting rifle steadied over a solid rest. The key to what I'd call a good blacktail rifle is accuracy, rather than fast handling, high velocity, and a heavy bullet.

Because blacktails don't take a lot for killing, a .270 with 130-grain loads or a .30/06 with 150-grain represent the upper limit of the lethality you need. I like something lighter, such as the .257 Roberts or .25/06. These offer the most useful combinations of accuracy, flat trajectory, long-range punch, and mild recoil for blacktail hunting. The .243 Winchester, 6mm Remington, and .240 Weatherby are also good choices for recoil-conscious hunters and, over the long haul, will put more blacktail venison in the freezer than a hard-thumping magnum. This is simply because they are "user friendly"—if I may borrow from computer jargon—and offer the average rifleman more precise bullet placement than is consistently possible with heavier harder-kicking calibers.

Bolt-action rifles are favored, of course; and, for hillside-to-hillside shooting, lightweight rifles offer no advantage. Thus, standard-weight bolt guns with sturdy full-length barrels in the 24-inch category are preferred by many expert blacktail hunters.

Because shots are regularly taken out to 300 yards, it's a smart idea to use scopes with plenty of power. Variables with $9 \times$ or $10 \times$ magnification on the high end are an especially good choice in blacktail country.

If I were much inclined to beat the midday brush for these deer, I'd go for a carbine-length bolt rifle with a reasonable compromise of fast handling, portability, and long-range accuracy. For this purpose the new bolt-action carbines are ideal.

By now you've probably decided that a good black-tail rifle isn't all that different from what you'd use on pronghorns. As a matter of fact, the rifle I've used to best advantage on blacktails also happens to be my favorite antelope rifle. It's a Model 70 Winchester with a stylish stock by Bob Winter and a slender 25-inch Douglas barrel in .25/06 chambering. With a 100-grain spitzer bullet over 53 grains of IMR 4831, the muzzle velocity is about 3,400 fps. Adjust your scope so that bullet impact is about 2½ inches above point-of-aim at 100 yards. This will put you almost dead on at 300 yards and eliminate most excuses for missing. Because some .25 caliber bullets have thin jackets and are liable to fragment at close range when fired at high-velocity level, it's a good idea to stay with tougher bullets such as the Speer Hot Core design and Nosler's solid-base or partition bullets.

### Mule Deer

Moving eastward into mule deer country, there's not much need to change one's rifle, but it's arguable that heavier calibers may be in order. Over the years, I've seen upwards of two score big-bodied mule deer shot with the .243 Winchester or the 6mm Remington by other hunters. With few exceptions, they went down as though zapped by a boulder from the slingshot of Zeus. A few didn't go down immediately but staggered around for a few moments before slumping to the ground. I don't remember any that got away, and I'm sure I would if any had. The people I hunt with are good shots, and a lost deer is loudly noted and long remembered. Of the 150 to 200 mule deer I've either shot myself or seen shot with all sorts of rifles and calibers, some went down in their tracks, some stumbled and fell, some ran off as if missed and then piled up after a few steps, and some went considerable distances.

The one certain thing I've learned from watching deer being shot is that it's impossible to judge what big-game caliber was used just by observing the immediate results. Specifically, I've seen deer shot with everything from a .243 to a .338 Magnum; and, regardless of caliber, some deer drop, some stay on their feet for a few seconds, and some walk or run off. Yet, I periodically get mail from disgruntled hunters who

*Shooting Editor Jim Carmichel chose a .30/06 to take this desert muley. Photograph by Jim Carmichel*

tell woeful tales of how they busted a deer with a .243 only to have it run into the next county. I'm usually unsympathetic because these tales don't dovetail with my personal experiences and observations.

The fact is that *missed* deer do have a habit of hightailing it out of the country. And a deer missed with a little .243 never seems to be all that much less injured than one missed with a blockbuster magnum. The only real difference is that when a deer is missed with a raging magnum, the hunter can soothe his tattered ego by blaming the cartridge, as if it were under a witch's curse that had caused it to bounce off a deer's ribs.

If you like the idea of using one of the accurate, softkicking 6mms, but fear it won't do the job on mule deer, by all means go to something bigger. Let's get

that potential alibi out of the way before it has a chance to mess up your thinking. The next step up from a .243 or 6mm is a .25, and the .257 Roberts or .25/06 Remington are superb for mule deer. But if you're afraid that the .243 isn't big enough, you probably won't get much consolation by increasing bullet diameter only .014 of an inch. So, play it safe and go all of the way to a .270, 7mm or a fast .30 caliber. The .270 with 130-grain slug provides no excuses or apologies when used on mule deer, and the .280 Remington with a 150-grain bullet in a factory load is at least as good. Better yet is a good .280 or 7mm handload with any of the superb 139 or 140-grain bullets offered by component bullet makers. It goes without saying that the .30/06 is unbeatable for the purpose. The everfaithful '06 with 150 or 165 grain bullets is accurate, fairly user-friendly, and it is the standard by which I judge all mule deer loads.

## A Texas Variation

In south-Texas whitetail country, a breed of gun is evolving that may become the most specialized of all deer rifles. This fascinating development is being brought about by some of the most awesome trophy deer ever hunted, combined with some of the most difficult terrain on which a hunter ever set foot. The high dense chaparral and cactus limit visibility to a few scant yards, so that hunting by traditional methods is out of the question. Therefore, south-Texas hunters have developed ingenious shooting towers that provide some visibility over thorny vegetation, and some hunters have even mounted high seats on vehicles with which they patrol the fringes of deer thickets. Before you condemn this technique as unsportsmanlike, let me promise you that it is the most difficult and uncomfortable way to hunt deer yet devised. Because most shots are fired at running targets at almost impossible distances, the degree of difficulty is easily three or four times greater than that encountered in many of the usual forms of deer hunting. When a south-Texas hunter says he missed six or eight shots during a morning's hunt, his fellow hunters only nod in solemn understanding.

And it's not just the shooting that makes it so tough. Even when a deer is known to have dropped in its tracks, locating it can be frustrating. This often requires the shooter to remain in the high seat or tower with his eye on the spot where the deer was last seen so that he can direct a couple of his buddies through a maze of head-high cactus. Picking your way through a tangle of the prickly growth sometimes results in a circuitous half-mile hike to find a spot only 200 yards away.

Naturally, if the deer manages to travel even a short distance after last being seen, the animal will be extremely difficult to find. It often takes hours to search a few acres. This problem has fostered appreciation for calibers that "wreck" a deer on the spot by doing such massive damage that the quarry is unable to move. In theory, this sounds great, but in practice it doesn't always work well. Sometimes, the results are less than satisfactory because the rifleman can't stand the recoil of a real magnum and actually uses something that isn't a real immobilizer. Other times, results are poor because the hunter is afraid of the big magnum and shoots poorly.

The bona fide class of game-paralyzing calibers is characterized by the .338 Magnum on the light end and the .375 H&H and .378 Weatherby Magnum on the heavy side. Many hunters find that it's difficult to shoot these steam rollering calibers accurately, and some of them note a significant drop in the number of bullets that find targets. The solution, therefore, may very well be to select an ultra-fast cartridge on the order of the .264 Winchester Magnum, or the Weath-erby magnums in .257, .270 or 7mm. The high velocity and flat trajectory of this kind of cartridge takes some of the guesswork out of distant shots, especially at moving targets. And the shock of the high-velocity bullet impact offers, to some extent, the desired "immobilizing" effect.

## Whitetails East

Crossing the Mississippi and traveling east, the dedicated deer hunter encounters dense-pack deer habitat ranging from brushy river bottoms to thick woodlots. In the Atlantic Coast states, he enters thick stands of second-growth and third-growth timber interspersed with meadows and farmland. With this observation comes the realization that when we talk about the rifles needed for the various North American deer, we aren't really matching the guns to the game. We are really selecting our firearms in terms of the terrain and the cover. If, for example, blacktails, mule deer, and whitetails all inhabited the Eastern forests, the best choice for all three would be a light fast-handling carbine in an adequate .30 or .35 caliber.

If, on the other hand, whitetails inhabited the open plains and mountains, the perfect whitetail rifle would be a medium to medium-heavy bolt gun in some far-ranging flat-shooting caliber. In fact, some savvy Southeastern hunters have found they get more and bigger bucks by abandoning the traditional Eastern "brush" rifle. These sportsmen shoot from tree stands and platforms situated around vast fields of soybeans and other deer-tempting crops. They snipe at big bucks that feed in the open fields. Sometimes they can shoot at close range, but more often, the distance is 200 yards or better, and a flat-shooting rifle has a distinct edge over the lumbering projectiles often characterized as "brush cartridges".

For most deer hunting in the Eastern forest, however, the hunter needs a fast-handling quick-shooter, and I have little patience with bolt-action snobs who look down their noses at autoloaders, pumps, and lever-action rifles. These fast-shooting designs result from matching the rifle to the land and the cover. An experienced rifleman can get off three aimed shots at a bounding buck in some three to four seconds with a fast repeater. Given the unavoidable error factor inherent in shooting at running game but adding the "learning advantage" of multiple shots (with every miss we learn where *not* to aim), the deer hunter who frequently shoots at running deer is better off with a fast-firing repeater. But that is true only if he doesn't succumb to the notion that speed is a desirable substitute for careful aiming.

I once heard the argument for fast-firing repeaters summed up very neatly during a debate on the merits of brush rifles. One hunter was quite sure that if allotted only three cartridges for a day's hunting, he would rather have one shot each at three different deer than three shots at one deer. "But tell me, Sonny," asked a weathered veteran of the Maine woods, "how many days have you had shots at three deer?"

# Quest for the Super Rifle

*By Tim Jones*

**A**kuliak Camp, Ungava Bay, far northern Quebec: Seven of us had traveled here for the hunt of a lifetime. The Torngat Mountains have produced most of the top Quebec/Labrador caribou in the Boone and Crockett Club record book. Akuliak Camp, run by Arctic Adventures, is one of only two camps that hunt the Torngats' legendary Korok herd.

As you might expect of hunters who had traveled thousands of miles and spent thousands of dollars to hunt trophy caribou, all of us were well-equipped. Only two of the seven rifles chosen for this trip of a lifetime were what you'd call "standard issue" models—one was a Winchester Model 70 in .30/06, the other a Ruger International M-77 in .308 Winchester. Both, of course, were time-proven hunting rifles.

The rest were what I call "trophy rifles"—firearms that are more accurate, more weatherproof, and more reliable than ordinary run-of-the-factory guns. A trophy rifle is one that you can count on when the trophy of a lifetime offers you that less-than-perfect shooting opportunity.

Back in the days of shooting editor Jack O'Connor, a trophy rifle was a custom rifle from Griffin & Howe or some other master of the rifle maker's art. With hand-tuned actions, the best barrels available, and

gracefully carved stocks of beautifully figured walnut, these artworks were priced far out of reach of the average hunter. They still are.

## SEMI-CUSTOM RIFLES

We can still dream about true custom guns, but most of us still can't afford them. And, by today's standards, a custom gun often isn't a trophy rifle, anyway. Beautiful wood carefully mated to engraved metal doesn't make a rifle easier to carry, more accurate, or tougher than ordinary—and accuracy, strength, and utility are what trophy rifles are all about.

Many manufacturers today—Dakota Arms, KDF, Kimber, McMillan, and Ultra Light Arms, just to name a few—offer "semi-custom" rifles. Sometimes these include a broader choice of calibers, including wildcats, barrel lengths, finishes, and stock styles, and materials. You also get a level of accuracy not

*Tim Jones and guides pose with trophy caribou and laminated-stock Ruger M-77 used to take the animal at Ungava Bay. Photograph by Ralph P. Stuart*

normally found in factory rifles. In other words, you can get a trophy rifle that has already been built for you by someone else—someone with similar ideas.

These semi-custom rifles are, of course, more expensive than standard factory guns, and $1,000 to $2,000 price tags are common for the "plain" versions of these uncommon firearms. But the custom performance features—premium barrels; stocks of either exceptional beauty or exceptional utility; smooth, polished, tuned actions; custom bedding; and crisp, adjustable triggers—are worth it—if, that is, you can afford the initially steep price tag. I wish I could.

## FACTORY RIFLES—WITH EXTRAS

Another, less expensive, option is to select a rifle that left the factory with some of the extra touches that make it right for a serious trophy hunt.

On the Akuliak trip, my hunting partner, OUTDOOR LIFE Senior Editor Ralph Stuart, was toting a prime example of a factory-issue trophy rifle. Ralph's Winchester Model 70 Winlite in .300 Winchester Magnum came from the factory equipped with a McMillan fiberglass stock, which enhances both the accuracy and the durability of the proven Model 70 rifle.

My own rifle, a Ruger M-77R in 7mm Remington Magnum, had left the factory with a camo-pattern laminated wood stock. Since I'd bought the gun, I'd had some tinkering done on its trigger, had had the bolt handle checkered for a better grip, and had had the bolt itself polished for smoother operation. Essentially, though, it was still a factory rifle with a better-than-standard stock for the anything-goes weather of the North Country.

Such straight-from-the-factory trophy rifles are common today. Virtually every big-name manufacturer of bolt-action rifles is now offering upgraded versions of its standard factory line. My laminated-stock Ruger and Ralph's Winlite from U.S. Repeating Arms are just two examples. Ruger also offers tough Zytel stocks for its new M-77 Mark II, and U.S. Repeating Arms has laminated stocks for its lightweight Model 70s—as well as a new synthetic stock in the works. Remington, Browning, Savage, Weatherby, Sako, and others each have similar rifles with their versions of more stable, stronger, tougher synthetic or laminated wood stocks added to the standard barreled actions. These factory-issue trophy rifles usually cost a couple of hundred dollars more than the factory wood-stocked guns, but they are worth more in the field.

Fortunately for those of us whose ambitions to own a perfect rifle outstrip our means to pay for even a factory trophy rifle, there's yet another alternative. That's to buy an ordinary run-of-the-factory gun and replace the various pieces as we are able. It's like buying a trophy rifle in installments. Even more money can be saved by purchasing a second-hand rifle (which should be checked for strength and reliability by a competent gunsmith before any cash is laid out) and renewing it over time.

The three other rifles on our caribou hunt had all started as standard factory rifles. One had started life as a wood-stocked Weatherby Mark V in .300 Weatherby Magnum. The other two were both Winchester Model 70s, one in .300 Winchester Magnum and the other in .338 Winchester Magnum. But none of these three looked—or performed—like factory rifles by the time they got to Akuliak. All three had had their factory wood stocks replaced with Bell & Carlson synthetic stocks. All had been Parkerized so that their metal surfaces wouldn't flash in the sunlight. The .338 had also been fitted with a KDF recoil arrestor muzzle brake to tame that caliber's hefty kick.

These were, obviously, rifles designed to do a job, long range or short, no matter what the weather. They were specifically designed to take some of the gamble out of an expensive quest for the trophy of a lifetime. They had also been assembled piece-by-piece as need arose and as time and money allowed.

## MODIFYING YOUR RIFLE PIECE-BY-PIECE

The process begins when you select a factory rifle to eventually convert into your trophy rifle. What you are really selecting is an action—the "lock" of your "lock, stock and barrel." It's comparatively easy to swap stocks and even barrels, but the action is the heart and soul of your rifle. Even the finest custom rifles are usually crafted on an existing factory action.

Take, for example, the trophy rifle made by a friend of mine. He wanted a highly accurate big-bore repeating hunting rifle that threw a fat slug at moderately high velocities. He couldn't find exactly what he wanted in a factory rifle, so he made one himself.

He took a Siamese Mauser action—strong and reliable, but hardly elegant—added a new barrel, chambered the barrel for the old war horse .45/70 Government, fitted the parts to a stock, glass-bedded the action, free-floated the barrel, topped things off with a 4× scope, and came up with a hunting rifle. This bolt-action will take much hotter loads than any factory-loaded .45/70 cartridge will deliver, and it will consistently group five shots inside of two inches at 200 yards!

Holding that rifle in your hands, you can just imagine looking through the scope at a trophy bull moose slashing a path through the Canadian bush as he answers your guide's seductive calls. Either that or you can picture ambushing a big fall bear—black or grizzly—and taking it down at handshaking range. You can also imagine the devastating effect of a 350-grain bullet lobbed in at about 2,000 fps (feet per second) with pinpoint accuracy. This is a hunting rifle; there's no doubt about it. And it's a very special one—one not available in any gun shop. It's a rifle that existed only in the mind of a skilled craftsman—until he made it real.

Unfortunately, very few of us have the tools, the time, or the know-how to take the various pieces of a rifle and fit them together into a working whole. Not all of us can complete the inletting of a stock and bed an action—let alone turn a barrel to perfect contour, thread it, chamber it, and fit it to an action. I have enough trouble loading and shooting a rifle, let alone building one from scratch. But we begin our quest for a trophy rifle by choosing the right action.

## THE RIGHT ACTION

Worldwide, probably the most popular action of all times for hunting rifles is the Model 98 Mauser and its dozens of incarnations. Most other modern actions borrow at least some of the features of Paul Mauser's original design: the strong, rigid (and therefore accurate) breeching system with two huge lugs, the positive extraction and ejection systems, and the dependable three-position safety, which allows the bolt to open while the firing pin is still deactivated.

Probably the most popular American-made action of all time for true custom rifles is the Winchester Model 70, with the "pre-64" Model 70 still being the most sought-after (and expensive). The pre-64 Model 70 retains the Mauser extraction system and positive ejection—in a more rigid overall receiver for greater inherent accuracy—but it has a faster lock time (the time interval between the instant the trigger breaks and when the firing pin strikes the primer) than the Mauser.

Model 70s built between 1964 and 1968 are not highly regarded in comparison with earlier and later models. (The major complaint is roughness in both finish and operation.) But the current Model 70 has a strong, smooth reliable action, and it is probably a better choice overall than the pre-64 for a modern trophy rifle.

The Remington Model 700, with its solid "ring of steel" supporting the entire cartridge head and its quick lock time, is a favorite with accuracy buffs. The Weatherby Mark V has nine small locking lugs instead of the Mauser design's two big ones, and it easily handles the most powerful cartridges in the world. The short, quick throw of the Browning A-Bolt appeals to some hunters for their trophy rifles. The highly accurate Sako, the classic Springfield, the slick Sauer, the solid, economical Savage Model 110, and a dozen other bolt-actions are all field-proven, and each can serve as the basis for a trophy rifle, too.

So far I've only mentioned bolt-actions because most hunters today rely on turnbolts. But there's no reason at all why your trophy rifle couldn't start life as an autoloader, lever-action, pump, or single-shot. I've got a super-accurate lever-action Savage Model 99 in .300 Savage in my gun cabinet that's a perfect candidate for a trophy deer rifle. If I ever get the money, it may end up with a shortened barrel and a new laminated stock.

The two rifles that I'm presently converting to trophy status are both Ruger M-77s. One is the long-action M-77R that I carried on that Quebec caribou hunt. The other is a short-action M-77RLS carbine in .308. I chose the Ruger factory rifles for two very simple reasons. First and foremost, I like the inherent strength of Ruger's integral scope mounts. Fewer screws mean fewer things to go wrong in the field. Second, I'm a shotgunner, and I like the M-77's tang safety (the new Ruger M-77 Mark II has a three-position safety like the Model 70). On such minor differences are personal choices made.

## CHOOSE CAREFULLY

When you choose a factory rifle as the basis for your trophy rifle, I'd recommend shooting it a lot at the range, and hunting with it a time or two "as is" before you decide to make major modifications. If the basic action and caliber don't fit you and your needs for a hunting rifle, the customized version probably won't, either. There's no sense in putting a lot of money into customizing a hard-hitting .338 when what you really want and need is a flat-shooting .270, or vice versa.

Incidentally, it doesn't hurt any trophy rifle to have some tuning done on the action. I've had the bolts of both my Rugers lapped and polished for smoother operation (a process that will cost anywhere from $25 to $50, depending on your gunsmith). And my M-77R is having installed a new lightweight titanium firing pin (available for $50 to $75 from Speedlock Systems, Canadian, Texas), which has a stronger firing-pin spring to reduce lock time and increase the force with which the pin strikes the primer. This should increase both the accuracy and reliability of my trophy rifle.

## A NEW BARREL?

Once you've got a "lock" on the rifle, it's time to consider exactly what you want from the barrel. When the benchrest boys and serious silhouette shooters set out to build the most accurate rifles in the world, they always rely on the precise craftsmanship of a premium barrel maker. For most hunters—even trophy hunters—that extreme level of accuracy just isn't necessary. So most trophy rifles wear factory barrels.

Besides, re-barreling any rifle is a major proposition, which, at from $300 to $500, often costs more than the original rifle, and there's always the risk, however slight, that the new barrel won't perform any better than the original. Fortunately, the quality of most factory rifle barrels today is excellent. Some, such as the hammer-forged barrels used by U.S. Repeating Arms on its Winchester rifles, are exceptional.

Still, there are several good reasons to consider a new barrel for your trophy rifle. The first, of course, is accuracy. If your rifle has a "Monday morning" barrel that isn't delivering the basic accuracy level you want, or if you are a good enough rifleman to take advantage of sub-minute-of-angle accuracy, go for it. That's when re-barreling is the only way to go.

Another reason to re-barrel is to gain durability. A stainless-steel tube (which will run $400 on the low side) will make your rifle more weatherproof. With a new barrel, you can choose from a wider range of calibers—including wildcats—too. You can also order your new barrel contoured slimmer to save weight

*Laminated-stock Ruger M-77RLS in .308 (right, center) is flanked by Ruger factory wood (far right) and Ram-Line injection-molded drop-ins. Photograph by Tim Jones*

Magnum re-barreled with a stainless-steel tube. But I'm getting acceptable accuracy from it with the standard Ruger factory barrel—three quick shots with any ammunition will group at less than 2 inches at 100 yards. With selected loads and by letting the barrel cool between shots, I can cut that to just more than 1 inch.

Given that level of accuracy to begin with, a new barrel just doesn't make that much sense. That's the way it is with many modern rifles. There are many other things you can do besides change the barrel. For example, you can have the muzzle recrowned for from $25 to $100. Any damage to the rifling at the muzzle of a barrel can severely impact the barrel's accuracy. Precision recrowning (which creates a new, indented muzzle for the barrel, with the rifling protected by a ring of steel) is a cheap alternative to a new barrel, and may indeed help the accuracy of your rifle.

Other options are to simply have the existing barrel glass-bedded (something I'll discuss later) or contoured slimmer (for between $100 and $200).

Another accuracy problem that can be cured with some barrel work is shooter flinch. By installing one of the new muzzle brake systems, you can cut recoil and your tendency to shy away at the shot. Mag-na-porting (which costs less than $100) involves cutting directly into the metal of the barrel. The KDF Slim Line Muzzle Brake (costing $180) is threaded on and can be removed and replaced with a screw-on collar. The only problem with a muzzle brake is that your rifle will sound louder than ever before.

## A NEW STOCK?

When you've got a barrel and an action that are right for your trophy rifle, the next step is to choose the stock. Because the stock, as much or more than any other component, affects a rifle's performance in the field, it pays to do some thinking before you make your selection.

At one time, a custom stock meant beautiful wood perfectly fitted to the metal of the action. Custom stocks still can mean this, but more and more, trophy rifles are sporting custom stocks of a different sort. It didn't surprise me at all that five of the seven rifles on that Akuliak caribou hunt wore synthetic or laminated wood stocks.

The reasons for switching are obvious. Though solid wood can be made more weatherproof than ever before with today's finishes (some of which glitter like diamonds in the sun), synthetic and laminated wood handles are more stable in all types of weather. And weather is one of the factors that you definitely can't control on a hunt.

Stocks made of either injection-molded plastic or layered composites (of fiberglass, Kevlar, graphite, and so on) are absolutely impervious to cold and moisture. (Some, however, will warp in extreme heat—so don't leave your rifle in the trunk of a car in the hot summer sun). Synthetic stocks are usually tougher than wood (something you'll appreciate if your guide,

or fatter for improved accuracy (the latter will prove especially effective as the barrel heats up with repeated shots).

Technically, if you are going to re-barrel, this should probably be the first step in your overall rifle remake, because a new barrel may require a new bedding job. In practice, however, unless you have either shot enough to wear out your old barrel (an extreme rarity, but it can happen, particularly with the hot magnum calibers), are changing calibers, or really want a stainless-steel tube, deciding on a new barrel is the last step you'll probably take.

I've been seriously considering having my 7mm

hunting partner, or horse happens to step on it), and are often lighter.

Remington, Browning, U.S. Repeating Arms (Winchester), Sako, Weatherby, and Ruger now offer straight-from-the-factory models with synthetic stocks. But, if you already own a rifle with a plain wood handle, many companies produce stocks that help turn factory guns into trophy rifles. For anywhere from $100 to $300 or so, you can get a synthetic handle made by Brown Precision, McMillan, Bell & Carlson, Ram-Line, Six Enterprises, and others. Chances are good that one can be found to fit your rifle's action.

Synthetic and composite stocks are not without faults, however. In my experience, most "drop-in" stocks don't replace as easily as the name suggests. It's sometimes possible to get good accuracy by simply unscrewing the factory wood stock and screwing on a new synthetic; but more often some bedding work is required to achieve maximum accuracy.

Also, synthetic stocks have one serious flaw in my book. I do much of my hunting for whitetail deer in thick Northern woods—spruce swamps being the favorite habitat of the big bucks I go after. Plastic and composite stocks are just too noisy for stalk hunting in brush.

That's why my two trophy rifles wear laminated wood stocks, which are nearly as strong and stable as plastic or fiberglass, but which are much quieter in brush. Though laminated stocks are sometimes a little heavier than factory wood, they feel good in your hands, and to my eye at least, look pretty good, too.

Ruger, U.S. Repeating Arms, Browning and Savage all offer factory rifles with laminated handles. In addition, E. C. Bishop & Son and Reinhart Fajen, both in Warsaw, Missouri, can fit a laminated stock to almost any rifle for between $200 and $500, depending on whether you're content with a pre-fit stock or want custom style, fit and finish.

To turn my little Ruger .308 carbine into a trophy rifle, I sent it off to Reinhart Fajen to be fitted with a laminated stock. With the clean lines and weatherproof stability of the laminated stock came some unexpected bonuses: The rounded cheekpiece and palm swell (in the pistol grip area) and the hard-rubber recoil pad make the rifle easier to handle and more comfortable to shoot. It's a whole lot closer to my ideal trophy rifle than I had expected, or even hoped.

## PUTTING TOGETHER IS THE KEY

Finding the right lock, stock, and barrel are important steps toward having a trophy rifle, but how well they are put together may make the ultimate difference in performance.

I don't know, for example, how much of the performance difference in my .308 carbine can be attributed to the new laminated stock, or how much is determined by the first-class glass-bedding job that Fajen did. But I do know that a rifle that was grouping in the 2-to-3-inch range (which is pretty standard for factory rifles) now groups any ammunition at less than 2 inches, and can come in at 1½ inches with its favorite Hornady 150-grain spire-point boattails in Frontier factory loads.

That kind of accuracy improvement isn't unusual. A glass-bedding job is something you can do yourself with kits that are available from most gun shops for less than $30. Or, you can turn the work over to a professional for from $50 to $100.

Phil Koehne, the accuracy wizard behind KDF Inc. in Seguin, Texas, makes a specialty of re-bedding rifles to improve their accuracy. According to Koehne, his $200 "Accurizing" process begins with re-bedding the action—Sakos, Colt/Sauers, and Ruger M-77s are glass-bedded; Weatherby, Winchester, and Remington rifles are "pillar"-bedded on special metal stock inserts at the action screws. "Accurizing" also includes crowning the muzzle and, if necessary, lapping the bolt lugs (for more precise lock-up) and polishing the chamber. According to Koehne, he expects his treatment to cut the group size of any rifle about in half.

That's why I've sent my Ruger M-77R off to KDF. My best groups with the rifle have run between 1¼ and 1½ inches at 100 yards. I'll be very happy to see those cut to less than 1 inch. Then I'll have a real trophy rifle.

## WHY BOTHER?

"Why bother?" you might ask. After all, everyone knows that, for all practical purposes, a rifle that groups its shots within a 3-inch circle at 100 yards is accurate enough for most hunting. Why spend the money to do better?

Well, maybe if I only hunted a few days a year in my own backyard I might feel that way. Then again, I might not. After all, I do hunt in my own backyard, and I don't want to blow a shot there, either. I want a rifle that will do the job. Period. I think that most serious hunters feel the same way.

Remember those rifles that showed up at Akuliak camp for that trophy caribou hunt? They were all chosen to do a job. And do the job they did. Our group of seven downed 10 huge trophy caribou, most with a single shot. One of our hunters took a 50-inch bull with a spectacular shot at much more than 300 yards—a shot that a standard factory rifle might not have made.

Interestingly, the only kill that required more than one shot and a finisher was made with the wood-stocked .30/06. When the gun's owner returned home, he found that the rifle's point-of-impact had shifted 6 inches during the course of the trip (despite the fact that he had sighted-in on the hunt's first day). He suspects that the wood stock is to blame, and he has just ordered a Weatherby Fibermark in .300 Weatherby Magnum to take on his next trophy hunt.

Of course, the most important component of any hunting rifle is the person holding it, but when the trophy of a lifetime is on the line, you want the best possible rifle to make that first shot count. That's why you want a trophy rifle.

# The .25 and Under Crowd

*By Warner Shedd*

Conventional wisdom. Conventional wisdom is simply the sum of many individual opinions, which can sometimes be poorly grounded in fact. In short, conventional wisdom can be wrong.

If you doubt this, consider that not too many years ago conventional wisdom touted heavy, slow-moving slugs as "brush-cutters," whereas small, speedy, pointed bullets supposedly were deflected even by tiny twigs. Well, with the advent of super-high-speed photography, roughly the opposite was found to be true—though we would all do well to remember that *any* projectile coming out of guns is a bullet and not a machete designed to chop its way through the jungle to its target!

Conventional wisdom. It isn't excessively kind to what I call "The .25 and Under Crowd"—guns of .25 caliber or less—as firearms for big-game hunting. In fact, conventional wisdom on this subject strikes me as somewhat condescending. "Good guns for women and youngsters," is a frequent comment. The unspoken corollary, of course, is that *real* men use heavier calibers. This conveniently overlooks the fact that many full size men are also sensitive to recoil—which I am, and I'm not in the least ashamed to admit it. Other comments less kind range from "marginal for deer" to "downright inadequate for all but outstanding marksmen."

A lot of experts don't share this view, of course. One of the items that triggered a good deal of thought on my part concerning this subject was a 1982 column entitled "Too Much Gun?" by Outdoor Life shooting editor Jim Carmichel. Carmichel's thesis was that accurate bullet placement is more important than overwhelming firepower, and that those who flinch from the recoil of heavy calibers might do much better with guns that are more pleasant to shoot.

Among other incidents, Carmichel told of neatly dropping four roe deer in Scotland at ranges up to 300

*Sure, .25-and-unders are fine firearms for women and youngsters but deer hunting is no place for chauvinism. Photograph by Jim Zumbo*

yards with four shots from a .222 Remington, while at the same time an overgunned fellow guest took 10 shots to do the same number of the animals. Now a .222 is regarded by many as a veritable popgun for shooting deer, so why did it perform so well? The answer, of course, is accurate bullet placement.

Carmichel also wrote that "three of the most effective whitetail cartridges I can name are the .243 Winchester, 6mm Remington, and .250 Savage." Nevertheless, hunters, guides, and writers often damn these cartridges with faint praise. Why the huge discrepancy? I can think of at least two reasons.

The first is perception. When a deer is wounded with a big-bore rifle, the incident is apt to be shrugged off as regrettable but one of those things that happens every once in a while. When a deer is wounded in the same way with a .243 or .250, however, prejudices come into play, and much finger-pointing ensues at what is presumed to be at best a marginal caliber for deer.

A corollary to this prejudice holds that young, inexperienced shooters—the ones for whom "The .25 and Under Crowd" is often recommended—are precisely the ones who should *not* use these calibers. Their inexperience and nervousness, the argument goes, make good bullet placement uncertain, so they should use heavier calibers to compensate for marginal shots.

This argument suggests that putting sheer firepower in the hands of the neophyte is the way to overcome inexperience and nervousness. It seems to me that this completely misses the point. Trying to compensate for an inexperienced hunter's problems by using a bigger gun can often compound the problem and simply create an inexperienced hunter who now flinches.

The whole point of the lighter calibers is that many people—veterans and neophytes alike—will shoot better with them. If they don't, using a bigger gun won't help a whole lot. A bad shot is a bad shot is a bad shot, and a poorly hit deer is a wounded deer, regardless of whether it was shot with a .243 or a .30/06. Granted, there are some situations in which a shot of marginal placement will succeed with a heavy caliber where it would fail with a light one, but those few instances must be balanced against the many times when hunters who are sensitive to recoil will shoot lighter calibers more accurately.

The second reason for the poor ratings often given to the lighter calibers is very likely related to bullets, rather than firepower. There are two major ways in which bullets can cause problems. The first is through the use of varmint-type bullets, which are too light for deer. The second is through the use of either bullets that are too lightly jacketed and that fail to penetrate adequately, or conversely, bullets that are too heavily jacketed and that zip right through a deer without expanding. When light, high-speed bullets are used on big game, it is critical that the bullet expand properly—not too quickly and not too slowly.

However, the need for proper bullet performance is by no means confined to the smaller bores: witness the following tale.

Our veterinarian, Dr. Stanley Pekala, is an outstanding deer hunter and a thoroughly reliable individual. Last fall he shot a buck twice in the shoulder with his .280 Remington—hardly a lightweight caliber in anyone's book. The deer kept running and dropped only after another shot through the lungs. The first two shots had hit the scapula (shoulder blade) and disintegrated, causing only superficial wounds. What makes this incident so frightening is the fact that Pekala was using factory ammunition produced by a major manufacturer, with bullets of the ideal weight for deer hunting. A bad batch of bullets? Read on.

Shortly thereafter, Pekala's son downed a buck with a neck shot from his .270 Winchester—again, a powerful cartridge. He was using the same type and brand of ammunition that his father had, with a bullet weight appropriate for big game. There was no exit wound, which seemed surprising. A little autopsy work revealed the identical problem: The bullet had disintegrated when it struck the spinal column, though it had broken the spine and killed the deer. When similar incidents happen with the smaller bores, skeptics are wont to blame the caliber, rather than faulty bullets, for the problem.

Still, the question lingers: Do these smaller calibers really have adequate power for clean, one-shot kills on big game, particularly deer? Let's look at a few ballistics to see what they have to offer.

The most widely used of "The .25 and Under Crowd" are the .243 Winchester, the 6mm Remington, the .250 Savage (formerly the .250/3000), the .257 Roberts, and the .25/06 Remington. The high-speed .22 centerfires are even more controversial, and considering that they are also illegal in a number of states, I'm going to leave those for another day.

The .25/06 is the most powerful of the five mentioned, and therefore, it seems to draw the least flak from critics. It's a wonderful, flat-shooting cartridge for things such as antelope, and with 100-grain bullets in commercial loads, it exceeds 3,200 fps (feet per second) muzzle velocity and 1,800 foot-pounds of energy at 100 yards. With 120-grain bullets, which might be a good choice for larger game, muzzle velocity is almost 3,000 fps, and energy at 100 yards is close to 2,000 foot-pounds. With maximum handloads (which should always be approached with caution), both the 100-grain and 120-grain bullets can yield better than 2,000 foot-pounds of energy at 100 yards.

Nor are the other calibers in this group far behind. The .257 Roberts and the .250 Savage (which is actually .257 caliber) are so similar ballistically as to make little practical difference, though the Roberts is a bit better on paper. In commercial loads with 100-grain bullets, the Roberts goes at close to 3,000 fps muzzle velocity and exceeds 1,550 foot-pounds of energy at

*This assortment of .25-and-under calibers are potent medicine for deer-size game. Photograph by Warner Shedd*

100 yards; with the same bullet, the .250 Savage tops 2,800 fps at the muzzle and delivers about 1,450 foot-pounds of energy at 100 yards. With handloads, 100-yard energy can be pushed to more than 1,800 and 1,600 foot-pounds, respectively, for the .257 and .250.

With 120-grain bullets, handloaders can achieve muzzle velocities of approximately 2,800 fps for the .250 and almost 2,900 fps for the .257; these translate into energies of roughly 1,800 and 1,900 foot-pounds, respectively, at 100 yards.

Not to be outdone, the .243 Winchester and 6mm Remington offer some impressive figures in their own right. As the fond owner of a .243 in Ruger's M-77, I'm delighted to see that Federal has just come out with a new load utilizing the 100-grain Nosler partition bullet—a projectile that has a sterling reputation for controlled expansion without breaking up. Muzzle velocity of this load is 2,960 fps, and energy at 100 yards is in excess of 1,700 foot-pounds. For 6mm Remington fans, Winchester puts out a 100-grain load that tops 3,100 fps at the muzzle and 1,800 foot-pounds of energy at the 100-yard mark.

With handloads, these two little gems can do even better. Muzzle velocities for the 6mm with either the Speer 100-grain boattail or the Speer 105-grain spitzer top 3,100 fps at the muzzle and develop 1,900 foot-pounds of energy at 100 yards. The .243 with the 100-grain Nosler partition bullet cranks up to a remarkable 3,250 fps at the muzzle and close to 2,000 foot-pounds of energy at 100 yards!

Are these .25-and-unders capable of quick, humane, one-shot kills on deer? Just consider that the venerable .30/30 Winchester, which almost everyone agrees has done in more North American deer than any other cartridge, with a 170-grain bullet produces a muzzle velocity of roughly 2,200 fps, an energy of 1,300 foot-pounds at 100 yards, and an energy of less than 1,000 foot-pounds at 200 yards. All of the calibers listed above substantially exceed these figures, often by about 50 percent. That's a far cry from being margi-

nal or barely adequate. Yes, I recognize the larger channel size of the .30 caliber bullets, but if a .257 or .243 bullet is of good design and it expands properly, it's all anyone needs to stop a deer in its tracks.

What about larger game, such as elk and moose? That grand old marksman and sportsman Col. Townsend Whelen tested the .257 Roberts extensively and pronounced it excellent for moose and other big game. Certainly, Whelen was a fine shot and realized the limitations of his gun, but isn't that what hunting is—or ought to be—all about?

I certainly wouldn't recommend the lighter calibers as ideal for everyone to use on elk and moose. On the other hand, recoil-conscious hunters who can shoot well with the .25s and .243s can certainly do the job efficiently *if* they use the right bullets and exercise reasonable restraint in their choice of shots. Here, the .25/06, .250 Savage and .257 Roberts offer a slight advantage; with a 117 or 120-grain bullet, these calibers can ensure a bit better penetration on big animals. On the other hand, by being a little selective in my shots, I wouldn't hesitate to go after elk with a .243 or 6mm Remington firing a 100-grain Nosler partition bullet with a 3,000-fps-or-better muzzle velocity.

The .25-and-unders, then, combine plenty of killing power—assuming bullets of reliable expansion and proper weight are used—with modest recoil, even in lightweight rifles. This is no merely theoretical advantage, either. The practicality of this combination becomes all too apparent after trudging up and down ridges that grow increasingly steeper with every passing hour, while each extra pound of rifle begins to feel like five!

There are always trade-offs in selecting a big-game rifle, and the wisdom of those trade-offs is a source of legitimate debate. To me, the gain of a light, flat-shooting gun whose unobtrusive recoil makes it a pleasure to shoot—even on the target range—is well worth the lesser (though still excellent) fire-power of "The .25 and Under-Crowd."

# Home-Brewed Shotgun Slugs

*By George H. Haas*

I f you shoot conventional one-ounce shotgun-slug cartridges, it costs you 77¢ every time you pull the trigger. A five-pack of ordinary Foster-type 12-gauge slug loads lists for $3.50. Add sales tax, say 10 percent, and divide by five. Fancy loads such as the Brenneke and even fancier ones with the slug encased in a two-part plastic sabot that drops away a short distance from the muzzle cost even more.

The high prices charged for slug cartridges is evidenced by the fact that standard 12-gauge slug cartridges are packed five to the box. If a gun shop confronted the average shooter with slug loads packed 25 to a box like ordinary birdshot cartridges, the $19.25 price (including sales tax) would cause deteriorating customer relations.

The high cost of slug loads makes it difficult for the average gunner to sight his slug gun in and to practice often enough so that he can hit his deer. Make no mistake—careful sighting in with adjustable sights or a scope are needed because a heavy slug's trajectory is very curved. Because of the money involved, most slug shooters practice very little, and this can only result in a lot of missed shots and some wounded game, which is a dirty shame.

If I told you that it is possible to cast your own slugs just like a youngster casting "tin" soldiers, and then handload them in fired cases by using simple, inexpensive equipment, thereby reducing the cost to 23¢ per load, would you believe me? I thought you would not, so I'll prove it. The accompanying table lists the unit prices for the components I recently used to load 12-gauge slugs, plus a few incidental costs.

| Component | Unit Cost | Minimum Quantities Available |
|---|---|---|
| Primer | 2.000 | 1,000 shotshell primers at $20 |
| Powder | 8.414 | $19 per pound of powder used |
| Gas-seal over-powder wad | 3.180 | $7.95 for one bag of 250 |
| Half-inch fiber filler wads | 1.390 | $6.95 for 500 |
| Hard card wad | 0.695 | $6.95 for 1000 |
| Shotshell case | 2.000 | Based on six reloads—see text |
| Scrap lead for cast slug | 1.700 | Pure lead scrap at 25¢ per pound. Junkyard price—475-grain slug |
| Sales tax | 1.614 | 10 percent (non-mail-order items only) |
| Mail-order delivery of wads | 1.900 | Based on most recent delivery |
| **Total** | 22.893 | |

*A batch of slugs cast in a home workshop is ready for loading in fired shotgun cases, in this case, Winchester AA compression-formed cases that formerly held 1⅛ ounces of shot for Skeetshooting. All photographs by Mary H. Haas*

These unit prices are fairly straightforward, except for the cost of the case. I use low-brass, compression-formed 12-gauge cases that I have fired once at the Skeet range. This type of case, made by several companies, is the very best for any form of reloading because there is no separate base wad inside the shell to come loose after several reloadings and wind up as a bore obstruction. Fancy, high-brass cases are not needed. The high brass has nothing to do with the strength of the case. In fact, most high-brass cases have separate base wads; and I therefore prefer to avoid reloading them.

New, unfired cases without a primer of the kind I prefer are available at about $12 per 100. If you invest 12¢ in a new hull but load it six times (a fair average), your unit cost sinks to the 2¢ listed in the table. Actually, I avoid new hulls entirely by reloading fired Skeet shells. It's easier because the cases have been factory-crimped and reforming an established crimp is a breeze compared with crimping an entirely new case. I have endless quantities of fired Skeet shells. You can easily scrounge them from claybird shooters who do not reload. If you scrounge, your cost falls to zero.

Of course, the most important component of any handload is reliable data that tells the handloader what to put into the case. The best source of data for home-cast slug loads is the Lyman *Shotshell Handbook*, Third Edition, available through your local gun shop for $17.95 and also available in some public libraries. This manual contains data for many different slug loads. Each listing specifies the correct case by brand name and type, the correct primer, powder type and charge, the components of the wad column, and the type of crimp that should be used to close the case mouth—roll crimp or folded crimp. Most of the listings call for the Lyman 475-grain cast slug, though a few listings call for the well-known Brenneke slug.

Only 12-gauge and 20-gauge loads are listed.

It is essential to use only the combinations of components listed in the manual. *Do not substitute other components*. For instance, you might be tempted to use 375 ½-grain (one-ounce) slugs instead of the 475-grain Lyman slugs. If you do, you're risking damage to your gun and yourself. Never, never use a powder that is not listed for the load you select from the manual, and make sure that you load the listed amount of powder. Substitutions of any kind can cause trouble in many different ways. For instance, wad columns are carefully designed to fit the case length perfectly when using the Lyman slug. If you substitute other wads, the length of the wad column changes, and it will be impossible to close the case mouth over the slug or the case will be forced inward around the slug because the wad column is too short.

The Lyman manual includes a discussion of shotshell cases. The various cases are illustrated with lengthwise cross-sectional drawings of the cases that clearly show whether or not the base wad is integral with the case wall. If you have any doubts about a batch of cases, saw a fired case in half lengthwise with a hacksaw and check it against the drawings. Do not simply look into the case mouth. You cannot see a separate base wad that way.

Loading home-cast slugs is a lot like loading birdshot or claybird cartridges. You can use almost any shotshell press or set of hand tools to do the job. The method is shown in the photographs with this article. Don't however, ignore the operator's manuals supplied with your shotshell press or hand tools because they may include essential safety precautions peculiar to your equipment.

The finished loads differ from commercial Foster-slug cartridges in several ways, the most important being that the cast slug does not have angled vanes on its circumference. In the minds of most slug users, this automatically makes the home-cast slug inferior. Many believe that a smooth-sided slug cannot possibly rotate in the air when fired from a smoothbore shotgun barrel and so acquire gyroscopic stabilization similar to that of a rifle bullet in flight. It can't, of course, but ask yourself if commercial rifled slugs rotate when fired from smoothbores. If the commercial slugs do not rotate, they are inherently no more accurate than smooth slugs.

It is often said that when the angled vanes of commercial slugs hit the air, atmospheric drag causes the slug to rotate. OK—prove it. Apparently, no one has done so. You would think that some investigator would be able to prove this widely accepted "fact" of ballistic life, but no one so far has published any proof, much less slow-motion photographs of a rotating slug in flight. A small minority of gun writers boldly state that commercial rifled slugs do not spin, but they do not offer any proof either.

By the way, the cast Lyman slug works well in tight chokes, but why take a chance? Passing through a tight choke certainly does not increase the accuracy of any slug load. It's really best not to fire them through anything tighter than Improved Cylinder. No choke whatsoever, as in specialized slug barrels with adjustable sights, is best and may also increase your safety margin.

One gunner recently asked me why it isn't a good idea to simply buy commercial slugs as handloading components and load them in fired cases. That would reduce costs substantially, though not as much as casting your own. However, Remington, Federal, and Winchester do not sell their rifled slugs separately as handloading components. Fancy slugs such as the Brenneke are available, but the prices are so high that loading them costs almost as much as buying loaded factory ammunition. Check the catalogs if you don't believe me. About the only inexpensive plain lead slug (without attached wads or sabot) available to handloaders is the Ballistics Products Incorporated (BPI) "Slugster," which costs $5.95 for 25, or a unit price of 23.8¢. The well-known Brenneke slug with attached wads in 12, 16, or 20 gauge costs $11 for 25, with a unit cost of 44¢, which is typical of "luxury" slugs.

About the only reason for buying fancy handloading slugs is that accuracy may be improved in a particular gun. That has to be a great improvement to justify the cost. BPI's comparatively inexpensive Slugster is described as having "fracture lines" that cause the slug to break into three parts on impact. That may be useful in some forms of deer hunting, but dividing the projectile into three parts on impact certainly lessens the depth of penetration, which is an important consideration indeed.

The Lyman cast slug also differs from commercial Foster-type slugs in that it does not have a hollow point. This does not bother me one bit. A 12-gauge slug has a diameter of almost three-quarters of an inch. That's a big projectile, and if it hits a deer, the slug would cause considerable damage without any

expansion whatsoever. In fact, however, the home-cast slug without hollow point does expand. In duct-seal tests and when fired into wood, these slugs expanded to about $1\frac{1}{16}$ inches in diameter.

The Lyman manual lists loads with a folded crimp identical to the crimp used with birdshot. It also lists loads that call for a roll crimp such as those used in factory-loaded slug cartridges. I prefer the folded crimp, and it is shown in the accompanying photographs. It is equal to the roll crimp in every way and holds the slug firmly in place within the cartridge case. The reasons for using the fold crimp are that it is easier to do and requires less equipment. To make a roll crimp, you need a roll crimper (available from BPI for $14.95) and a shell vise to hold the hull very firmly in place while you crimp it. The shell vise, also from BPI, costs $29.95. With a folded crimp, you can use the ordinary crimping gear incorporated in a shotshell press. *Warning: The folded crimp develops more pressure than the roll crimp, other things being equal, so make sure that you use the Lyman data that is correct for the crimp that you have selected*. Again, don't substitute.

The fold crimp results in a shell that looks and weighs almost exactly the same as a birdshot load. With the roll crimp, you can see the nose of the slug in the loaded cartridge, so there's little excuse for confusion. With a fold crimp, it's impossible to tell a slug load from a birdshot load. If you make this mistake, you could fire a slug load at a high angle by mistake. After you finish loading a batch, it's therefore essential to distinctively mark your slug loads. I use quick-drying paint to make a white circle right around the plastic portion of the hull, but even after doing so, I keep the slug loads carefully segregated from my birdshot and Skeet cartridges.

All shotgun slugs are made of commercial-grade pure lead because the slug must swage down to fit tight bore diameters and to pass through tight chokes. If you buy casting lead from a plumber-supply house, you're on pretty safe ground as long as you specify exactly what you want. If you buy your lead in a junkyard, as I do, or scrounge it, you should do some tests. Many different lead alloys are made, and some of them are considerably harder than pure lead, particularly those that contain zinc. Slugs cast with these hard alloys could blow up your gun.

In the presence of air, pure commercial lead quickly combines with oxygen and turns from fresh-cast silvery to battleship gray, just like the gray of an old lead sinker. Avoid silvery lead because it's probably a hard alloy. At the junkyard or other supplier, scratch the lead with your thumbnail. If that cuts a silvery line in the patina, you have one indication that the metal is all right for slugs. At home, chop off a small piece with a mallet and wood chisel or a hatchet and put it on a flat metal surface. Then pound it with a hammer. If the lead easily spreads out and forms a thin sheet, it's almost certainly commercial-grade pure lead. Then, take the sheet and put it in a vise with some sticking out. Whack the protruding portion with a hammer. If it bends easily to a right angle, you have another indication that the metal is all right. If it breaks off, leaving a crystalline surface on the edges, you probably have a very hard alloy, useless for casting slugs and dangerous, too. Take it back, complain, and try another batch or get a refund.

Another good test that you really can't avoid when you cast slugs is temperature. Pure lead melts at 327.43°C, a much lower temperature than the melting points of hard-lead alloys. It melts on an ordinary electric kitchen stove or gas stove or on a wood fire. Test-melt some of your batch. If it won't melt over these heat sources, and even if it does melt but takes a long time and pours as slowly and thickly as molasses, steer clear of it. I make all these tests whenever I buy casting metal.

Handling molten lead can be dangerous. For instance, a single drop of water in molten lead causes instantaneous steam, which throws droplets of lead into your face and all over the place. Be cautious and always wear eye protection, long sleeves, and thick gloves when you are casting.

The proper handling of casting metal is discussed in some detail in Lyman's *Reloading Handbook*, 46th edition. This includes a description of various alloys. Much of the information is for riflemen who cast their own bullets and involves such things as gas checks for the bullets and bullet lubrication. But the information on casting pure lead is valuable and many safety tips are included. The discussion also includes material on fluxing the molten metal to burn out impurities. This manual is also available through your local gun shop ($18.95). Don't even think about casting slugs without reading this material first. You may be able to borrow the publication from another handloader—it's very popular among riflemen—or locate one in a public library.

By the way, casting alloyed bullets makes a sophisticated and rather expensive electric handloader's melting pot an essential. It's not needed for pure lead, though it's convenient. Also, you can get away with a plain plumber's lead ladle when you use pure lead, so don't jump at the chance to buy a fancy pouring ladle. This will keep your equipment costs down. Put to the choice, I'd rather have the two manuals than fancy, convenient, but unnecessary, equipment.

All of the components, except wads, are available in gun stores. The best supplier of wads is Ballistics Products Inc. (2106 Daniels St. Box 408, Long Lake, MN 55356). This company issues a catalog for $1 through the mail. It includes drawings of various wads, the roll crimper, the shell vise, and other useful items. This company also offers numerous reloading manuals with data for a variety of slug loads. Some of them are quite remarkable. For instance, one load calls for two one-ounce Slugster projectiles mounted on top of one another in the shotshell hull! Another calls for six 00 buckshot and one 12-gauge slug in the same case. You can have a lot of fun experimenting with these special loads, but I take no responsibility whatsoever for the results. I take no responsibility for your use of the Lyman data either, because I have no control over your reloading procedures or the degree of care you exercise.

Everyone who has had experience with shotgun slugs will tell you that accuracy is much more mysterious with these projectiles than it is with metallic rifle ammunition. For instance, seemingly identical shotguns often differ in the accuracy with which they handle shotgun slugs. Also, a single shotgun may fire one brand of factory slugs with fine accuracy and another with dismal results. It takes an expert to find out why, and numerous gun writers advise their readers to experiment with different factory brands until they find the one that shoots most accurately in their particular guns. In fact, you may sometimes be forced to conclude that a given gun doesn't fire any slug load with acceptable accuracy. The only recourse then is to acquire a gun that does.

Much the same applies to home-brewed loads. The first load that you select from the Lyman manual may shoot all over the target and may even produce flyers that don't hit the paper. If so, try other listed loads until you find the one that works best. The Lyman *Shotshell Handbook* lists 38 different loads for 12-gauge cast slugs and eight 20-gauge using one-piece cases. If one of them doesn't shoot accurately in your gun, something is wrong with the gun insofar as shooting slugs is concerned. By the way, the Lyman cast slugs work well in the new rifled shotgun barrels. Recovered slugs were clearly engraved with rifling lands and grooves.

Finally, I have to say that the photographs and captions in this article are intended only to tell you what you are getting into before you lay out any money. This material is not a substitute for the Lyman manual or the manufacturers' instructions furnished with reloading equipment and components. Be safe when you're handloading, and you'll be safer when you're shooting.

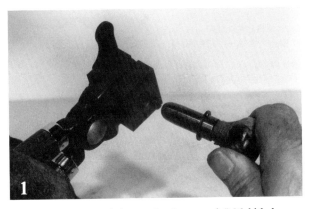

*Mold consists of two halves and a "top punch." Mold halves are attached to hinged handles. These Lyman molds are available in 12 and 20 gauge. Here, the top punch, which forms the large hollow in the base of the slug, is being inserted in the mold. Mold assembly must be hot to cast good slugs with smooth surfaces. Preheat on your heat source, but don't set fire to wooden handle of top punch.*

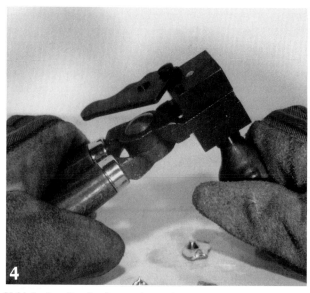

Hold the handles firmly together to keep the cast slug stationary within the mold and rotate the top punch about a quarter-turn to free it from the newly cast slug. But don't apply much force if the top punch won't turn. You could damage it.

Lead is poured into the mold from an ordinary plumber's lead ladle. Rest top-punch handle on the bench for steadiness. Be generous with the metal so that it overflows a bit and forms a sprue. This ensures that the mold is really full.

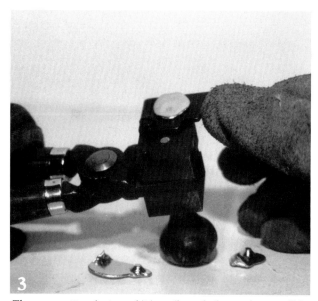

The sprue cutter pivots, and it is easily pushed around to cut off the sprue, if sprue is still hot. If not, tap sprue cutter with wooden stick or mallet, never metal. Sprues from previous slugs lie on the bench. Melt them down from time to time and use for casting.

The mold has been opened. The slug usually drops out easily, but here it has remained on top punch. Place soft cloth or carpeting on bench to cushion the slug, which is very hot and easily marred by hitting a hard bench. On the bench are two new slugs. The one on its side shows the large base cavity. If slug sticks in mold, tap one-piece end of hinge pin in handles with wooden or plastic mallet, never metal.

If the top punch is hot, the cast slug easily comes away from it. If punch is cool, slug may stick. Don't use a lot of force, and never use a metal tool to dislodge it. Here a homemade wooden jig that closely fits around the shank of the top punch is being used to remove a stuck slug. If that doesn't work, melt the slug off the top punch by placing it in the molten lead in your ladle on your heat source. Again, don't set fire to the wooden handle. After a little experience, you'll know how to control the heat.

Temporarily removed from the press, here are the flexible plastic wad fingers that guide wads into the case.

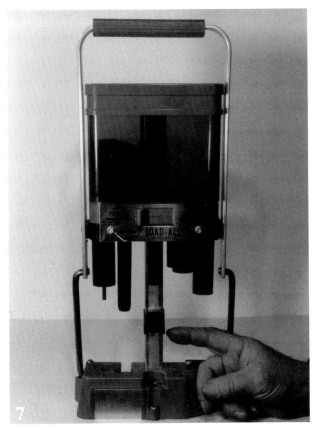

With a batch of slugs ready, you can begin loading. Almost any shotgun reloading tool can be used. This is a very inexpensive Lee Load-All II. The instruction manual supplied with a shotshell press tells how to resize, de-prime, prime, and charge your cases with powder. At this station, the spout (also used as a ram to seat the wads) is used first to charge the cases with powder from the powder hopper (upper left). I'm pointing to wad fingers at Station 3.

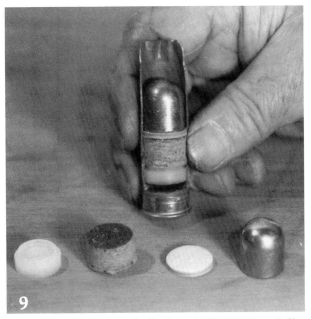

From left to right are: Ballistics Products Gas Seal plastic wad, fiber filler wad, card wad and a 12-gauge cast slug. Each wad in the column has a purpose: to contain expanding powder gas, to fill out the column to the correct length, to prevent the soft filler wad from being driven into the hollow base of the slug, which would impair accuracy. Cutaway shotshell shows wads and slugs in their proper positions.

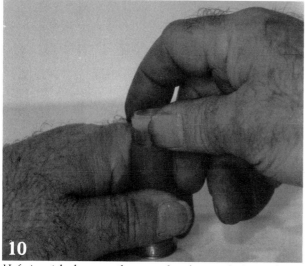

10

Unfortunately, however, the gas-seal wad cannot be inserted with the plastic wad fingers. It is too hard and too short and often jams in the fingers. Instead, insert the wad manually by pressing it against one side of the original crimp and then pushing the other side down into the case mouth. Plastic cases are slightly elastic. Inspect to make sure that wad is in the correct position just below case mouth. Large cavity in the wad must be down toward the powder.

Now we're ready to use the wad fingers. Place the case on Station 3, making sure that the plastic wad fingers go inside the case mouth.

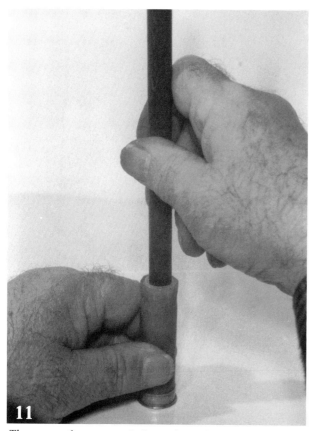

11

13

Then use a three-quarter-inch wooden rod to push the gas seal down onto the power. That size rod fits neatly into the small cavity in the top of the gas seal. Inspect to make sure that the wad is in correct position. If it is not, you can get it out of the case by using a corkscrew, which, of course, pierces the wad. Discard it and insert a new one.

Put a fiber wad in the wad fingers. Press it down until it is just below the top of the plastic wad-finger guide.

**14**

Now place a white, hard card wad on top of the fiber wad.

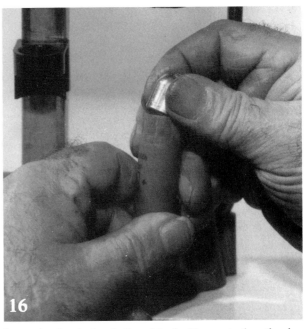

**16**

Insert the slug by hand. Surprisingly, it's easy to drop the slug right down on the wads because the diameter of the projectile is less than the interior diameter of the case.

**15**

Use the operating crank to lower the ram and push both wads down on the top of the gas seal. Do not apply enough force to compress the fiber wad, but make sure that all of the wads are down far enough to allow proper seating of the slug. The chosen wad column is carefully designed to take up the right amount of space in the case.

**17.**

Move the case to Station 4. Modern plastic cases with an eight-segment folded crimp go on the front position at this station. Rear position is for six-point crimps—almost always paper cases. Don't try to load slugs in paper cases. It's a real mess. The plastic case must be placed so that an inward fold in the case mouth is centered to the front. This aligns the folds in the case mouth with the vanes inside the tool.

Lowering the tool with the operating crank pushes the crimp-starting ram down over the case mouth. Don't press too hard or you will bulge or distort the case below the crimp. All you want to do is start the folds of the star crimp.

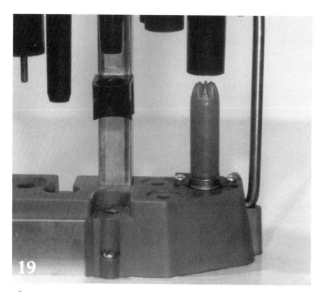

Case is now placed on Station 5. Ram is lowered to form the final crimp. This is the point where a little force should be applied to slightly dish in the folds of the crimp to make it just as secure as a factory crimp.

Nicely formed crimp just like a factory-loaded birdshot shell is the result. If the crimp folds down inside the case, exposing the slug, the wad column is too short or your powder charge is too little. If you cannot close the case mouth, the wad column is too long (wrong components), or there is too much powder—which is very dangerous. Make sure that you track down the cause of such troubles and correct it. Safely discard all defective rounds. Folded crimp is just as good as a roll crimp, and it's easier to do. See text.

# Conicals or Balls?

*By Rick Hacker*

It has become the perennial campfire debate among muzzleloading hunters: Which is more effective for big game, the round ball or the conical? This one question has been responsible for the disruption of more friendships than any other single subject, with the possible exceptions of politics or football.

What's the big deal, you ask? Who cares what you ram down your smokepole, just so it comes out the muzzle? Actually, the subject is a bit more complicated than that and does merit some in-depth discussion. For one thing, every blackpowder hunter has a choice to make every autumn—should he use round balls or conicals in his frontloader?

Of the two, the round ball is by far the more "traditional" hunting projectile. Its basic spherical form has been used ever since the Chinese touched off the first matchlock. Up until the early 1800s, American hunters knew of nothing else. Because they were easy to cast and required less lead, round balls remained the favorite bullet for backwoods hunters even after the advent of the conical.

Conicals came about because a faster-loading, harder-hitting bullet was needed for the larger game animals that were being encountered in the Far West. Using nothing but round balls, Lewis and Clark's 1803–05 journals are filled with accounts of wounded bears requiring four or five shots to finally bring them down. By contrast, many later blackpowder hunting books, most of them written by men who hunted for sport rather than survival, tell of using conicals for big game such as elk and bears and making one-shot kills.

Although the first hunting conicals began to appear around the 1850s, the elongated bullet was catapulted into popularity during the Civil War, when the undersize Mini-Ball won praise for its quick loading and hard-hitting characteristics. Of course, hollow-based Minis were hard to cast, required more lead per bullet, and were best shot in guns that were specially rifled for them, such as the U.S. Springfields. Conicals entered the shooting scene about the same time and the metallic cartridge was finally perfected, and the "bullet" shape was quickly adopted for the newfangled breechloading cartridges. But even in breechloaders, the conical bullet never achieved maximum accuracy until the advent of larger cases (and later on, in the 1890s, with the introduction of smokeless powders), when higher stabilizing velocities could finally be obtained. With sportsmen's attention focused on the self-contained metallic cartridge, the conical, as far as muzzleloading was concerned, was largely ignored. In fact, there were no significant design changes in muzzleloading bullets until the 1980s.

Meanwhile, the tried and true round ball had already reached the zenith of design. After all, how do you improve upon a perfect sphere? The only advancement modern technology has made was to create the swaged ball, thus eliminating any air pockets that could affect the weight and, hence, the accuracy of the round ball. Thus, the round ball has had plenty of time to rack up an impressive history of hunting successes and untold leagues of devotees.

Recently, the growth of muzzleloading hunting has

*Relative position to the bull's-eye was not as important as the group size in the OUTDOOR LIFE test. Round balls were clearly more accurate but have less knockdown power. Photographs by Rick Hacker*

paralleled the increased interest in perfecting the effectiveness of the conical bullet as a hunting projectile. As a result, there are no fewer than four major companies (and an untold number of minor ones) producing variations of the conical bullet for hunting. Yet, it is interesting to note that most of these companies also produce the traditional round ball. Obviously, they are not willing to take sides in a century-old controversy. However, I can certainly give you some insight into my own hunting experience with round balls and conicals.

First, the round ball. On the plus side: When a proper hunting load is worked up, the round ball can be extremely accurate in barrels with slow-twist rifling, such as the Dixie Gun Works Tennessee Mountain Rifle, the Navy Arms Ithaca Hawken, and the Thompson/Center Pennsylvania Hunter. Five-shot cloverleaf groups at 50 yards are often the norm rather than the exception. Round balls also shoot flatter than conicals, which means that there will be less deviation (i.e., Kentucky windage) needed for your sight picture when you touch off a shot at 100 yards with a rifle that was zeroed in for 50 yards. On the minus side: Round balls must be patched in the rifling, which means that they take longer to load. (Pre-lubed, pre-cut patches can ease this chore somewhat.) Because they weigh less than conicals, round balls are also more susceptible to windage variations; at 100 yards, a stiff breeze can push your shot off its mark just enough to make you miss a heart-size target. And, as the hunting range increases, round balls lose energy dramatically.

Now let's talk about conicals. Caliber for caliber, they carry more grain weight than round balls (as an example, a .50 caliber round ball contains 180 grains of lead while a .50 Thompson/Center Maxi-Hunter

weighs 355 grains—and that's with a hollowpoint). Thus, though round balls travel at higher velocities because of their lighter weight, the heavier conicals hit with far greater striking energy. For example, a 220-grain .54 round ball backed by 100 grains of RS Pyrodex has a muzzle velocity of 1,740 fps (feet per second) and a 100-yard striking energy of 549 foot-pounds. By contrast, a 410-grain .54 conical, backed with the same 100-grain charge of RS Pyrodex, has a muzzle velocity of 1,525 fps and a 100-yard striking energy of 1,218 foot-pounds. Thus, using the same powder charge, even though the conical travels at slightly less velocity than the round ball, it hits with more than twice the energy. In muzzleloading hunting, what matters most is how hard the bullet hits, not how quickly it reaches the target. (Remember, you cannot apply smokeless powder rules to black-powder.)

Another factor in favor of conicals is that they require no patching, thereby making loading easier and faster than round balls, which must be patched to create the tight gas seal that gives the ball its accuracy and velocity. (For the record, unpatched round balls are not capable of hunting accuracy beyond 15 to 20 yards and striking energy suffers appreciably; therefore, they are not recommended for any type of hunting activities.) Undersize versions of the conical, such as Buffalo Bullets and Minis, can be started in the bore with mere finger pressure, requiring just a ramrod to complete the loading process. By contrast, patched round balls first require a short-starter to force the tightly patched ball into the bore and then a ramrod to firmly seat it against the powder charge. This separate loading step takes extra time and equipment.

The only conicals that require a separate short-starting procedure akin to that for round balls are the oversize rifling-engraved-at-loading projectiles such as the Lee R.E.A.L. bullets and Thompson/Center's Maxi-Ball. Because the soft lead of these bullets is literally swaged into the rifling as they are forced into the bore, these particular conicals form a very tight gas seal. This translates into more breech pressure, greater velocity, and increased recoil. These oversize conicals can approach the round ball's accuracy. (Note: Because of this extra pressure buildup, Thompson/Center recommends that the Maxi-Ball only be used in guns of their manufacture.)

The rifling-engraved-at-loading conicals are not a practical choice for the hunter. They are often difficult to load, requiring extra force to get them started down the bore. In fact, some rifles, such as Cimarron Arms' Hawken, may require the use of a hammer to get these bullets started. Definitely not a choice for cold-weather hunting or when a fast follow-up shot is required. For the hunter, the slightly undersize, smooth-sliding conicals definitely have the advantage.

It should be noted that, unless they hit bone, both round balls and conicals, when backed by normal hunting charges of 75 to 100 grains of blackpowder, have the ability to shoot clean through a big-game animal, especially when fired at close range. However, when a bone or dense tissue is hit, both of these soft-lead projectiles can flatten out admirably, often doubling their diameter and producing tremendous shock effect. In thick-bodied game such as elk, a conical will penetrate twice as deep as a round ball, and with twice the striking energy. This is why a conical is so much more effective on hard-to-kill game.

It would seem that the harder-hitting, easier-loading conical would be the optimum choice for hunting. Yet, up until the mid-1980s, the hunter wishing to use conicals had to rely on the fragile Mini

(which does not shoot well in rifles with slow twists and which often keyholes when heavy hunting charges blow past the thin-skirted base) or specially cast bullets from firms such as Lyman and Dixie Gun Works. Then came what can best be described as the Conical Revolution. Most notable was the appearance of the Buffalo Bullet, a thick-based, self-lubricated conical that came in various weights, in both hollow-points and solids, for the three most popular hunting calibers (.45, .50 and .54; a new .58 was added in 1990).

A few years after the Buffalo Bullet, Hornady came out with its Great Plains Maxi-Bullet, a hollow-base, hollow-point conical available in .45, .50 and .54 calibers. About that same time, Thompson/Center announced its flat-based, hollow-point Maxi-Hunter, offering "maximum expansion on deer-size game." It is this qualification that sets the lighter Thompson/Center and Hornady hollow-points apart from the heavier, solid-nosed bullets. At relatively low blackpowder velocities, hollow-points do not expand appreciably unless they hit bone or heavy tissue. Their lighter weight makes them ideal for deer-size animals, but they would not be my first choice on thicker-bodied game, where penetration is vital. For elk, moose, and similar-size animals, including dangerous game such as bears and mountain lions, I opt for solid-nosed conicals backed by stiff blackpowder charges of 100 grains or more.

The majority of today's frontloaders feature slow-twist rifling, which is best suited for the round ball. However, even in these guns, some of the lighter-weight conicals can be made to print 2-inch groups at 50 yards (opening up to 4 or 6 inches at 100 yards—which is still acceptable big-game accuracy) with a little careful experimentation with powder charges. Recognizing the need for hunting rifles capable of handling conicals for big game, a number of new

*With the growth of muzzleloading hunting has come the perennial debate: conicals or balls? Photograph by Rick Hacker*

muzzleloaders have been introduced with faster-twist rifling. Most notable are the Lyman Deerstalker, the CVA Plainsman, the .50 Traditions Hunter, and the White Mountain Carbine from Thompson/Center. Even in states where smoothbores are required and a patched round ball might seem to be the only logical choice, using a conical rifled shotgun slug can increase your muzzleloader's striking energy considerably.

With round balls already at their peak of perfection, conicals continue to inspire a new wave of research and development each year. Hornady has announced what may be the ultimate conical—its Muzzleloading Magnum Sabot that features a plastic cup affixed to its new jacketed XTP cartridge-type bullet. Test results of the sabot, as well as a comparison between conicals and round balls, is given in the box.

For small game and medium-size deer, a round ball may suffice, but for hunters going after anything larger and heavier where penetration and striking energy are the keys to success with a muzzleloader, the conical is by far the optimum choice for the sportsman who is serious about making one-shot kills. Judging from their journals, Lewis and Clark would have used 'em if they'd had 'em! 🦌

## FIELD TEST

Even though I have seen the end result of the conical's effectiveness on scores of game animals, practical field tests help prove a point. They also offer some interesting comparisons between various types of hunting projectiles available to the muzzleloader of today.

I started off with a basic "control gun," a .54 caliber custom Hawken made for me years ago by Ozark Mountain Arms. This gun features a premium barrel that is rifled one turn in 66 inches, making it ideally suited for round balls. However, since I switched over to conicals, I have developed a practical hunting load for this gun, using 100 grains of blackpowder or RS Pyrodex backing a 435-grain Buffalo Bullet. With this load, I have made one-shot kills on game animals ranging in size and stamina from 90-pound whitetail deer to an angered 300-pound wild boar.

To establish a basis for comparison, I began by using my Hawken control gun to fire a three-shot, round-ball group into a target posted at 50 yards. The rifle bore was cleaned after every shot to achieve maximum accuracy. For this test, my goal was to establish the tightest three-shot group for each type of projectile; rather than trying to shoot a perfect 10× score. Thus, for the purposes of this test, it did not matter where on the target the shots hit, as long as the same point-of-reference hold and powder charge was used for all three shots.

Using 100 grains of RS Pyrodex and a swaged Speer .54 caliber round ball in the slow-twist Hawken, my first three shots printed a nice, tight 1½-inch group, with two of the shots touching. Certainly, the round ball was accurate!

Next, using the same rifle and a 100-grain powder charge, I switched to my tried and true 435-grain Buffalo Bullet, a load that I know prints consistent 2-inch groups at this range. The fist two shots printed a tight 1-inch group, but the third shot was a flier, striking the target 3½ inches high. Miffed at this deviation from the norm, I thought back and suddenly realized that I had not cleaned the bore between the second and third shots. Thus, this target served as a practical and somewhat embarrassing reminder of the effect blackpowder/Pyrodex fouling can have upon bullet trajectory.

It should be noted that although Buffalo Bullets come in a variety of weights and calibers, I have found that the lighter-weight bullets will generally shoot tighter groups in slow-twist barrels, while the heavier-grained offerings perform best in rifles with fast-twist barrels.

Taking this discovery one step further, I then proceeded to shoot a three-shot group with Hornady's 425-grain hollow-point, hollow-based Great Plains Bullet using the same custom Hawken and 100-grain powder charge. This produced a 2½-inch group. It is interesting to note that I have shot similar groups with this bullet in fast-twist barrels. Thus, overall bullet design as well as weight plays an important role in muzzleloading accuracy.

Continuing the trend of shooting the newest variations of conical bullets, I next tested Buffalo Bullet's latest rendition of the original .58 Mini-Ball. Using my replica Dixie Gun Works 1861 Springfield and a standard charge of 70 grains of powder (which produces 4-inch groups with standard Minis), I was able to shoot a 3½-inch group, which is quite remarkable for a regulation-style military arm. Of course, part of the secret to this success is the fact that these .58 Buffalo Bullets are available in four different diameters (to compensate for the great variations in bore diameters among the .58 replicas). Thus, .58 shooters can experiment with .576, .578, .580 and .582 diameter bullets. For the Dixie Gun Works replica, I found that the .580 bullet worked best and used it for this test.

Then, I decided to test the new Hornady Sabot, a two-piece projectile that consists of a plastic outer sleeve that contains one of Hornady's copper-jacketed XTP bullets normally intended for handgun cartridges. Thus, a .45 caliber sabot is fitted with a .357 bullet, and the .50 and .54 sabots each contain a .44 XTP bullet. For our test, I used the .54 Thompson/Center Renegade, Hornady's .54 sabot (which comes with a .44 Jacketed Flat Point bullet), powered by Hornady's recommended charge of 80 grains of blackpowder or Pyrodex.

My first observation was that the bullets proved extremely difficult to load, even in a clean bore. In fact, a special unbreakable "sabot-loader" sold by Mountain State Muzzleloading had to be used just to get this bullet started down the bore. After that, an Uncle Mike's heavy duty stainless-steel ramrod was used to make sure that the sabot was firmly seated all the way down against the powder charge. Otherwise, there could be the possibility of a dangerous air gap between the bullet and the powder, the results of which could have disastrous effects upon the barrel and the shooter. Once everything was in place, the sabot shot the best group of the day, producing a 1¼-inch cluster. However, due to the difficulty of in-the-field loading (especially if a fast follow-up shot is needed), I cannot recommend the sabot concept for hunting, unless it is only used for a first shot.

Using the same 100-grain powder charge, the 220-grain round ball had the least amount of penetration (5½ inches), while the 425-grain Hornady Great Plains bullet had the most (7 inches). The slightly heavier 435-grain Buffalo Bullet hit with greater force; it noticeably knocked the newspaper-filled box back upon impact. In a separate test, using only 80 grains of powder, the Hornady Sabot had slightly greater penetration (7¼ inches). However as evidenced by the recovered bullets, the smaller-caliber sabot retains the least amount of mass.

# Over-the-Counter Accuracy

*By Tim Williams*

It's odd how hunters get caught in a rut. You know, they hunt the same place every year, with the same rifle and the same ammunition. I know how it is, because I've had it happen to me.

For example, I have a Savage Model 99 in .300 Savage that I use for most of my deer and black bear hunting near my home in New Hampshire. I inherited the old Savage from a favorite uncle, one of the men who taught me to hunt. It has a lot of sentimental value, which is why I use it around home. If it didn't shoot well, though, all of the sentiment in the world wouldn't make me take it out of the gun rack come deer season.

It turns out that the old Savage is a real shooter—just like most Savage 99s. It's no trick at all to hold five shots below three inches at 100 yards from a rest. With the right ammunition, the groups get smaller. Much smaller. For years, when I was so poor I did all my hunting near home and this Savage was the only deer rifle I owned, the right ammunition for me was a 180-grain roundnose load. Every year, just before deer season, I'd use up last year's remaining ammo fine-tuning the sights. Then I'd scrape together the money for a fresh box, fire one three-shot group with it to make sure that it still shot all right, and carry the remaining 17 shells while hunting. Often, I ended the season with a deer hanging and 16 shells left for the next year's sighting in.

Usually, my groups ran between 2¼ and 2¾ inches if I did my part. Not bad for an old lever gun. Any deer that stood still within 200 yards of me and the old Savage ran a very good chance of becoming venison. At one point, I'd taken eight deer with nine shots.

One year, however, my local gun shop didn't have the roundnose loads. I was feeling flush that year, so I bought a box of 150-grain ammunition and a box of 180-grain pointed softpoints, just to try something different. The 150-grain ammunition didn't do quite as well as my old favorite roundnose loads—five shot groups expanded a little, still staying under 3 inches. The new, pointed loads did even better, though, shrinking my groups to where I could be pretty sure of putting my first three shots inside of 3 inches at *200* yards. Impressive. My old 200-yard rifle was now a 300-yard rifle.

Aha, you might say. You found a good manufacturer of ammunition. You'd be wrong. All three loads—150, 180 roundnose, and 180 spitzer—were all the same brand. The truth of the matter is that Federal, Remington, Winchester, PMC, Hornady, Norma, CCI, and others all make good, reliable factory ammo. It all depends on the rifle.

Factory ammo today is better than ever, offering a degree of accuracy and consistency that you once had to handload to achieve. In fact, today's factory ammunition will do just about anything any hunter requires, *if* it's properly matched to the rifle.

This business of matching rifle and ammunition is critical, however, because every rifle is different. Even if you took two rifles from the same production line with consecutive serial numbers, you'd find they differed—still well within today's tight manufacturing tolerances, but different. The chamber throat might be a hundredth of an inch longer in one, the bore might be a thousandth of an inch tighter in the other, the headspace differing slightly in each. Individually, these differences might not matter—might not even be measurable—but, together, they add up to the fact that different rifles like different ammunition.

Just as rifles are different so, too, are the people who use them. Some riflemen are once-a-year duffers who never check the sights on their rifles. Others are fanatics who live and breathe velocity tables, handloads, and sub-minute-of-angle accuracy. Somewhere in between live the vast majority of us. Our rifles are important to us because we hunt with them. Some of us handload, but many of us don't. Whether we handload or not, we want our rifles to shoot well because we want our best chance at taking game.

As I discovered with the old Savage, different brands of factory ammunition, with different styles and weights of bullets, behave differently in different rifles. If I'd never tried anything but that 150-grain ammo, I might have believed that my rifle was only capable of 3-inch groups at 100 yards. That's perfectly acceptable hunting accuracy, but I like the confidence of knowing that my rifle is doing its best. Since that first experiment, I've tried every other brand and bullet weight of .300 Savage factory ammunition, just to make sure. Some worked well, some didn't; that particular 180-grain pointed softpoint still works best of all. I found it by accident. Since then, I've made it a policy to search for the right brand of factory ammunition for each rifle. If, for some reason, I run out of ammo far from a reloading bench, I know what will work best in my rifle.

I tried some side-by-side comparisons of factory ammo in some of my other rifles. I wanted to see which, if any, worked better in these rifles. I believe that the results I obtained in this test are similar to the results any hunter would find with his pet rifles. I also believe that any hunter can improve his chances of bringing home game just by trying out different brands of factory ammunition.

The rifles I used are the straight-from-the-factory models that I use for hunting. I tested my newest all-around deer rifle, a Ruger M-77RLS bolt-action .308 carbine with a Swarovski 3×-to-9× scope; a heavy-barreled Ruger M-77V .22/250 with a Swarovski 2.2×-to-9× scope; and two .22s, an old Mossberg Model 44 U.S. target .22 (a World War II vintage training rifle that I learned to shoot with that's far more accurate than it has any business being) and a Ruger Model-77/22, both with Bushnell Banner scopes.

I selected only appropriate hunting loads. In the rimrifles, I tested high-velocity Long Rifle solids and hollow-points; in the varmint rifle the ammo had 40 to 55-grain expanding bullets. And in the .308, I tested a variety of loads with solidly constructed expanding bullets between 150 and 180 grains.

I used very little equipment for this test, nothing the average rifleman doesn't own or have available. I set up on a good solid benchrest at a range with 50 and 100-yard target stands. Two sandbags homemade from empty shot bags served for a rifle rest. A P.A.S.T. recoil pad helped tame the .308 (a sissy bag with five pounds of lead shot would have worked as well) because a 6½-pound .308 kicks hard enough to get your attention. I also used Bilsom muff-type hearing protectors over foam-insert earplugs, because excess noise can permanently damage your hearing and can cause flinching, which destroys accuracy. A sheaf of paper targets completed my equipment. Nothing fancy.

The rifles were sighted in with the ammo I had been using for hunting. I didn't resight each rifle for each ammo, but rather shot for groups. I had decided to resight later with a fresh box of the ammo that proved itself best.

For the .308, I started with a clean rifle, a fresh box of 20 cartridges, and a target with five bull's-eyes. I first fired a five-shot group on the center bull's-eye, followed by four three-shot groups at the smaller surrounding bull's-eyes. The light barrel of the little carbine heats up quickly, and the five-shot groups spread, on average, much wider than the three-shot groups. This doesn't bother me at all in a hunting firearm, because hunting situations rarely demand five fast shots.

With the heavy-barreled .22/250, I simply fired three five-shot groups. This particular rifle seems to become more consistently accurate as it heats up. I suspect that sustained firing would have produced tighter groups. In a five-shot group, it was generally the first and second shots that determined the maximum outside spread.

I alternated between firearms, allowing each to cool between groups because the first shot in hunting, which is the one that counts, is generally fired from a cool rifle. Between boxes, I gave each rifle's bore a cleaning with brush and solvent because my rifles are clean when I take them afield.

All centerfire shooting was done at 100 yards.

The rimfires were easier. I simply fired five 10-shot groups with each type of ammunition on the 50-yard range, cleaning the barrels between boxes of ammunition. The heavy-barreled Mossberg target rifle took to the sustained firing better. The Ruger M-77/22 generally did slightly better with the first five shots.

I spread the testing over several days and took frequent breaks to avoid shooter fatigue. I also shot only in the calm of morning and evening, so wind wasn't a factor in group size.

I did take one step the average shooter probably wouldn't. To prevent any subconscious bias toward any brand of ammo, bullet style, or bullet weight, I had my wife empty the boxes into brown paper bags labeled with a letter—A, B, C and so on. I didn't know until the test was over which manufacturer was which. (No, I didn't peek.)

To check the results, I simply measured the greatest spread of the groups—outside point to outside point—and averaged the results. I can't think of any fairer way to check ammunition performance.

There were times, especially with the .308, when I was sure that shooter error had added a flier to the proceedings. I shoot enough to know when I've blown a shot. Because the purpose of this test was to check the ammo, not the shooter, I simply hid my mistake

*It's dumb to take accuracy lightly. Different brands of ammo shoot better in some guns. Photograph by Tim Williams*

with a piece of tape and used one of the remaining shells to correct the error.

As I looked over the charts, the one thing I could see at a glance was the amazing quality of modern factory ammunition. None of the brands and loads tested performed badly. All were consistent performers, each brand repeating its particular performance from group to group—when the shooter did his part.

Some of the results were predictable. I assumed that different brands and bullet weights would work better in different rifles, and that proved true. Otherwise, the test wouldn't have been worth doing.

Some of the results took me by surprise, however. I had always assumed, for example, that .22 Match ammunition was the most accurate. I threw a box in to test with the hunting loads in the .22s, just to check it out. Well, it ranked right up there, but in both of my .22s, at least one brand (different in each) of high-velocity ammunition produced significantly better accuracy.

I had also convinced myself over the years that 165-grain bullets were the best for the .308, simply because of the excellent retained energy and sectional density figures for that weight bullet. Maybe that's true, but not in my .308. My rifle likes all 150-grain ammo better than any 165. It also handled some 180-grain bullets better than some 165s. Doesn't make sense, does it? But the groups don't lie. A couple of the 150-grain loads performed very well. In that case, I'll choose the load with what I believe is the best-performing hunting bullet.

The .22/250 was the most persnickety of the lot—more so that I expected. A 2-inch group at 100 yards is perfectly acceptable in most rifles, but not in a heavy-barreled varminter. Only two of the factory loads approached acceptable accuracy with the first two shots from a cold barrel. Those first shots count on critters such as coyotes, woodchucks, and marmots. In a prairie dog town, where the action is continuous, most of the factory cartridges settled into acceptable accuracy.

Generally, though, all of the ammunition I tested was accurate enough for hunting. Which means, probably, that you could buy any brand at random and expect to get reasonable accuracy from your rifle. The best loads, however, frequently cut average group sizes almost in half. Think about that. Your rifle may be twice as accurate as you think it is.

That kind of clear accuracy makes a difference when your target is a squirrel's skull at 50 yards, a woodchuck sticking its head out of its hole at 250 yards, or a buck skulking through the softwoods at 90 yards.

The test also had some other benefits. I spent a lot of time with my rifles. Each time I handled them, I grew more familiar with the actions, magazines, safeties, and triggers. Such a familiarity is important when hunting.

Any handloader will tell you that he can concoct a special load that will wring the last bit of accuracy from any rifle. Maybe that's true. But the hunter who has done his homework—who has found the right factory load for his rifle—can have confidence that his choice will work at the moment of truth.

# Index